WEST-E

Middle Level Humanities (010/011) Part 2 of 2

SECRETS

Study Guide
Your Key to Exam Success

WEST-E Test Review for the Washington Educator Skills Tests - Endorsements

Written and edited by the Mometrix Exam Secrets Test Prep Team
Printed in the United States of America

TABLE OF CONTENTS

U.S. and World History - Continued

Roosevelt administration

Roosevelt's "New Deal"

Franklin D. Roosevelt was elected president in 1932 with his promise of a "New Deal" for Americans. His goals were to provide government work programs to provide jobs, wages and relief to numerous workers throughout the beleaguered US. Congress gave Roosevelt almost free rein to produce relief legislation. The goals of this legislation were:

- Relief—creating jobs for the high numbers of unemployed
- Recovery—stimulating the economy through the National Recovery Administration
- Reform—passing legislation to prevent future, similar economic crashes

The Roosevelt Administration also passed legislation regarding ecological issues, including the Soil Conservation Service, aimed at preventing another Dust Bowl.

Roosevelt's "alphabet organizations"

So-called "alphabet organizations" set up during Roosevelt's administration included:

- Civilian Conservation Corps (CCC)—provided jobs in the forestry service
- Agricultural Adjustment Administration (AAA)—increased agricultural income by adjusting both production and prices
- Tennessee Valley Authority (TVA)—organized projects to build dams in the Tennessee River for flood control and production of electricity, resulting in increased productivity for industries in the area, and easier navigation of the Tennessee River
- Public Works Administration (PWA) and Civil Works Administration (CWA)—provided a multitude of jobs, initiating over 34,000 projects
- Works Progress Administration (WPA)—helped unemployed persons to secure employment on government work projects or elsewhere

Actions taken to prevent future crashes and stabilize the economy

The Roosevelt administration passed several laws and established several institutions to initiate the "reform" portion of the New Deal, including:

- Glass-Steagall Act—separated investment from commercial banking
- Securities Exchange Commission (SEC)—helped regulate Wall Street investment practices, making them less dangerous to the overall economy
- Wagner Act—provided worker and union rights to improve relations between employees and employers
- Social Security Act of 1935—provided pensions as well as unemployment insurance

Other actions focused on insuring bank deposits and adjusting the value of American currency. Most of these regulatory agencies and government policies and programs still exist today.

Labor regulations

Three major regulations regarding labor that were passed after the Great Depression are:

- The Wagner Act (1935)—also known as the National Labor Relations Act, it established that unions were legal, protected members of unions, and required collective bargaining. This act was later amended by the Taft-Hartley Act of 1947 and the Landrum-Griffin Act of 1959, which further clarified certain elements.
- Davis-Bacon Act (1931)—provided fair compensation for contractors and subcontractors
- Walsh-Healey Act (1936)—established a minimum wage, child labor laws, safety standards, and overtime pay

World War II

Interventionist and Isolationist approaches to involvement

When war broke out in Europe in 1939, President Roosevelt stated that the US would remain neutral. However, his overall approach was considered "interventionist," as he was willing to provide aid to the Allies without actually entering the conflict. Thus the US supplied a wide variety of war materials to the Allied nations in the early years of the war.

Isolationists believed the US should not provide any aid to the Allies, including supplies. They felt Roosevelt, by assisting the Allies, was leading the US into a war for which it was not prepared. Led by Charles Lindbergh, the Isolationists believed that any involvement in the European conflict endangered the US by weakening its national defense.

> **Review Video:** World War II: An Overview
> *Visit **mometrix.com/academy** and enter **Code**:* **759402**

US entry into the war

In 1937, Japan invaded China, prompting the US to eventually halt exports to Japan. Roosevelt also did not allow Japanese interests to withdraw money held in US banks. In 1941, General Tojo rose to power as the Japanese prime minister. Recognizing America's ability to bring a halt to Japan's expansion, he authorized the bombing of Pearl Harbor on December 7. The US responded by declaring war on Japan. Partially because of the Tripartite Pact among the Axis Powers, Germany and Italy then declared war on the US, later followed by Bulgaria, Hungary, and other Axis nations.

Surrender of Germany

In 1941, Hitler violated the non-aggression pact he had signed with Stalin two years earlier by invading the USSR. Stalin then joined the Allies. Stalin, Roosevelt and Winston Churchill planned to defeat Germany first, then Japan, bringing the war to an end. In 1942-1943, the Allies drove Axis forces out of Africa. In addition, the Germans were soundly defeated at Stalingrad.

The Italian Campaign involved Allied operations in Italy between July 1943 and May 1945, including Italy's liberation. On June 6, 1944, known as D-Day, the Allies invaded France at Normandy. Soviet troops moved on the eastern front at the same time, driving German forces back. By April 25, 1945, Berlin was surrounded by Soviet troops. On May 7, Germany surrendered.

➤ **Review Video:** World War II: Germany
Visit ***mometrix.com/academy*** *and enter* ***Code*****: 951452**

Surrender of Japan
War continued with Japan after Germany's surrender. Japanese forces had taken a large portion of Southeast Asia and the Western Pacific, all the way to the Aleutian Islands in Alaska. General Doolittle bombed several Japanese cities while American troops scored a victory at Midway. Additional fighting in the Battle of the Coral Sea further weakened Japan's position. As a final blow, the US dropped two atomic bombs on Japan, one on Hiroshima and the other on Nagasaki. This was the first time atomic bombs had been used in warfare, and the devastation was horrific and demoralizing. Japan surrendered on September 2, 1945, which became V-J Day in the US.

➤ **Review Video:** World War II: Japan
Visit ***mometrix.com/academy*** *and enter* ***Code*****: 313104**

442nd Regimental Combat Team, the Tuskegee Airmen, and the Navajo Code Talkers
The 442nd Regimental Combat Team consisted of Japanese-Americans fighting in Europe for the US. The most highly decorated unit per member in US history, they suffered a 93% casualty rate during the war. The Tuskegee Airmen were African-American aviators, the first black Americans allowed to fly for the military. In spite of being ineligible to become official navy pilots, they flew over 15,000 missions and were highly decorated. The Navajo Code Talkers were native Navajo who used their traditional language to transmit information among Allied forces. Because Navajo is a language and not simply a code, the Axis powers were never able to translate it. Use of Navajo Code Talkers to transmit information was instrumental in the taking of Iwo Jima and other major victories of the war.

Women during World War II
Women served widely in the military during WWII, working in numerous positions, including the Flight Nurses Corps. Women also moved into the workforce while men were overseas, leading to over 19 million women in the US workforce by 1944. Rosie the Riveter stood as a symbol of these women and a means of recruiting others to take needed positions. Women, as well as their families left behind during wartime, also grew Victory Gardens to help provide food.

Atomic bomb
The atomic bomb, developed during WWII, was the most powerful bomb ever invented. A single bomb, carried by a single plane, held enough power to destroy an entire city. This devastating effect was demonstrated with the bombing of Hiroshima and Nagasaki in 1945 in what later became a controversial move, but ended the war. The bombings resulted in as many as 150,000 immediate deaths and many more as time passed after the bombings, mostly due to radiation poisoning.

Whatever the arguments against the use of "The Bomb," the post WWII era saw many countries develop similar weapons to match the newly expanded military power of the US. The impact of those developments and use of nuclear weapons continues to haunt international relations today.

Yalta Conference and the Potsdam Conference

In February 1945, Joseph Stalin, Franklin D. Roosevelt and Winston Churchill met in Yalta to discuss the post-war treatment of the Axis nations, particularly Germany. Though Germany had not yet surrendered, its defeat was imminent. After Germany's official surrender, Joseph Stalin, Harry Truman (Roosevelt's successor), and Clement Attlee (replacing Churchill partway through the conference) met to formalize those plans.

This meeting was called the Potsdam Conference. Basic provisions of these agreements included:

- Dividing Germany and Berlin into four zones of occupation
- Demilitarization of Germany
- Poland remaining under Soviet control
- Outlawing the Nazi Party
- Trials for Nazi leaders
- Relocation of numerous German citizens
- The USSR joining the United Nations, established in 1945
- Establishment of the United Nations Security Council, consisting of the US, the UK, the USSR, China and France

Agreements made with post-war Japan

General Douglas MacArthur led the American military occupation of Japan after the country surrendered. The goals of the US occupation included removing Japan's military and making the country a democracy. A 1947 constitution removed power from the emperor and gave it to the people, as well as granting voting rights to women. Japan was no longer allowed to declare war, and a group of 28 government officials were tried for war crimes. In 1951, the US finally signed a peace treaty with Japan. This treaty allowed Japan to rearm itself for purposes of self-defense, but stripped the country of the empire it had built overseas.

Alien Registration Act and treatment of Japanese immigrants

In 1940, the US passed the Alien Registration Act, which required all aliens older than fourteen to be fingerprinted and registered. They were also required to report changes of address within five days.

Tension between whites and Japanese immigrants in California, which had been building since the beginning of the century, came to a head with the bombing of Pearl Harbor in 1941. Believing that even those Japanese living in the US were likely to be loyal to their native country, the president ordered numerous Japanese to be arrested on suspicion of subversive action and isolated in exclusion zones known as War Relocation Camps. Approximately 120,000 Japanese-Americans, two-thirds of them US citizens, were sent to these camps during the war.

General state of the US after World War II

Following WWII, the US became the strongest political power in the world, becoming a major player in world affairs and foreign policies. The US determined to stop the spread of communism, having named itself the "arsenal of democracy" during the war. In addition, America emerged with a greater sense of itself as a single, integrated nation, with many regional and economic differences diminished. The government worked for greater equality and the growth of communications increased contact among different areas of the country. Both the aftermath of the Great Depression and the necessities of WWII had given the government greater control over various institutions as well as the economy. This also meant that the American government took on greater responsibility for the well-being of its citizens, both in the domestic arena, such as providing basic needs, and in protecting them from foreign threats. This increased role of providing basic necessities for all Americans has been criticized by some as "the welfare state."

Harry S. Truman

Harry S. Truman took over the presidency from Franklin D. Roosevelt near the end of WWII. He made the final decision to drop atomic bombs on Japan and played a major role in the final decisions regarding treatment of post-war Germany. On the domestic front, Truman initiated a 21-point plan known as the Fair Deal. This plan expanded Social Security, provided public housing, and made the Fair Employment Practice Committee permanent. Truman helped support Greece and Turkey (which were under threat from the USSR), supported South Korea against communist North Korea, and helped with recovery in Western Europe. He also participated in the formation of NATO, the North Atlantic Treaty Organization.

Korean War

The Korean War began in 1950 and ended in 1953. For the first time in history, a world organization—the United Nations—played a military role in a war. North Korea sent communist troops into South Korea, seeking to bring the entire country under communist control. The UN sent out a call to member nations, asking them to support South Korea. Truman sent troops, as did many other UN member nations. The war ended three years later with a truce rather than a peace treaty, and Korea remains divided at the 38th parallel north, with communist rule remaining in the North and a democratic government ruling the South.

Dwight D. Eisenhower

Eisenhower carried out a middle-of-the-road foreign policy and brought the US several steps forward in equal rights. He worked to minimize tensions during the Cold War, and negotiated a peace treaty with Russia after the death of Stalin. He enforced desegregation by sending troops to Little Rock Central High School in Arkansas, as well as ordering the desegregation of the military. Organizations formed during his administration included the Department of Health, Education and Welfare, and the National Aeronautics and Space Administration (NASA).

John F. Kennedy

Although his term was cut short by his assassination, JFK instituted economic programs that led to a period of continuous expansion in the US unmatched since before WWII. He formed the Alliance for Progress and the Peace Corps, organizations intended to help developing nations. He also oversaw the passage of new civil rights legislation, and drafted plans to attack poverty and its causes, along with support of the arts. Kennedy's presidency ended when he was assassinated by Lee Harvey Oswald in 1963.

Cuban Missile Crisis

The Cuban Missile Crisis occurred in 1962, during John F. Kennedy's presidency. Russian Premier Nikita Khrushchev decided to place nuclear missiles in Cuba to protect the island from invasion by the US. An American U-2 plane flying over the island photographed the missile bases as they were being built. Tensions rose, with the US concerned about nuclear missiles so close to its shores, and the USSR concerned about American missiles that had been placed in Turkey. Eventually, the missile sites were removed, and a US naval blockade turned back Soviet ships carrying missiles to Cuba. During negotiations, the US agreed to remove their missiles from Turkey and agreed to sell surplus wheat to the USSR. A telephone hotline between Moscow and Washington was set up to allow instant communication between the two heads of state to prevent similar incidents in the future.

Lyndon B. Johnson

Kennedy's Vice President, Lyndon Johnson, assumed the presidency after Kennedy's assassination. He supported civil rights bills, tax cuts, and other wide-reaching legislation that Kennedy had also supported. Johnson saw America as a "Great Society," and enacted legislation to fight disease and poverty, renew urban areas, support education and environmental conservation. Medicare and Medicaid were instituted under his administration. He continued Kennedy's support of space exploration and he is also known, although less positively, for his handling of the Vietnam War.

Civil Rights Movement

In the 1950s, post-war America was experiencing a rapid growth in prosperity. However, African-Americans found themselves left behind. Following the lead of Mahatma Gandhi, who led similar class struggles in India, African-Americans began to demand equal rights. Major figures in this struggle included:

- Rosa Parks—often called the "mother of the Civil Rights Movement," her refusal to give up her seat on the bus to a white man served as a seed from which the movement grew.
- Martin Luther King, Jr.—the best-known leader of the movement, King drew on Gandhi's beliefs and encouraged non-violent opposition. He led a march on Washington in 1963, received the Nobel Peace Prize in 1964, and was assassinated in 1968.
- Malcolm X—espousing less peaceful means of change, Malcolm X became a Black Muslim, and supported black nationalism.
- Stokely Carmichael—Carmichael originated the term "Black Power" and served as head of the Student Nonviolent Coordinating Committee. He believed in black pride

and black culture, and felt separate political and social institutions should be developed for blacks.

- Adam Clayton Powell—chairman of the Coordinating Committee for Employment, he led rent strikes and other actions, as well as a bus boycott, to increase the hiring of blacks.
- Jesse Jackson—Jackson was selected to head the Chicago Operation Breadbasket in 1966, and went on to organize boycotts and other actions. He also had an unsuccessful run for President.

Three major events of the Civil Rights Movement are:

- Montgomery Bus Boycott—in 1955, Rosa Parks refused to give her seat on the bus to a white man. As a result, she was tried and convicted of disorderly conduct and of violating local ordinances. A 381-day bus boycott ensued, protesting segregation on public buses.
- Desegregation of Little Rock—in 1957, after the Supreme Court decision on Brown v. Board of Education, which declared "separate but equal" unconstitutional, the Arkansas school board voted to desegregate their schools. Even though Arkansas was considered progressive, its governor brought in the Arkansas National Guard to prevent nine black students from entering Central High School in Little Rock. President Eisenhower responded by federalizing the National Guard and ordering them to stand down.
- Birmingham Campaign—protestors organized a variety of actions such as sit-ins and an organized march to launch a voting campaign. When the City of Birmingham declared the protests illegal, the protestors, including Martin Luther King, Jr., persisted and were arrested and jailed.

Three major pieces of legislation passed as a result of the Civil Rights movement are:

- Brown v. Board of Education (1954)—the Supreme Court declared that "separate but equal" accommodations and services were unconstitutional.
- Civil Rights Act of 1964—this declared discrimination illegal in employment, education, or public accommodation.
- Voting Rights Act of 1965—this act ended various activities practiced, mostly in the South, to bar blacks from exercising their voting rights. These included poll taxes and literacy tests.

Vietnam War

After World War II, the US pledged, as part of its foreign policy, to come to the assistance of any country threatened by communism. When Vietnam was divided into a communist North and democratic South, much like Korea before it, the eventual attempts by the North to unify the country under Communist rule led to intervention by the US. On the home front, the Vietnam War became more and more unpopular politically, with Americans growing increasingly discontent with the inability of the US to achieve the goals it had set for the Asian country. When President Richard Nixon took office in 1969, his escalation of the war led to protests at Kent State in Ohio, during which several students were killed by National Guard troops. Protests continued, eventually resulting in the end of the compulsory draft in 1973. In that same year, the US departed Vietnam. In 1975, the south surrendered, and Vietnam became a unified country under communist rule.

US Cold War foreign policy acts

The following are US Cold War foreign policy acts and how they affected international relationships, especially between the US and the Soviet Union:

- Marshall Plan—this sent aid to war-torn Europe after WWII, largely focusing on preventing the spread of communism.
- Containment Policy—proposed by George F. Kennan, the containment policy focused on containing the spread of Soviet communism.
- Truman Doctrine—Harry S. Truman stated that the US would provide both economic and military support to any country threatened by Soviet takeover.
- National Security Act—passed in 1947, this act reorganized the government's military departments into the Department of Defense, as well as creating the Central Intelligence Agency and the National Security Council.

The combination of these acts led to the Cold War, with Soviet communists attempting to spread their influence and the US and other countries trying to contain or stop this spread.

> **Review Video:** The Cold War: The United States and Russia
> *Visit **mometrix.com/academy** and enter **Code**:* **981433**

NATO, the Warsaw Pact, and the Berlin Wall

NATO, the North Atlantic Treaty Organization, came into being in 1949. It essentially amounted to an agreement among the US and Western European countries that an attack on any one of these countries was to be considered an attack against the entire group.

Under the influence of the Soviet Union, the Eastern European countries of the USSR, Bulgaria, East Germany, Poland, Romania, Albania, Hungary, and Czechoslovakia responded with the Warsaw Pact, which created a similar agreement among those nations.

In 1961, a wall was built to separate communist East Berlin from democratic West Berlin. This was a literal representation of the "Iron Curtain" that separated the democratic and communist countries through the world.

Arms race

After World War II, major nations, particularly the US and USSR, rushed to develop highly advanced weapons systems such as the atomic bomb and later the hydrogen bomb. These countries seemed determined to outpace each other with the development of numerous, deadly weapons. These weapons were expensive and extremely dangerous, and it is possible that the war between US and Soviet interests remained "cold" due to the fear that one side or the other would use these powerful weapons.

End of the Cold War

In the late 1980s, Mikhail Gorbachev led the Soviet Union. He introduced a series of reform programs. Ronald Reagan famously urged Gorbachev to tear down the Berlin Wall as a gesture of growing freedom in the Eastern Bloc, and in 1989 it was demolished, ending the separation of East and West Germany. The Soviet Union relinquished its power over the various republics in Eastern Europe, and they became independent nations with their own individual governments. In 1991, the USSR was dissolved and the Cold War also came to an end.

> ➤ **Review Video:** The Cold War: Resolution
> *Visit **mometrix.com/academy** and enter **Code:*** **278032**

Technological advances after WWII

Numerous technological advances after the Second World War led to more effective treatment of diseases, more efficient communication and transportation, and new means of generating power. Advances in medicine increased the human lifespan in developed countries, and near-instantaneous communication opened up a myriad of possibilities. Some of these advances include:

- Discovery of penicillin (1928)
- Supersonic air travel (1947)
- Nuclear power plants (1951)
- Orbital satellite leading to manned space flight (Sputnik, 1957)
- First man on the moon (1969)

US policy toward immigrants after World War II

Prior to WWII, the US had been limiting immigration for several decades. After WWII, policy shifted slightly to accommodate political refugees from Europe and elsewhere. So many people were displaced by the war that in 1946, the UN formed the International Refugee Organization to deal with the problem. In 1948, the US Congress passed the Displaced Persons Act, which allowed over 400,000 European refugees to enter the US, most of them concentration camp survivors and refugees from Eastern Europe. In 1952, the United States Escapee Program (USEP) increased the quotas, allowing refugees from communist Europe to enter the US, as did the Refugee Relief Act, passed in 1953. At the same time, however, the Internal Security Act of 1950 allowed deportation of declared communists, and Asians were subjected to a quota based on race, rather than country of origin. Later changes included:

- Migration and Refugee Assistance Act (1962)—provided aid for refugees in need
- Immigration and Nationality Act (1965)—ended quotas based on nation of origin
- Immigration Reform and Control Act (1986)—prohibited the hiring of illegal immigrants, but also granted amnesty to about three million illegals already in the country

Expansion of minority rights

Several major acts have been passed, particularly since WWII, to protect the rights of minorities in America. These include:

- Civil Rights Act (1964)
- Voting Rights Act (1965)
- Age Discrimination Act (1967)
- Americans with Disabilities Act (1990)

Other important movements for civil rights included a prisoner's rights movement, movements for immigrant rights, and the women's rights movement. The National Organization for Women (NOW) was established in 1966 and worked to pass the Equal Rights Amendment. The amendment was passed, but not enough states ratified it for it to become part of the US Constitution.

Richard Nixon (R, 1969-1974)

Richard Nixon is best known for the Watergate scandal during his presidency, but other important events marked his tenure as president, including:

- End of the Vietnam War
- Improved diplomatic relations between the US and China, and the US and the USSR
- National Environmental Policy Act passed, providing for environmental protection
- Compulsory draft ended
- Supreme Court legalized abortion in Roe v. Wade
- Watergate

The Watergate scandal of 1972 ended Nixon's presidency. Rather than face impeachment and removal from office, he resigned in 1974.

Gerald Ford (R, 1974-1977)

Gerald Ford was appointed to the vice presidency after Nixon's vice president Spiro Agnew resigned in 1973 under charges of tax evasion. With Nixon's resignation, Ford became president.Ford's presidency saw negotiations with Russia to limit nuclear arms, as well as struggles to deal with inflation, economic downturn, and energy shortages. Ford's policies sought to reduce governmental control of various businesses and reduce the role of government overall. He also worked to prevent escalation of conflicts in the Middle East.

Jimmy Carter (D, 1977-1981)

Jimmy Carter was elected as president in 1976. Faced with a budget deficit, high unemployment, and continued inflation, Carter also dealt with numerous matters of international diplomacy including:

- Torrijos-Carter Treaties—the US gave control of the Panama Canal to Panama.
- Camp David Accords—negotiations between Anwar el-Sadat, the president of Egypt, and Menachem Begin, the Israeli Prime Minister, led to a peace treaty between Egypt and Israel.
- Strategic Arms Limitation Talks (SALT)—these led to agreements and treaties between the US and the Soviet Union.
- Iran Hostage Crisis—after the Shah of Iran was deposed, an Islamic cleric, Ayatollah Khomeini, came to power. The shah came to the US for medical treatment and Iran demanded his return so he could stand trial. In retaliation, a group of Iranian students stormed the US Embassy in Iran. Fifty-two American hostages were held for 444 days.
- Jimmy Carter was awarded the Nobel Peace Prize in 2002.

Ronald Reagan (R, 1981-1989)

Ronald Reagan, at 69, became the oldest American president. The two terms of his administration included notable events such as:

- Reaganomics, also known as supply-side, trickle-down, or free-market economics, major tax cuts
- Economic Recovery Tax Act of 1981
- First female justice appointed to the Supreme Court—Sandra Day O'Connor
- Massive increase in the national debt – from $1 trillion to $3 trillion
- Reduction of nuclear weapons via negotiations with Mikhail Gorbachev
- Iran-Contra scandal—cover-up of US involvement in revolutions in El Salvador and Nicaragua
- Deregulation of savings and loan industry
- Loss of the space shuttle *Challenger*

George H. W. Bush (R, 1989-1993)

Reagan's presidency was followed by a term under his former Vice President, George H. W. Bush. Bush's run for president included the famous "thousand points of light" speech, which was instrumental in increasing his standing in the election polls. During Bush's presidency, numerous international events took place, including:

- Fall of the Berlin wall and Germany's unification
- Panamanian dictator Manuel Noriega captured and tried on drug and racketeering charges
- Dissolution of the Soviet Union
- Gulf War, or Operation Desert Storm, triggered by Iraq's invasion of Kuwait
- Tiananmen Square Massacre in Beijing, China
- Ruby Ridge
- The arrival of the World Wide Web

Bill Clinton (D, 1993-2001)

William Jefferson "Bill" Clinton was the second president in US history to be impeached, but he was not convicted, and maintained high approval ratings in spite of the impeachment. Major events during his presidency included:

- Family and Medical Leave Act
- Don't Ask, Don't Tell, a compromise position regarding homosexuals serving in the military
- North American Free Trade Agreement, or NAFTA
- Defense of Marriage Act
- Oslo Accords
- Siege at Waco, Texas, involving the Branch Davidians led by David Koresh
- Bombing of the Murrah Federal Building in Oklahoma City, Oklahoma
- Troops sent to Haiti, Bosnia and Somalia to assist with domestic problems in those areas

George W. Bush (R, 2001-2009)

George W. Bush, son of George Herbert Walker Bush, became president after Clinton. Major events during his presidency included:

- September 11, 2001, al-Qaeda terrorists hijack commercial airliners and fly into the World Trade Center towers and the Pentagon, killing nearly 3000 Americans
- US troops sent to Afghanistan to hunt down al-Qaeda leaders, including the head of the organization, Osama Bin Laden; beginning of the War on Terror
- US troops sent to Iraq, along with a multinational coalition, to depose Saddam Hussein and prevent his deployment of suspected weapons of mass destruction
- Subprime mortgage crisis and near collapse of the financial industry, leading to the Great Recession; first of multiple government bailouts of the financial industry

Barack Obama (D, 2009-2017)

Barack Obama, a first-term senator from Illinois, became the first African-American president. Major events included:

- Multiple bailout packages and spending efforts, in an attempt to inject more money into a stagnant economy
- Massive increase in the national debt – from $10 trillion to $18 trillion
- Reinforcement of the War on Terror in Afghanistan and Iraq; additional deployment of troops in Libya and Syria
- Capture and execution of Osama Bin Laden
- Passage of the Affordable Care Act, legislation that greatly increased government involvement in the healthcare industry, and required every person living in the US to maintain health insurance coverage
- Moves to broaden gay rights, including the repeal of Clinton's Don't Ask, Don't Tell policy for homosexuals serving in the military

Donald Trump (R, 2017-)

Donald Trump, a billionaire real estate tycoon with no prior political experience, was elected to the presidency in a surprise victory over former First Lady and Secretary of State (under Obama) Hillary Clinton. His platform focused on increasing immigration enforcement to curb illegal immigration, restricting foreign trade to improve the dwindling American manufacturing industry, and repealing the Affordable Care Act passed during the prior administration.

Nez Perce tribe

The Nez Perce people lived in what is now southeast Washington, northeast Oregon, and Idaho. The name Nez Perce was given to the tribe by French trappers; it means "pierced nose." The members of the tribe refer to themselves as Nimiipuu. The Nez Perce caught salmon and small game to sustain themselves. In the 18th century, the tribe acquired horses, and became noted breeders and riders. At this point, they began to participate in buffalo hunts in the Great Plains. In 1855, the Nez Perce signed away much of their territory to the United States. As the American population grew in the succeeding decades, pressure was put on the tribe to give up even more land. When they resisted, a fraudulent treaty was drawn up, and the tribe was relocated to a reservation in northwest Idaho. At this point, there was an unsuccessful uprising led by Chief Joseph. There are currently only a few thousand Nez Perce in the United States.

Interactions between Native Americans and settlers

The Native American tribes of what would become Washington State were known for their totem poles, canoes, and masks. These tribes survived mainly by hunting salmon and small game, although some of the tribes along the Puget Sound also hunted whale. These tribes were often in armed conflict with settlers, but perhaps the most devastating blow to the native peoples was inflicted in the 1770s by smallpox. After this, the settlers slowly began to dominate the Native American tribes. The settlers forced many of the tribes to sign disadvantageous treaties and relinquish their lands, and the Native Americans who fought back were subdued by the settlers, who possessed greater numbers and superior weapons.

Oregon Country

The Oregon Country was the region of North America bordered on the west by the Pacific, on the east by the Rockies, on the south by the 42nd parallel, and on the north by Alaska, which at that time was owned by Russia. Before 1810, the region was mainly populated by Native Americans and British and French Canadian fur traders. In 1818, the U.S. and Great Britain agreed to share this property for ten years. This treaty ended up staying in effect until 1846, when the 49th parallel became the northern border. In 1853, the Washington Territory was established. Washington took on its present borders in 1863, when the Idaho Territory was created.

Oregon Trail

The Oregon Trail was the 2000-mile route along which many of the first non-Native American Washington inhabitants made their way west. The precise endpoints of the Oregon Trail are indistinct, but it is generally considered to have started around Independence, Missouri, and ended up in either Oregon City or on the coast of California, depending on whether the travelers took the northern or southern route. Use of the Oregon Trail began in the late 1830s, and by 1841 numerous wagon trains were making their way annually. There was a chain of forts to protect against raids by Native Americans. The Oregon Trail was used until the 1870s, when it fell into disrepair and was no longer passable. At this point, travel westward was accomplished mainly by train.

Chinook tribe

The Chinook tribe consisted of several smaller groups that resided in what is now Washington and Oregon. The Chinook mainly lived in the Columbia River valley. These people survived mainly as traders, traveling as far east as the Great Plains to make their exchanges. Their most popular wares included canoes, dried salmon, and, occasionally, slaves. The religion of the Chinook centered on the salmon, which they relied on for sustenance. Lewis and Clark described interactions with the Chinook. Smallpox decimated the tribe in the early 19th century, and the Chinook people who were left joined other tribes or moved to reservations. There are now just over a thousand Chinook in the United States.

Great Migration on Washington State

From 1915 to 1930, over a million African Americans moved from the Southeast to the major cities of the Northeast, the Midwest, and the West. Although California received many more African American immigrants than Washington, the northwestern-most state saw a sharp increase in its African American population. In particular, many new citizens moved to inner-city Seattle, where they competed for manufacturing jobs. African Americans also sought better schools and a more tolerant society than they had found in the South. Although this move was a good economic decision for most African Americans, there were instances of employee abuse. African Americans tended to live in close proximity to one another, and did not integrate into the preexisting business and government leadership hierarchies.

Conflicts between Great Britain and the United States

In the early 19th century, the United States became increasingly interested in taking control of the Pacific Northwest. However, Great Britain's Hudson Bay Company had a well-established operation in what was then called the Columbia District. After the War of 1812, the United States and Great Britain decided to share ownership of the Oregon Territory, which included the Columbia District. At around the same time, both Spain and Russia relinquished any claims to this region. American settlers and British fur traders continued to step on each other's toes, however, and eventually it became necessary to split the territory. The United States took everything below the 49th parallel, and Great Britain kept everything above.

Stevens treaties

In the mid-nineteenth century, advances in transportation accelerated the pace of settlement in Washington. During this period, there was relatively little conflict with Native Americans. One exception was the campaigns of Isaac Stevens, the first governor of Washington Territory. Stevens aggressively negotiated with Native American leaders, essentially forcing them to sign over the rights to land at gunpoint. Indeed, many of the tribes who resisted Stevens' treaties were massacred by federal troops. Despite numerous complaints from other settlers, President Franklin Pierce refused to remove Stevens from his post. Many scholars believe that even though he was already deceased, Stevens was responsible for the bloody war with the Nez Perce.

Early settlements in eastern Washington

The early settlements of eastern Washington were mainly populated by missionaries and farmers. Most of these settlements were in what is now known as the Walla Walla Valley. American and British Christians sought to convert Native Americans, despite the natives' general reluctance. There were occasional conflicts between Native Americans and missionaries like Mr. and Mrs. Marcus Whitman, who were blamed when natives died en masse from smallpox. The Whitmans are believed to have been killed by members of the Cayuse tribe. Eventually, these conflicts led the federal government to force Native Americans into disadvantageous treaties and onto reservations. Even these arrangements were subsequently violated when gold was found on the Yakima reservation.

Early settlements around the Puget Sound

The Oregon Trail led many settlers to the area around the Puget Sound. Fort Nisqually was a major early farm and trading post in this area. In 1846, George Washington Bush, an African American, established a small settlement called New Market. There were occasional conflicts between settlers and indigenous people, but for the most part the opposing sides coexisted peacefully. Soon, the extensive lumber around the Puget Sound attracted business. Seattle, originally known as Duwamps, was established in 1853 as an outpost of the burgeoning lumber industry. These small towns were notorious for their lawlessness and incivility. The Gold Rush in British Columbia and Alaska in the late 19th century only accelerated the pace of migration to the Puget Sound area, which prospectors used as a way station on their journey to the frontier.

Washington's achievement of statehood

The boundary between Washington and Canada was established in an 1846 treaty with Great Britain. Washington became a territory in 1853, and was redefined to its present borders in 1863. This property was acquired by the United States in the 1846 Oregon Treaty. The Washington Territory was originally known as the Columbia Territory, but Congressman Richard Stanton of Kentucky passed a measure to name it after the first president. Washington was finally admitted to the union in 1889, along with North Dakota, South Dakota, and Montana. This move was, in part, a response to the rapidly increasing population in the region. Between 1880 and 1890, the population of Washington nearly quadrupled. Washington is considered the 42nd state; its capital is in Olympia.

Seattle General Strike of 1919

During the Seattle General Strike of February, 1919, approximately 65,000 workers protested low wages and the loss of shipyard jobs due to demobilization after World War I. The strike was organized by the Industrial Workers of the World, which had been a major influence in logging camps and farms, and the American Federation of Labor. In the years before the strike, both of these organizations were very powerful among workers. The Seattle General Strike lasted for less than one week. After the federal government moved troops into the area, the organizers of the strike decided to relent. Afterwards, the IWW and AFL lost the public relations battle; their opponents warned people that a Communist takeover of the working class was underway. This climate of paranoia paved the way for repressive anti-labor policies.

Columbia Basin

Over the last two centuries, the Columbia Basin has been transformed from an arid plain into one of the more productive pieces of farmland in North America. In the 19th century, efforts were made to irrigate the valleys around the Columbia River. Once this was done, farmers were successful in cultivating fruit (particularly apples), vegetables, and hay. The most striking step in the development of the Columbia Basin was the construction of the Grand Coulee Dam, which was completed in 1942. This enormous structure continues to provide hydroelectric power and water, and has made the Columbia Basin even more fertile. These days, wheat, fruit, and dairy products are the main goods produced in the region.

Gilded Age, World War I, and the Great Depression on Washington State

Washington became the 42nd state in 1889. During the first years of its statehood, it was perhaps best known as the chief port for Alaska, which was in the middle of a gold rush. For the first 40 years, Republicans dominated the state government. During this period, the state made a number of progressive policy changes, including a direct primary (1907), women's suffrage (1910), workmen's compensation (1911), and initiative, referendum, and recall (1913). The city of Tacoma became known as a prime smelter of precious metals. During World War I, the shipbuilding and lumber industries thrived in western Washington. The Great Depression, however, hit Washington hard, and many of the industries that had thrived during wartime were no longer profitable. It was during this period that the state undertook many of its greatest infrastructure projects, including the Grand Coulee Dam.

Hanford Engineering Works for Washington State

The Hanford Engineering Works was a nuclear power plant along the Columbia River operated by the federal government. This complex was established in 1943, and played a crucial role in the Manhattan Project, which resulted in the production of the first atomic bombs. The Hanford site was responsible for the first reactor capable of producing weapons-grade plutonium. Some of the plutonium made there ended up in the bomb detonated over Nagasaki. After World War II, Hanford continued to produce plutonium for the American nuclear arsenal. Unfortunately, the safety measures used during Hanford's early days were inadequate, and the land and people of the area suffered from exposure to harmful radiation. The Hanford Engineering Works is no longer in operation. The site is currently mainly used to research the effects of radiation on the environment.

Boeing Company for Washington State

The Boeing Company is the largest aerospace company in the world, and is one of the largest employers in Washington State. The company was first incorporated by William Boeing in 1916, although it did not become the Boeing Airplane Company until 1934. It quickly became one of the largest manufacturers of planes for both the military and private sectors. Boeing also supplies much of the equipment used by NASA. Indeed, the Apollo 11 mission that put the first man on the moon was in large part accomplished with parts made by Boeing. At present, the Boeing Company employs approximately 75,000 people in Washington State. The company has dozens of subsidiaries throughout the world, and now maintains its headquarters in Chicago.

Microsoft for Washington State

Microsoft is the world's largest software manufacturer. For all intents and purposes, it has a monopoly on operating systems for personal computers. Microsoft Windows is the operating system which most people must learn in order to become computer literate. Microsoft was founded in 1975 by Bill Gates and Paul Allen. Gates and Allen were young men from Seattle who believed that computers had the potential to revolutionize daily life. From the beginning, the company specialized in developing computer operating systems. The first of these was known as BASIC. This system made personal computing possible. In Washington State, Microsoft is the biggest example of a thriving high-tech industry. The corporation is headquartered in Redmond, WA.

Economic development of Washington State since the end of World War II

Even after World War II, Washington remained a major provider of military supplies for the federal government. The need to maintain an arsenal competitive with that of the Soviet Union ensured major growth for Boeing during the Cold War. During this period, the Hanford site continued to produce weapons-grade plutonium for the American nuclear arsenal. In the 1970s and 80s, Washington became known as a haven for technology businesses. The state has also taken advantage of its location to set up lucrative trade deals with Asia. Throughout the postwar period, lumber, apples, and fish continued to be major exports of Washington State. Continued irrigation of the Columbia Basin has made that region among the most fertile pieces of farmland in the nation.

Boldt Decision

In *United States v. Washington* (1974), commonly known as the Boldt Decision, the United States District Court ruled that Native American tribes in Washington State had the right to harvest salmon. The ruling declared that when the Native Americans signed over their ownership of the land, they retained the right to continue fishing. Indeed, most of the relevant treaties contained specific language granting Native Americans continued access to salmon. The case followed a long period during which the Washington State government had restricted the fishing rights of Native Americans. According to the district court's ruling, Native American fishermen had the right to harvest up to 50% of the available salmon in Washington State. The Boldt Decision, named after the judge who wrote it, remains in effect today.

Globalization

The positive and negative consequences of globalization have been important topics during the last few decades in Washington State. Boeing and Microsoft are just two large Washington-based businesses that have offices and factories all over the world. Although many manufacturing jobs have gone overseas, Washington has benefited from the tech boom of the last decade, as many California businesses have moved north. Still, there remains a staunch anti-globalization movement in the Pacific Northwest. In 1999, the controversy came to a head when the World Trade Organization held meetings in Seattle. At least 40,000 people gathered in the streets to protest the WTO's role in promoting globalization. There were also some violent altercations between police and protesters in this so-called "Battle of Seattle."

Environmental protection

The abundant natural resources and astounding scenic beauty of Washington State have underscored the need for environmental protection. Over the past few decades, government officials have instituted policies to protect both lumber and salmon. For a time, there was concern that salmon had been overfished to the point that it might be impossible for the population to recover. In addition, the Environmental Protection Agency has done extensive work to maintain the timber of the Cascade region while still allowing the logging industry to thrive. There are three national parks in the state: Mount Rainier, North Cascades, and Olympic. In addition, there are two national monuments (Mount Saint Helens and Hanford Reach), as well as numerous national forests and other protected lands.

Immigration and migrant labor

Washington State has always had a diverse population. In 2004, it was estimated that 631,500 foreign-born citizens and 100,000 illegal aliens were living in Washington. The largest self-identified ethnic group in the state is Germans, although most of these people are second- or third-generation citizens. There is a large population of Mexican migrant workers in the southeast-central part of Washington. Washington also has the fourth largest population of Asian Americans of any state. In 1997, Gary Locke became the first Asian American governor in the nation's history. Businesses have taken advantage of this demographic to trade with Japan, China, and Korea. Finally, there is considerable commercial traffic between Washington State and the Canadian province of British Columbia.

Prehistory

Prehistory is the period of human history before writing was developed. The three major periods of prehistory are:

- Lower Paleolithic—Humans used crude tools.
- Upper Paleolithic—Humans began to develop a wider variety of tools. These tools were better made and more specialized. They also began to wear clothes, organize in groups with definite social structures, and to practice art. Most lived in caves during this time period.
- Neolithic—Social structures became even more complex, including growth of a sense of family and the ideas of religion and government. Humans learned to domesticate animals and produce crops, build houses, start fires with friction tools, and to knit, spin and weave.

Anthropology

Anthropology is the study of human culture. Anthropologists study groups of humans, how they relate to each other, and the similarities and differences between these different groups and cultures. Anthropological research takes two approaches: cross-cultural research and comparative research. Most anthropologists work by living among different cultures and participating in those cultures in order to learn about them. There are four major divisions within anthropology:

- Biological anthropology
- Cultural anthropology
- Linguistic anthropology
- Archaeology

Archeology

Archeology studies past human cultures by evaluating what they leave behind. This can include bones, buildings, art, tools, pottery, graves, and even trash. Archeologists maintain detailed notes and records of their findings and use special tools to evaluate what they find. Photographs, notes, maps, artifacts, and surveys of the area can all contribute to evaluation of an archeological site. By studying all these elements of numerous archeological sites, scientists have been able to theorize that humans or near-humans have existed for about 600,000 years. Before that, more primitive humans are believed to have appeared about one million years ago. These humans eventually developed into Cro-Magnon man, and then Homo sapiens, or modern man.

Human development from the Lower Paleolithic to the Iron Age

Human development has been divided into several phases:

- Lower Paleolithic or Early Stone Age, beginning two to three million years ago—early humans used tools like needles, hatchets, awls, and cutting tools.
- Middle Paleolithic or Middle Stone Age, beginning approximately 300,000 B.C.E.—sophisticated stone tools were developed, along with hunting, gathering, and ritual practices.
- Upper Paleolithic or Late Stone Age, beginning approximately 40,000 B.C.E.—including the Mesolithic and Neolithic eras, textiles and pottery are developed. Humans of this era discovered the wheel, began to practice agriculture, made polished tools, and had some domesticated animals.
- Bronze Age, beginning in approximately 3,000 B.C.E.—metals are discovered and the first civilizations emerge as humans become more technologically advanced.
- Iron Age, beginning in 1,200 to 1,000 B.C.E.—metal tools replace stone tools as humans develop knowledge of smelting.

Civilizations

Civilizations are defined as having the following characteristics:

- Use of metal to make weapons and tools
- Written language
- A defined territorial state
- A calendar

The earliest civilizations developed in river valleys where reliable, fertile land was easily found, including:

- The Nile River Valley in Egypt
- Mesopotamia
- The Indus Valley
- Hwang Ho in China

The very earliest civilizations developed in the Tigris-Euphrates valley in Mesopotamia, which is now part of Iraq, and in Egypt's Nile valley. These civilizations arose between 5,000 and 3,000 B.C.E. The area where these civilizations grew is known as the Fertile Crescent. Geography and the availability of water made large-scale human habitation possible.

<u>Importance of rivers and water</u>

The earliest civilizations are also referred to as fluvial civilizations because they were founded near rivers. Rivers and the water they provide were vital to these early groupings, offering:

- Water for drinking, cultivating crops, and caring for domesticated animals
- A gathering place for wild animals that could be hunted
- Rich soil deposits as a result of regular flooding

Irrigation techniques helped direct water where it was most needed, to sustain herds of domestic animals and to nourish crops of increasing size and quality.

Fertile Crescent

James Breasted, an archeologist from the University of Chicago, popularized the term "Fertile Crescent" to describe the area in the Near East where the earliest civilizations arose. The region includes modern day Iraq, Syria, Lebanon, Israel, Palestine, and Jordan. It is bordered on the south by the Syrian and Arabian Deserts, the west by the Mediterranean Sea, and to the north and east by the Taurus and Zagros Mountains respectively. This area not only provided the raw materials for the development of increasingly advanced civilizations, but also saw waves of migration and invasion, leading to the earliest wars and genocides as groups conquered and absorbed each other's cultures and inhabitants.

Sumerian, Egyptian, Babylonian, and Assyrian cultures

The Sumerians were the first to invent the wheel, and also brought irrigation systems into use. Their cuneiform writing was simpler than Egyptian hieroglyphs, and they developed the timekeeping system we still use today.

> ➢ **Review Video:** Early Mesopotamia: The Sumerians
> *Visit **mometrix.com/academy** and enter **Code**:* **939880**

The Egyptians were one of the most advanced ancient cultures, having developed construction methods to build the great pyramids, as well as a form of writing known as hieroglyphics. Their religion was highly developed and complex, and included advanced techniques for the preservation of bodies after death. They also made paper by processing papyrus, a plant commonly found along the Nile, invented the decimal system, devised a solar calendar, and advanced overall knowledge of mathematics.

> ➢ **Review Video:** Egyptians
> *Visit **mometrix.com/academy** and enter **Code**:* **398041**

The Babylonians are best known for the Code of Hammurabi, an advanced law code.

> ➢ **Review Video:** Early Mesopotamia: The Babylonians
> *Visit **mometrix.com/academy** and enter **Code**:* **340325**

The Assyrians developed horse-drawn chariots and an organized military.

Hebrew, Persian, Minoan, and Mycenaean cultures

The Hebrew or ancient Israelite culture developed the monotheistic religion that eventually developed into modern Judaism and Christianity.

The Persians were conquerors, but those they conquered were allowed to keep their own laws, customs, and religious traditions rather than being forced to accept those of their conquerors. They also developed an alphabet and practiced Zoroastrianism and Mithraism, religions that have influenced modern religious practice.

The Minoans used a syllabic writing system and built large, colorful palaces. These ornate buildings included sewage systems, running water, bathtubs, and even flushing toilets. Their script, known as Linear A, has yet to be deciphered.

The Mycenaeans practiced a religion that grew into the Greek pantheon, worshipping Zeus and other Olympian gods. They developed Linear B, a writing system used to write the earliest known form of Greek.

Phoenicians and early culture in India and ancient China

Skilled seafarers and navigators, the Phoenicians used the stars to navigate their ships at night. They developed a purple dye that was in great demand in the ancient world, and worked with glass and metals. They also devised a phonetic alphabet, using symbols to represent individual sounds rather than whole words or syllables.

In the Indus Valley, an urban civilization arose in what is now India. These ancient humans developed the concept of zero in mathematics, practiced an early form of the Hindu religion, and developed the caste system which is still prevalent in India today. Archeologists are still uncovering information about this highly developed ancient civilization.

In ancient China, human civilization developed along the Yangtze and Yellow Rivers. These people produced silk, grew millet, and made pottery, including Longshan black pottery.

Civilizations of Mesopotamia

The major civilizations of Mesopotamia, in what is now called the Middle East, were:

- Sumerians
- Amorites
- Hittites
- Assyrians
- Chaldeans
- Persians

These cultures controlled different areas of Mesopotamia during various time periods, but were similar in that they were autocratic: a single ruler served as the head of the government and often was the main religious ruler as well. These rulers were often tyrannical, militaristic leaders who controlled all aspects of life, including law, trade, and religious activity. Portions of the legacies of these civilizations remain in cultures today. These include mythologies, religious systems, mathematical innovations and even elements of various languages.

Sumer

Sumer, located in the southern part of Mesopotamia, consisted of a dozen city-states. Each city-state had its own gods, and the leader of each city-state also served as the high priest. Cultural legacies of Sumer include:

- The invention of writing
- Invention of the wheel
- The first library—established in Assyria by Ashurbanipal

- The Hanging Gardens of Babylon—one of the Seven Wonders of the Ancient World
- First written laws—Ur-Nammu's Codes and the Codes of Hammurabi
- The *Epic of Gilgamesh*—the first recorded epic story

Kushite culture

Kush, or Cush, was located in Nubia, south of ancient Egypt, and the earliest existing records of this civilization were found in Egyptian texts. At one time, Kush was the largest empire on the Nile River, ruling not only Nubia but Upper and Lower Egypt as well.

In Neolithic times, Kushites lived in villages, with buildings made of mud bricks. They were settled rather than nomadic, and practiced hunting and fishing, cultivated grain, and also herded cattle. Kerma, the capital, was a major center of trade.

Kush determined leadership through matrilineal descent of their kings, as did Egypt. Their heads of state, the Kandake or Kentake, were female. Their polytheistic religion included the primary Egyptian gods as well as regional gods, including a lion-headed god, which is commonly found in African cultures.

Archeological evidence indicates the Kushites were a mix of Mediterranean and Negroid peoples. Kush was conquered by the Aksumite Empire in the 4th century CE.

Minoan civilization

The Minoans lived on the island of Crete, just off the coast of Greece. This civilization reigned from approximately 4000 to 1400 B.C.E. and is considered to be the first advanced civilization in Europe. The Minoans developed writing systems known to linguists as Linear A and Linear B. Linear A has not yet been translated; Linear B evolved into classical Greek script. "Minoans" is not the name they used for themselves, but is instead a variation on the name of King Minos, a king in Greek mythology believed by some to have been a denizen of Crete. The Minoan civilization subsisted on trade, and their way of life was often disrupted by earthquakes and volcanoes. Much is still unknown about the Minoans, and archeologists continue to study their architecture and archeological remains. The Minoan culture eventually fell to Greek invaders and was supplanted by the Mycenaean civilization.

Influences of ancient Indian civilization

The civilizations of ancient India gave rise to both Hinduism and Buddhism, major world religions that have influenced countries far from their place of origin. Practices such as yoga, increasingly popular in the West, can trace their roots to these earliest Indian civilizations, and the poses are still formally referred to by Sanskrit names. Literature from ancient India includes the *Mahabharata* containing the *Bhagavad Gita*, the *Ramayana*, *Arthashastra*, and the *Vedas*, a collection of sacred texts. Indo-European languages, including English, find their beginnings in these ancient cultures. Ancient Indo-Aryan languages such as Sanskrit are still used in some formal Hindu practices.

Earliest civilizations in China

Many historians believe Chinese civilization is the oldest uninterrupted civilization in the world. The Neolithic age in China goes back to 10,000 B.C.E., with agriculture in China beginning as early as 5,000 B.C.E. Their system of writing dates to 1,500 B.C.E. The Yellow River served as the center for the earliest Chinese settlements. In Ningxia, in northwest China, there are carvings on cliffs that date back to the Paleolithic Period, indicating the extreme antiquity of Chinese culture. Literature from ancient China includes Confucius' *Analects*, the *Tao Te Ching*, and a variety of poetry.

Ancient American cultures

Less is known of ancient American civilizations since less was left behind. Some of the more well-known cultures include:

- The Norte Chico civilization in Peru, an agricultural society of up to 30 individual communities, existed over 5,000 years ago. This culture is also known as the Caral-Supe civilization, and is the oldest known civilization in the Americas.
- The Anasazi, or Ancestral Pueblo People, lived in what is now the southwestern United States. Emerging about 1200 B.C.E., the Anasazi built complex adobe dwellings and were the forerunners of later Pueblo Indian cultures.
- The Maya emerged in southern Mexico and northern Central America as early as 2,600 B.C.E. They developed a written language and a complex calendar.

> **Review Video:** American Civilizations: Early Cultures
> *Visit **mometrix.com/academy** and enter **Code**:* **575452**

> **Review Video:** American Civilizations: The Mayas
> *Visit **mometrix.com/academy** and enter **Code**:* **556527**

Mycenaean civilization

In contrast to the Minoans, whom they displaced, the Mycenaeans relied more on conquest than on trade. Mycenaean states included Sparta, Athens, and Corinth. The history of this civilization, including the Trojan War, was recorded by the Greek poet, Homer. His work was largely considered mythical until archeologists discovered evidence of the city of Troy in Hisarlik, Turkey. Archeologists continue to add to the body of information about this ancient culture, translating documents written in Linear B, a script derived from the Minoan Linear A. It is theorized that the Mycenaean civilization was eventually destroyed in either a Dorian invasion or an attack by Greek invaders from the north.

Dorian invasion

A Dorian invasion does not refer to an invasion by a particular group of people, but rather is a hypothetical theory to explain the end of the Mycenaean civilization and the growth of classical Greece. Ancient tradition refers to these events as "the return of the Heracleidae," or the sons (descendents) of Hercules. Archeologists and historians still do not know exactly who conquered the Mycenaeans, but it is believed to have occurred around 1200 B.C.E., contemporaneous with the destruction of the Hittite civilization in what is now modern Turkey. The Hittites speak of an attack by people of the Aegean Sea, or the "Sea People." Only Athens was left intact.

Spartans and Athenians

Both powerful city-states, Sparta and Athens fought each other in the Peloponnesian War (431-404 B.C.E.). Despite their proximity, the Spartans and the Athenians nurtured contrasting cultures:

- The Spartans, located in Peloponnesus, were ruled by an oligarchic military state. They practiced farming, disallowed trade for Spartan citizens, and valued military arts and strict discipline. They emerged as the strongest military force in the area, and maintained this status for many years. In one memorable encounter, a small group of Spartans held off a huge army of Persians at Thermopylae.
- The Athenians were centered in Attica, where the land was rocky and unsuitable for farming. Like the Spartans, they descended from invaders who spoke Greek. Their government was very different from Sparta's; it was in Athens that democracy was created by Cleisthenes of Athens in 508 B.C.E. Athenians excelled in art, theater, architecture, and philosophy.

Contributions of ancient Greece

Ancient Greece made numerous major contributions to cultural development, including:

- Theater—Aristophanes and other Greek playwrights laid the groundwork for modern theatrical performance.
- Alphabet—the Greek alphabet, derived from the Phoenician alphabet, developed into the Roman alphabet, and then into our modern-day alphabet.
- Geometry—Pythagoras and Euclid pioneered much of the system of geometry still taught today. Archimedes made various mathematical discoveries, including calculating a very accurate value of pi.
- Historical writing—much of ancient history doubles as mythology or religious texts. Herodotus and Thucydides made use of research and interpretation to record historical events.
- Philosophy—Socrates, Plato, and Aristotle served as the fathers of Western philosophy. Their work is still required reading for philosophy students.

Alexander the Great

Born to Philip II of Macedon and tutored by Aristotle, Alexander the Great is considered one of the greatest conquerors in history. He conquered Egypt, the Achaemenid/Persian Empire, a powerful empire founded by Cyrus the Great that spanned three continents, and he traveled as far as India and the Iberian Peninsula. Though Alexander died from malaria at age 32, his conquering efforts spread Greek culture into the east. This cultural diffusion left a greater mark on history than did his empire, which fell apart due to internal conflict not long after his death. Trade between the East and West increased, as did an exchange of ideas and beliefs that influenced both regions greatly. The Hellenistic traditions his conquest spread were prevalent in Byzantine culture until as late as the 15th century.

Hittite Empire

The Hittites were centered in what is now Turkey, but their empire extended into Palestine and Syria. They conquered the Babylonian civilization, but adopted their religion, laws, and literature. Overall, the Hittites tended to tolerate other religions, unlike many other contemporary cultures, and absorbed foreign gods into their own belief systems rather than forcing their religion onto peoples they conquered. The Hittite Empire reached its peak in 1600-1200 B.C.E. After a war with Egypt, which weakened them severely, they were eventually conquered by the Assyrians.

Persian Wars

The Persian Empire, ruled by Cyrus the Great, encompassed an area from the Black Sea to Afghanistan, and beyond into Central Asia. After the death of Cyrus, Darius I became king in 522 B.C.E. The empire reached its zenith during his reign and Darius attempted to conquer Greece as well. From 499-449 B.C.E., the Greeks and Persians fought in the Persian Wars. The Peace of Callias brought an end to the fighting, after the Greeks were able to repel the invasion.

Battles of the Persian Wars included:

- The Battle of Marathon—heavily outnumbered Greek forces managed to achieve victory.
- The Battle of Thermopylae—a small band of Spartans held off a throng of Persian troops for several days before Persia defeated the Greeks and captured an evacuated Athens.
- The Battle of Salamis—this was a naval battle that again saw outnumbered Greeks achieving victory.
- The Battle of Plataea—this was another Greek victory, but one in which they outnumbered the Persians. This ended the invasion of Greece.

Maurya Empire

The Maurya Empire was a large, powerful empire established in India. It was one of the largest ever to rule in the Indian subcontinent, and existed from 322 to 185 B.C.E., ruled by Chandragupta Maurya after the withdrawal from India of Alexander the Great. The Maurya Empire was highly developed, including a standardized economic system, waterways, and private corporations. Trade to the Greeks and others became common, with goods including silk, exotic foods, and spices. Religious development included the rise of Buddhism and Jainism. The laws of the Maurya Empire protected not only civil and social rights of the citizens, but also protected animals, establishing protected zones for economically important creatures such as elephants, lions and tigers. This period of time in Indian history was largely peaceful, perhaps due to the strong Buddhist beliefs of many of its leaders.

The empire finally fell after a succession of weak leaders, and was taken over by Demetrius, a Greco-Bactrian king who took advantage of this lapse in leadership to conquer southern Afghanistan and Pakistan around 180 B.C.E., forming the Indo-Greek Kingdom.

Chinese dynasties

In China, history was divided into a series of dynasties. The most famous of these, the Han dynasty, existed from 206 B.C.E. to 220 CE. Accomplishments of the Chinese Empires included:

- Building the Great Wall of China
- Numerous inventions, including paper, paper money, printing, and gunpowder
- High level of artistic development
- Silk production

The Chinese dynasties were comparable to Rome as far as their artistic and intellectual accomplishments, as well as the size and scope of their influence.

Roman Republic and Empire

Rome began humbly, in a single town that grew out of Etruscan settlements and traditions, founded, according to legend, by twin brothers Romulus and Remus, who were raised by wolves. Romulus killed Remus, and from his legacy grew Rome. A thousand years later, the Roman Empire covered a significant portion of the known world, from what is now Scotland, across Europe, and into the Middle East. Hellenization, or the spread of Greek culture throughout the world, served as an inspiration and a model for the spread of Roman culture. Rome brought in belief systems of conquered peoples as well as their technological and scientific accomplishments, melding the disparate parts into a Roman core. Rome began as a republic ruled by consuls, but after the assassination of Julius Caesar, it became an empire led by emperors. Rome's overall government was autocratic, but local officials came from the provinces where they lived. This limited administrative system was probably a major factor in the long life of the empire.

Byzantine Empire

In the early fourth century, the Roman Empire split, with the eastern portion becoming the Eastern Empire, or the Byzantine Empire. In 330 CE, Constantine founded the city of Constantinople, which became the center of the Byzantine Empire. Its major influences came from Mesopotamia and Persia, in contrast to the Western Empire, which maintained traditions more closely linked to Greece and Carthage. Byzantium's position gave it an advantage over invaders from the west and the east, as well as control over trade from both regions. It protected the Western empire from invasion from the Persians and the Ottomans, and practiced a more centralized rule than in the West. The Byzantines were famous for lavish art and architecture, as well as the Code of Justinian, which collected Roman law into a clear system. The Byzantine Empire finally fell to the Ottomans in 1453.

Nicene Creed

The Byzantine Empire was Christian-based but incorporated Greek language, philosophy and literature and drew its law and government policies from Rome. However, there was as yet no unified doctrine of Christianity, as it was a relatively new religion that had spread rapidly and without a great deal of organization. In 325, the First Council of Nicaea addressed this issue. From this conference came the Nicene Creed, addressing the Trinity and other basic Christian beliefs. The Council of Chalcedon in 451 further defined the view of the Trinity.

Fall of the Western Roman Empire

Germanic tribes, including the Visigoths, Ostrogoths, Vandals, Saxons and Franks, controlled most of Europe. The Roman Empire faced major opposition on that front. The increasing size of the empire also made it harder to manage, leading to dissatisfaction throughout the empire as Roman government became less efficient. Germanic tribes refused to adhere to the Nicene Creed, instead following Arianism, which led the Roman Catholic Church to declare them heretics. The Franks proved a powerful military force in their defeat of the

Muslims in 732. In 768, Charlemagne became king of the Franks. These tribes waged several wars against Rome, including the invasion of Britannia by the Angles and Saxons. Far-flung Rome lost control over this area of its Empire, and eventually Rome itself was invaded.

Iconoclasm and conflict between Roman Catholic and Eastern Orthodox churches

Emperor Leo III ordered the destruction of all icons throughout the Byzantine Empire. Images of Jesus were replaced with crosses, and images of Jesus, Mary or other religious figures were considered blasphemy on grounds of idolatry. Pope Gregory II, called a synod to discuss the issue. The synod declared that the images were not heretical, and that strong disciplinary measures would result for anyone who destroyed them. Leo's response was an attempt to kill Pope Gregory, but this plan ended in failure.

Viking invasions

Vikings invaded Northern France in the tenth century, eventually becoming the Normans. Originating in Scandinavia, the Vikings were accomplished seafarers with advanced knowledge of trade routes. With overpopulation plaguing their native lands, they began to travel. From the eighth to the eleventh centuries, they spread throughout Europe, conquering and colonizing. Vikings invaded and colonized England in several waves, including the Anglo-Saxon invasions that displaced Roman control. Their influence remained significant in England, affecting everything from the language of the country to place names and even the government and social structure. By 900, Vikings had settled in Iceland. They proceeded then to Greenland and eventually to North America, arriving in the New World even before the Spanish and British who claimed the lands several centuries later. They also traded with the Byzantine Empire until the eleventh century when their significant level of activity came to an end.

Tenth century events in the West and the East

In Europe, the years 500-1000 CE are largely known as the Dark Ages. In the tenth century, numerous Viking invasions disrupted societies that had been more settled under Roman rule. Vikings settled in Northern France, eventually becoming the Normans. By the eleventh century, Europe would rise again into the High Middle Ages with the beginning of the Crusades.

In China, wars also raged. This led the Chinese to make use of gunpowder for the first time in warfare.

In the Americas, the Mayan Empire was winding down while the Toltec became more prominent. Pueblo Indian culture was also at its zenith.

In the East, the Muslims and the Byzantine Empire were experiencing a significant period of growth and development.

European feudalism in the Middle Ages

A major element of the social and economic life of Europe, feudalism developed as a way to ensure European rulers would have the wherewithal to quickly raise an army when necessary. Vassals swore loyalty and promised to provide military service for lords, who in return offered a fief, or a parcel of land, for them to use to generate their livelihood. Vassals could work the land themselves, have it worked by peasants or serfs—workers who had few rights and were little more than slaves—or grant the fief to someone else. The king legally owned all the land, but in return promised to protect the vassals from invasion and war. Vassals returned a certain percentage of their income to the lords, who in turn passed a portion of their income on to the king. A similar practice was manorialism, in which the feudal system was applied to a self-contained manor. These manors were often owned by the lords who ran them, but were usually included in the same system of loyalty and promises of protection that drove feudalism.

Influence of the Roman Catholic Church

The Roman Catholic Church extended significant influence both politically and economically throughout medieval society. The church supplied education, as there were no established schools or universities. To a large extent, the church had filled a power void left by various invasions throughout the former Roman Empire, leading it to exercise a role that was far more political than religious. Kings were heavily influenced by the Pope and other church officials, and churches controlled large amounts of land throughout Europe.

Black Death

The Black Death, believed to be bubonic plague, most likely came to Europe on fleas carried by rats on sailing vessels. The plague killed more than a third of the entire population of Europe and effectively ended feudalism as a political system. Many who had formerly served as peasants or serfs found different work, as a demand for skilled labor grew. Nation-states grew in power, and in the face of the pandemic, many began to turn away from faith in God and toward the ideals of ancient Greece and Rome for government and other beliefs.

Crusades

The Crusades began in the eleventh century and continued into the fifteenth. The major goal of these various military ventures was to slow the progression of Muslim forces into Europe and to expel them from the Holy Land, where they had taken control of Jerusalem and Palestine. Alexius I, the Byzantine emperor, called for helped from Pope Urban II when Palestine was taken. In 1095, the Pope, hoping to reunite Eastern and Western Christianity, encouraged all Christians to help the cause. Amidst great bloodshed, this Crusade recaptured Jerusalem, but over the next centuries, Jerusalem and other areas of the Holy Land changed hands numerous times. The Second Crusade (1147-1149) consisted of an unsuccessful attempt to retake Damascus. The Third Crusade, under Pope Gregory VIII, attempted to recapture Jerusalem, but failed. The Fourth Crusade, under Pope Innocent III, attempted to come into the Holy Land via Egypt. The Crusades led to greater power for the Pope and the Catholic Church in general and also opened numerous trading and cultural routes between Europe and the East.

Developments through the eleventh century

<u>Politics in India</u>
After the Mauryan dynasty, the Guptas ruled India, maintaining a long period of peace and prosperity in the area. During this time, the Indian people invented the decimal system as

well as the concept of zero. They produced cotton and calico, as well as other products in high demand in Europe and Asia, and developed a complex system of medicine. The Gupta Dynasty ended in the sixth century. First the Huns invaded, and then the Hephthalites (an Asian nomadic tribe) destroyed the weakened empire.

In the fourteenth century, Tamerlane, a Muslim who envisioned restoring Genghis Khan's empire, expanded India's borders and founded the Mogul Empire. His grandson Akbar promoted freedom of religion and built a wide-spread number of mosques, forts, and other buildings throughout the country.

Chinese and Japanese governments

After the Mongols, led by Genghis Khan and his grandson Kublai Khan, unified the Mongol Empire, China was led by the Ming Dynasty (1368-1644) and the Manchu (also known as Qing) Dynasty (1644-1912). Both dynasties were isolationist, ending China's interaction with other countries until the eighteenth century. The Ming Dynasty was known for its porcelain, while the Manchus focused on farming and road construction as the population grew.

Japan developed independently of China, but borrowed the Buddhist religion, the Chinese writing system, and other elements of Chinese society. Ruled by the divine emperor, Japan basically functioned on a feudal system led by daimyo, or warlords, and soldiers known as samurai. Japan remained isolationist, not interacting significantly with the rest of the world until the 1800s.

Africa

Much of Africa was difficult to traverse early on, due to the large amount of desert and other inhospitable terrain. Egypt remained important, though most of the northern coast became Muslim as their armies spread through the area. Ghana rose as a trade center in the ninth century, lasting into the twelfth century, primarily trading in gold, which it exchanges for Saharan salt. Mali rose somewhat later, with the trade center Timbuktu becoming an important exporter of goods such as iron, leather and tin. Mali also dealt in agricultural trade, becoming one of the most significant trading centers in West Africa. The Muslim religion dominated, and technological advancement was sparse. African culture was largely defined through migration, as Arab merchants and others settled on the continent, particularly along the east coast. Scholars from the Muslim nations gravitated to Timbuktu, which in addition to its importance in trade, had also become a magnet for those seeking Islamic knowledge and education.

Islam

Born in 570 CE, Muhammad began preaching around 613, leading his followers in a new religion called Islam, which means "submission to God's will." Before this time, the Arabian Peninsula was inhabited largely by Bedouins, nomads who battled amongst each other and lived in tribal organizations. But by the time Muhammad died in 632, most of Arabia had become Muslim to some extent.

Muhammad conquered Mecca, where a temple called the Kaaba had long served as a center of the nomadic religions. He declared this temple the most sacred of Islam, and Mecca as the holy city. His writings became the Koran, or Qur'an, divine revelations he said had been delivered to him by the angel Gabriel.

Muhammad's teachings gave the formerly tribal Arabian people a sense of unity that had not existed in the area before. After his death, the converted Muslims of Arabia conquered a vast territory, creating an empire and bringing advances in literature, technology, science and art as Europe was declining under the scourge of the Black Death. Literature from this period includes the *Arabian Nights* and the *Rubaiyat* of Omar Khayyam. Later in its development, Islam split into two factions, the Shiite and the Sunni Muslims. Conflict continues today between these groups.

➢ **Review Video:** Islam
Visit ***mometrix.com/academy*** *and enter* ***Code*****: 359164**

➢ **Review Video:** The Islamic Empire
Visit ***mometrix.com/academy*** *and enter* ***Code*****: 511181**

Geography and Social Studies Concepts

Geography

Geography literally means the study of the earth. Geographers study physical characteristics of the earth as well as man-made borders and boundaries. They also study the distribution of life on the planet, such as where certain species of animals can be found or how different forms of life interact. Major elements of the study of geography include:

- Locations
- Regional characteristics
- Spatial relations
- Natural and manmade forces that change elements of the earth

These elements are studied from regional, topical, physical and human perspectives. Geography also focuses on the origins of the earth as well as the history and backgrounds of different human populations.

Physical and cultural geography

Physical geography is the study of the physical characteristics of the earth: how they relate to each other, how they were formed, and how they develop. These characteristics include climate, land, and water, and also how they affect human population in various areas. Different landforms in combination with various climates and other conditions determine characteristics of various cultures.

Cultural geography is the study of how the various aspects of physical geography affect individual cultures. Cultural geography also compares various cultures: how their lifestyles and customs are affected by their geographical location, climate, and other factors, and how they interact with their environment.

Divisions of geographical study

The four divisions of geographical study and tools used are:

- Topical—the study of a single feature of the earth or one specific human activity that occurs world-wide.
- Physical—the various physical features of the earth, how they are created, the forces that change them, and how they are related to each other and to various human activities.
- Regional—specific characteristics of individual places and regions.
- Human—how human activity affects the environment. This includes study of political, historical, social, and cultural activities.

Tools used in geographical study include special research methods like mapping, field studies, statistics, interviews, mathematics, and use of various scientific instruments.

Ancient geographers

The following are three important ancient geographers and their contributions to the study of geography:

- Eratosthenes lived in ancient Greek times, and mathematically calculated the circumference of the earth and the tilt of the earth's axis. He also created the first map of the world.
- Strabo wrote a description of the ancient world called *Geographica* in seventeen volumes.
- Ptolemy, primarily an astronomer, was also an experienced mapmaker. He wrote a treatise entitled *Geography*, which was used by Christopher Columbus in his travels.

Analysis of areas of human population

In cities, towns, or other areas where many people have settled, geographers focus on distribution of populations, neighborhoods, industrial areas, transportation, and other elements important to the society in question. For example, they would map out the locations of hospitals, airports, factories, police stations, schools, and housing groups. They would also make note of how these facilities are distributed in relation to the areas of habitation, such as the number of schools in a certain neighborhood, or how many grocery stores are located in a specific suburban area. Another area of study and discussion is the distribution of towns themselves, from widely spaced rural towns to large cities that merge into each other to form a megalopolis.

Cartographers and maps

A cartographer is a mapmaker. Mapmakers produce detailed illustrations of geographic areas to record where various features are located within that area. These illustrations can be compiled into maps, charts, graphs, and even globes. When constructing maps, cartographers must take into account the problem of distortion. Because the earth is round, a flat map does not accurately represent the correct proportions, especially if a very large geographical area is being depicted. Maps must be designed in such a way as to minimize this distortion and maximize accuracy. Accurately representing the earth's features on a flat surface is achieved through projection.

Map projections

The three major types of projection used in creating world maps are:

- Cylindrical projection—this is created by wrapping the globe of the Earth in a cylindrical piece of paper, then using a light to project the globe onto the paper. The largest distortion occurs at the outermost edges.
- Conical projection—the paper is shaped like a cone and contacts the globe only at the cone's base. This type of projection is most useful for middle latitudes.
- Flat-Plane projections—also known as a Gnomonic projection, this type of map is projected onto a flat piece of paper that only touches the globe at a single point. Flat-plane projections make it possible to map out Great-Circle Routes, or the shortest route between one point and another on the globe, as a straight line.

Four specific types of map projections that are commonly used today are:

- Winkel tripel projection—this is the most common projection used for world maps, since it was accepted in 1998 by the National Geographic Society as a standard. The Winkel tripel projection balances size and shape, greatly reducing distortion.
- Robinson projection—east and west sections of the map are less distorted, but continental shapes are somewhat inaccurate.
- Goode homolosine projection—sizes and shapes are accurate, but distances are not. This projection basically represents a globe that has been cut into connected sections so that it can lie flat.
- Mercator projection—though distortion is high, particularly in areas farther from the equator, this cylindrical projection is commonly used by seafarers.

Map elements

The five major elements of any map are:

- Title—this tells basic information about the map, such as the area represented.
- Legend—also known as the key, the legend explains what symbols used on a particular map represent, such as symbols for major landmarks.
- Grid—this most commonly represents the Geographic Grid System, or latitude and longitude marks used to precisely locate specific locations.
- Directions—a compass rose or other symbol is used to indicate the cardinal directions.
- Scale—this shows the relation between a certain distance on the map and the actual distance. For example, one inch might represent one mile, or ten miles, or even more depending on the size of the map.

➢ **Review Video:** Elements of a Map
Visit ***mometrix.com/academy*** *and enter* ***Code*****: 437727**

Equal area map and conformal map

An equal area map is designed such that the proportional sizes of various areas are accurate. For example, if one land mass is one-fifth the size of another, the lines on the map will be shifted to accommodate for distortion so that the proportional size is accurate. In many maps, areas farther from the equator are greatly distorted; this type of map compensates for this phenomenon. A conformal map focuses on representing the correct shape of geographical areas, with less concern for comparative size.

Consistent scale map and thematic map

With a consistent scale map, the same scale, such as one inch=ten miles, is used throughout the entire map. This is most often used for maps of smaller areas, as maps that cover larger areas, such as the full globe, must make allowances for distortion. Maps of very large areas often make use of more than one scale, with scales closer to the center representing a larger area than those at the edges.

A thematic map is constructed to show very specific information about a chosen theme. For example, a thematic map might represent political information, such as how votes were distributed in an election, or could show population distribution or climatic features.

Relief map

A relief map is constructed to show details of various elevations across the area of the map. Higher elevations are represented by different colors than lower elevations. Relief maps often also show additional details, such as the overall ruggedness or smoothness of an area. Mountains would be represented as ridged and rugged, while deserts would be shown as smooth. Elevation in relief maps can also be represented by contour lines, or lines that connect points of the same elevation.

Mountains, hills, plains, and valleys

- Mountains are elevated areas that measure 2,000 feet or more above sea level. Often steep and rugged, they usually occur in groups called chains or ranges. Six of the seven continents on Earth contain at least one range.
- Hills are of lower elevation than mountains, at about 500-2,000 feet. Hills are usually more rounded, and are found throughout every continent.
- Plains are large, flat areas and are usually very fertile. The majority of the Earth's population is supported by crops grown on vast plains.
- Valleys lie between hills and mountains. Depending on their location, their specific features can vary greatly, from fertile and habitable to rugged and inhospitable.

Plateaus, deserts, deltas, mesas, basins, foothills, marshes, and swamps

- Plateaus are elevated, but flat on top. Some plateaus are extremely dry, such as the Kenya Plateau, because surrounding mountains prevent them from receiving moisture.
- Deserts receive less than ten inches of rain per year. They are usually large areas, such as the Sahara Desert in Africa or the Australian Outback.
- Deltas occur at river mouths. Because the rivers carry sediment to the deltas, these areas are often very fertile.
- Mesas are flat, steep-sided mountains or hills. The term is also used to refer to plateaus.
- Basins are areas of low elevation where rivers drain.
- Foothills are the transitional area between the plains and the mountains, usually consisting of hills that gradually increase in size as they approach the mountain range.
- Marshes and swamps are also lowlands, but they are very wet and largely covered in vegetation such as reeds and rushes.

Bodies of water

- Oceans are the largest bodies of water on Earth, covering about two-thirds of the earth's surface. The five major oceans are the Atlantic, Pacific, Indian, Arctic, and Southern.
- Seas are generally also salt water, but are smaller than oceans and surrounded by land. Examples include the Mediterranean Sea, the Caribbean Sea, and the Caspian Sea.

- Lakes are bodies of freshwater found inland. Sixty percent of all lakes are located in Canada.
- Rivers are moving bodies of water that flow from higher elevations to lower. They usually start as rivulets or streams, and grow until they finally empty into a sea or an ocean.
- Canals, such as the Panama Canal and the Suez Canal, are manmade waterways connecting two large bodies of water.

➤ **Review Video:** Bodies of Water
*Visit **mometrix.com/academy** and enter **Code**:* **463122**

Communities

Communities, or groups of people who settle together in a specific area, typically gather where certain conditions exists. These conditions include:

- Easy access to resources such as food, water, and raw materials
- Ability to easily transport raw materials and goods, such as access to a waterway
- Room to house a sufficient work force

People also tend to form groups with others who are similar to them. In a typical community, people can be found who share values, a common language, and common or similar cultural characteristics and religious beliefs. These factors will determine the overall composition of a community as it develops.

Cities

Cities develop and grow as an area develops. Modern statistics show that over half of the world's people live in cities. That percentage is even higher in developed areas of the globe. Cities are currently growing more quickly in developing regions, and even established cities continue to experience growth throughout the world. In developing or developed areas, cities often are surrounded by a metropolitan area made up of both urban and suburban sections. In some places, cities have merged into each other and become a megalopolis—a single, huge city.

Cities develop differently in different areas of the world. The area available for cities to grow, as well as cultural and economic forces, drives how cities develop. For example, North American cities tend to cover wider areas. European cities tend to have better developed transportation systems. In Latin America, the richest inhabitants can be found in the city centers, while in North America wealthier inhabitants tend to live in suburban areas.

In other parts of the world, transportation and communication between cities is less developed. Recent technological innovations such as the cell phone have increased communication even in these areas. Urban areas must also maintain communication with rural areas in order to procure food, resources, and raw materials that cannot be produced within the city limits.

Weather and climate

Weather and climate are physical systems that affect geography. Though they deal with similar information, the way this information is measured and compiled is different. Weather involves daily conditions in the atmosphere that affect temperature, precipitation (rain, snow, hail, or sleet), wind speed, air pressure, and other factors. Weather focuses on the short-term—what the conditions will be today, tomorrow, or over the next few days.

In contrast, climate aggregates information about daily and seasonal weather conditions in a region over a long period of time. The climate takes into account average monthly and yearly temperatures, average precipitation over long periods of time, and the growing season of an area. Climates are classified according to latitude, or how close they lie to the earth's equator. The three major divisions are:

- Low Latitudes, lying from 0 to approximately 23.5 degrees latitude
- Middle Latitudes, found from approximately 23.5 to 66.5 degrees
- High Latitudes, found from approximately 66.5 degrees to the poles

Rainforests, savannas, and deserts occur in low latitudes:

- Rainforest climates, near the equator, experience high average temperatures and humidity, as well as relatively high rainfall.
- Savannas are found on either side of the rainforest region. Mostly grasslands, they typically experience dry winters and wet summers.
- Beyond the savannas lie the desert regions, with hot, dry climates, sparse rainfall, and temperature fluctuations of up to fifty degrees from day to night.

The climate regions found in the middle latitudes are:

- Mediterranean—the Mediterranean climate occurs between 30 and 40 degrees latitude, both north and south, on the western coasts of continents. Characteristics include a year-long growing season, hot, dry summers followed by mild winters, and sparse rainfall that occurs mostly during the winter months.
- Humid-subtropical—humid-subtropical regions are located on southeastern coastal areas. Winds that blow in over warm ocean currents produce long summers, mild winters, and a long growing season. These areas are highly productive, and support a larger part of the earth's population than any other climate.
- Humid-continental—the humid continental climate produces the familiar four seasons typical of a good portion of the US. Some of the most productive farmlands in the world lie in these climates. Winters are cold, summers are hot and humid.
- Marine—marine climates are found near water or on islands. Ocean winds help make these areas mild and rainy. Summers are cooler than humid-subtropical summers, but winters also bring milder temperatures due to the warmth of the ocean winds.
- Steppe—steppe climates, or prairie climates, are found far inland on large continents. Summers are hot and winters are cold, but rainfall is sparser than in continental climates.
- Desert—desert climates occur where steppe climates receive even less rainfall. Examples include the Gobi desert in Asia as well as desert areas of Australia and the southwestern US.

The high latitudes consist of two major climate areas, the tundra and taiga:

- Tundra means "marshy plain." Ground is frozen throughout long, cold winters, but there is little snowfall. During the short summers, it becomes wet and marshy.

Tundras are not amenable to crops, but many plants and animals have adapted to the conditions.

- Taigas lie south of tundra regions, and include the largest forest areas in the world, as well as swamps and marshes. Large mineral deposits exist here, as well as many animals valued for their fur. In the winter, taiga regions are colder than the tundra, and summers are hotter. The growing season is short.

A vertical climate exists in high mountain ranges. Increasing elevation leads to varying temperatures, growing conditions, types of vegetation and animals, and occurrence of human habitation, often encompassing elements of various other climate regions.

➢ **Review Video:** Weather and Climate
*Visit **mometrix.com/academy** and enter **Code**:* **237380**

Factors that affect climate

Because the earth is tilted, its rotation brings about changes in seasons. Regions closer to the equator, and those nearest the poles, experience very little change in seasonal temperatures. Mid-range latitudes are most likely to experience distinct seasons. Large bodies of water also affect climate. Ocean currents and wind patterns can change the climate for an area that lies in typically cold latitude, such as England, to a much more temperate climate. Mountains can affect both short-term weather and long-term climates. Some deserts occur because precipitation is stopped by the wall of a mountain range. Over time, established climate patterns can shift and change. While the issue is hotly debated, it has been theorized that human activity has also led to climate change.

Human systems

Human systems affect geography in the way in which they settle, form groups that grow into large-scale habitations, and even create permanent changes in the landscape. Geographers study movements of people, how they distribute goods among each other and to other settlements or cultures, and how ideas grow and spread. Migrations, wars, forced relocations, and trade can all spread cultural ideas, language, goods and other practices to wide-spread areas. Some major migrations or the conquering of one people by another have significantly changed cultures throughout history. In addition, human systems can lead to various conflicts or alliances to control access to and the use of natural resources.

North America

North America consists of 23 countries, including (in decreasing population order) the United States of America, Mexico, Canada, Guatemala, Cuba, Haiti, and the Dominican Republic. The US and Canada support similarly diverse cultures, as both were formed from groups of native races as well as large numbers of immigrants. Many North American cultures come from a mixture of indigenous and colonial European influences. Agriculture is important to North American countries, while service industries and technology also play a large part in the economy. On average, North America supports a high standard of living and a high level of development and supports trade with countries throughout the world.

South America

Including Brazil (largest in area and population), Colombia, Argentina, Venezuela, Peru, and 10 more countries or territories, South America is largely defined by its prevailing languages. The majority of countries in South America speak Spanish or Portuguese. Most of South America has experienced a similar history, having been originally dominated by Native cultures, conquered by European nations. The countries of South America have since gained independence, but there is a wide disparity between various countries' economic and political factors. Most South American countries rely on only one or two exports, usually agricultural, with suitable lands often controlled by rich families. Most societies in South America feature major separations between classes, both economically and socially. Challenges faced by developing South American countries include geographical limitations, economic issues, and sustainable development, including the need to preserve the existing rainforests.

Europe

Europe contains a wide variety of cultures, ethnic groups, physical geographical features, climates, and resources, all of which have influenced the distribution of its varied population. Europe in general is industrialized and developed, with cultural differences giving each individual country its own unique characteristics. Greek and Roman influences played a major role in European culture, as did Christianity. European countries spread their beliefs and cultural elements throughout the world by means of migration and colonization. They have had a significant influence on nearly every other continent in the world. While Western Europe has been largely democratic, Eastern Europe functioned under communist rule for many years. The recent formation of the European Union (EU) has increased stability and positive diplomatic relations among European nations. Like other industrialized regions, Europe is now focusing on various environmental issues.

Russia

After numerous conflicts, Russia became a Communist state, known as the USSR. With the collapse of the USSR in 1991, the country has struggled in its transition to a market-driven economy. Attempts to build a workable system have led to the destruction of natural resources as well as problems with nuclear power, including accidents such as Chernobyl. To complete the transition to a market economy, Russia needs to improve its transportation and communication systems, and find a way to more efficiently use its natural resources.

The population of Russia is not distributed evenly, with three quarters of the population living west of the Ural Mountains. The people of Russia encompass over a hundred different ethnic groups. Over eighty percent of the population is ethnically Russian, and Russian is the official language of the country.

North Africa and Southwest and Central Asia

The largely desert climate of these areas has led most population centers to rise around sources of water, such as the Nile River. This area is the home of the earliest known civilizations and the origin of Christianity, Judaism, and Islam. After serving as the site of huge, independent civilizations in ancient times, North Africa and Southwest and Central Asia were largely parceled out as European colonies during the eighteenth and nineteenth centuries. The beginning of the twentieth century saw many of these countries gain their independence. Islam has served as a unifying force for large portions of these areas, and many of the inhabitants speak Arabic. In spite of the arid climate, agriculture is a large business, but the most valuable resource is oil. Centuries of conflict throughout this area have led to ongoing political problems. These political problems have also contributed to environmental issues.

Sub-Saharan Africa

South of the Sahara Desert, Africa is divided into a number of culturally diverse nations. The inhabitants are unevenly distributed due to geographical limitations that prevent settlement in vast areas. AIDS has become a major plague throughout this part of Africa, killing millions, largely due to restrictive beliefs that prevent education about the disease, as well as abject poverty and unsettled political situations that make it impossible to manage the pandemic. The population of this area of Africa is widely diverse due to extensive migration. Many of the people still rely on subsistence farming for their welfare. Starvation and poverty are rampant due to drought and political instability. Some areas are far more stable than others due to greater availability of resources. These have been able to begin the process of industrialization.

<u>South Asia</u>
South Asia is home to one of the first human civilizations, which grew up in the Indus River Valley. With a great deal of disparity between rural and urban life, South Asia has much to do to improve the quality of life for its lower classes. Two major religions, Hinduism and Buddhism, have their origins in this region. Parts of South Asia, most notably India, were subject to British rule for several decades, and are still working to improve independent governments and social systems. Overall, South Asia is very culturally diverse, with a wide mix of religions and languages throughout. Many individuals are farmers, but a growing number have found prosperity in the spread of high-tech industries. Industrialization is growing in South Asia, but continues to face environmental, social, religious and economic challenges.

<u>East Asia</u>
Governments in East Asia are varied, ranging from communist to democratic governments, with some governments that mix both approaches. Isolationism throughout the area limited the countries' contact with other nations until the early twentieth century. The unevenly distributed population of East Asia consists of over one and a half billion people with widely diverse ethnic backgrounds, religions and languages. More residents live in urban areas than in rural areas, creating shortages of farm workers at times. Japan, Taiwan and South Korea are overall more urban, while China and Mongolia are more rural. Japan stands as the most industrial country of East Asia. Some areas of East Asia are suffering from major environmental issues. Japan has dealt with many of these problems and now has some of the strictest environmental laws in the world.

<u>Southeast Asia</u>
Much of Southeast Asia was colonized by European countries during the eighteenth and nineteenth centuries, with the exception of Siam, now known as Thailand. All Southeast Asian countries are now independent, but the twentieth century saw numerous conflicts between communist and democratic forces.

Southeast Asia has been heavily influenced by both Buddhist and Muslim religions. Industrialization is growing, with the population moving in large numbers from rural to urban areas. Some have moved to avoid conflict, oppression, and poverty.

Natural disasters, including volcanoes, typhoons, and flash flooding, are fairly common in Southeast Asia, creating extensive economic damage and societal disruption.

<u>The South Pacific</u>

South Pacific cultures originally migrated from Southeast Asia, creating hunter-gatherer or sometimes settled agricultural communities. European countries moved in during later centuries, seeking the plentiful natural resources of the area. Today, some South Pacific islands remain under the control of foreign governments, and culture in these areas mixes modern, industrialized society with indigenous culture. Population is unevenly distributed, largely due to the inhabitability of many parts of the South Pacific, such as the extremely hot desert areas of Australia. Agriculture still drives much of the economy, with tourism growing. Antarctica remains the only continent not claimed by a single country. There are no permanent human habitations in Antarctica, but scientists and explorers visit the area on a temporary basis.

Human-environment interaction

Geography also studies the ways people interact with, use, and change their environment. The effects, reasons, and consequences of these changes are studied, as are the ways the environment limits or influences human behavior. This kind of study can help determine the best course of action when a nation or group of people are considering making changes to the environment, such as building a dam or removing natural landscape to build or expand roads. Study of the consequences can help determine if these actions are manageable and how long-term, detrimental results can be mitigated.

Physical geography and climate

North America
The largest amount of North America is the US and Canada, which have a similar distribution of geographical features, mountain ranges in both east and west, stretches of fertile plains through the center, and lakes and waterways. Both areas were shaped by glaciers, which also deposited highly fertile soil. Because they are so large, Canada and the US experience several varieties of climate, including continental climates with four seasons in median areas, tropical climates in the southern part of the US, and arctic climes in the far north. The remaining area of North America is comprised primarily of islands, including the Caribbean Isles and Greenland.

South America
South America contains a wide variety of geographical features including high mountains such as the Andes, wide plains, and high altitude plateaus. The region contains numerous natural resources, but many of them have remained unused due to various obstacles, including political issues, geographic barriers, and lack of sufficient economic power. Climate zones in South America are largely tropical, with rainforests and savannas, but vertical climate zones and grasslands also exist in places.

Europe
Europe spans a wide area with a variety of climate zones. In the east and south are mountain ranges, while the north is dominated by a plains region. The long coastline and the island nature of some countries, such as Britain, mean the climate is often warmer than other lands at similar latitudes, as the area is warmed by ocean currents. Many areas of western Europe have a moderate climate, while areas of the south are dominated by the classic Mediterranean climate. Europe carries a high level of natural resources. Numerous waterways help connect the inner regions with the coastal areas. Much of Europe is industrialized, and agriculture has been developed for thousands of years.

Russia
Russia's area encompasses part of Asia and Europe. From the standpoint of square footage alone, Russia is the largest country in the world. Due to its size, Russia encompasses a wide variety of climatic regions, including plains, plateaus, mountains, and tundra.

Russia's climate can be quite harsh, with rivers that are frozen most of the year, making transportation of the country's rich natural resources more difficult. Siberia, in northern Russia, is dominated by permafrost. Native peoples in this area still follow a hunting and gathering lifestyle, living in portable yurts and subsisting largely on herds of reindeer or caribou. Other areas include taiga with extensive, dense woods in north central Russia and more temperate steppes and grasslands in the southwest.

North Africa and Southwest and Central Asia
This area of the world is complex in its geographical structure and climate, incorporating seas, peninsulas, rivers, mountains, and numerous other features. Earthquakes are common, with tectonic plates in the area remaining active. Much of the world's oil lies in this area. The tendency of the large rivers of North Africa, especially the Nile, to follow a set pattern of drought and extreme fertility, led people to settle there from prehistoric times. As technology has advanced, people have tamed this river, making its activity more predictable and the land around it more productive. The extremely arid nature of many other parts of this area has also led to human intervention such as irrigation to increase agricultural production.

Sub-Saharan Africa
South of the Sahara Desert, the high elevations and other geographical characteristics have made it very difficult for human travel or settlement to occur. The geography of the area is dominated by a series of plateaus. There are also mountain ranges and a large rift valley in the eastern part of the continent. Contrasting the wide desert areas, Sub-Saharan Africa contains numerous lakes, rivers, and world-famous waterfalls. The area has tropical climates, including rainforests, savannas, steppes, and desert areas. The main natural resources are minerals, including gems and water.

South Asia
The longest alluvial plain, a plain caused by shifting floodplains of major rivers and river systems over time, exists in South Asia. South Asia boasts three major river systems in the Ganges, Indus, and Brahmaputra. It also has large deposits of minerals, including iron ore that is in great demand internationally. South Asia holds mountains, plains, plateaus, and numerous islands. The climates range from tropical to highlands and desert areas. South Asia also experiences monsoon winds that cause a long rainy season. Variations in climate, elevation and human activity influence agricultural production.

East Asia
East Asia includes North and South Korea, Mongolia, China, Japan, and Taiwan. Mineral resources are plentiful but not evenly distributed throughout. The coastlines are long, and while the population is large, farmlands are sparse. As a result, the surrounding oceans have become a major source of sustenance. East Asia is large enough to also encompass several climate regions. Ocean currents provide milder climates to coastal areas, while monsoons provide the majority of the rainfall for the region. Typhoons are somewhat common, as are

earthquakes, volcanoes and tsunamis. The latter occur because of the tectonic plates that meet beneath the continent and remain somewhat active.

Southeast Asia
Southeast Asia lies largely on the equator, and roughly half of the countries of the region are island nations. These countries include Indonesia, the Philippines, Vietnam, Thailand, Myanmar, and Malaysia (which is partially on the mainland and partially an island country). The island nations of Southeast Asia feature mountains that are considered part of the Ring of Fire, an area where tectonic plates remain active, leading to extensive volcanic activity as well as earthquakes and tsunamis. Southeast Asia boasts many rivers as well as abundant natural resources, including gems, fossil fuels and minerals. There are basically two seasons—wet and dry. The wet season arrives with the monsoons. In general, Southeast Asia consists of tropical rainforest climates, but there are some mountain areas and tropical savannas.

Australia, Oceania and Antarctica
In the far southern hemisphere of the globe, Australia and Oceania present their own climatic combinations. Australia, the only island on earth that is also a continent, has extensive deserts as well as mountains and lowlands. The economy is driven by agriculture, including ranches and farms, and minerals. While the steppes bordering extremely arid inland areas are suitable for livestock, only the coastal areas receive sufficient rainfall for crops without using irrigation. Oceania refers to over 10,000 Pacific islands created by volcanic activity. Most of these have tropical climates with wet and dry seasons. New Zealand, Australia's nearest neighbor, boasts rich forests as well as mountain ranges and relatively moderate temperatures, including rainfall throughout the year. Antarctica is covered with ice. Its major resource consists of scientific information. It supports some wildlife, such as penguins, and little vegetation, mostly mosses or lichens.

Plate tectonics

According to the geological theory of plate tectonics, the earth's crust is made up of ten major and several minor tectonic plates. These plates are the solid areas of the crust. They float on top of the earth's mantle, which is made up of molten rock. Because the plates float on this liquid component of the earth's crust, they move, creating major changes in the earth's surface. These changes can happen very slowly over a long time period, such as in continental drift, or rapidly, such as when earthquakes occur. Interaction between the different continental plates can create mountain ranges, volcanic activity, major earthquakes, and deep rifts. Plate tectonics defines three types of plate boundaries, determined by the way in which the edges of the plates interact. These plate boundaries are:

- Convergent boundaries—the bordering plates move toward one another. When they collide directly, this is known as continental collision, which can create very large, high mountain ranges such as the Himalayas and the Andes. If one plate slides under the other, this is called subduction. Subduction can lead to intense volcanic activity. One example is the Ring of Fire that lies along the northern Pacific coastlines.
- Divergent boundaries—plates move away from each other. This movement leads to rifts such as the Mid-Atlantic Ridge and east Africa's Great Rift Valley.
- Transform boundaries—plate boundaries slide in opposite directions against each other. Intense pressure builds up along transform boundaries as the plates grind

along each other's edges, leading to earthquakes. Many major fault lines, including the San Andreas Fault, lie along transform boundaries.

➢ **Review Video:** Plate Tectonics
Visit ***mometrix.com/academy*** *and enter* ***Code*****: 535013**

Erosion, weathering, transportation and deposition

Erosion involves movement of any loose material on the earth's surface. This can include soil, sand, or rock fragments. These loose fragments can be displaced by natural forces such as wind, water, ice, plant cover, and human factors. Mechanical erosion occurs due to natural forces. Chemical erosion occurs as a result of human intervention and activities. Weathering occurs when atmospheric elements affect the earth's surface. Water, heat, ice, and pressure all lead to weathering. Transportation refers to loose material being moved by wind, water or ice. Glacial movement, for example, carries everything from pebbles to boulders, sometimes over long distances. Deposition is the result of transportation. When material is transported, it is eventually deposited, and builds up to create formations like moraines and sand dunes.

Effects of human interaction and conflict on geographical boundaries

Human societies and their interaction have led to divisions of territories into countries and various other subdivisions. While these divisions are at their root artificial, they are important to geographers in the discussion of interactions of various populations. Geographical divisions often occur through conflict between different human populations. The reasons behind these divisions include:

- Control of resources
- Control of important trade routes
- Control of populations

Conflict often occurs due to religious, political, language, or race differences. Natural resources are finite and so often lead to conflict over how they are distributed among populations.

State sovereignty

State sovereignty recognizes the division of geographical areas into areas controlled by various governments or groups of people. These groups control not only the territory, but also all its natural resources and the inhabitants of the area. The entire planet Earth is divided into political or administratively sovereign areas recognized to be controlled by a particular government with the exception of the continent of Antarctica.

Alliances

Alliances form between different countries based on similar interests, political goals, cultural values, or military issues. Six existing international alliances include:

- North Atlantic Treaty Organization (NATO)
- Common Market
- European Union (EU)
- United Nations (UN)

- Caribbean Community
- Council of Arab Economic Unity

In addition, very large companies and multi-national corporations can create alliances and various kinds of competition based on the need to control resources, production, and the overall marketplace.

Agricultural revolution

The agricultural revolution began approximately six thousand years ago when the plow was invented in Mesopotamia. Using a plow drawn by animals, people were able to cultivate crops in large quantities rather than gathering available seeds and grains and planting them by hand. Because large-scale agriculture was labor intensive, this led to the development of stable communities where people gathered to make farming possible. As stable farming communities replaced groups of nomadic hunter-gatherers, human society underwent profound changes. Societies became dependent on limited numbers of crops as well as subject to the vagaries of weather. Trading livestock and surplus agricultural output led to the growth of large-scale commerce and trade routes.

Modification of surrounding environments by human populations

The agricultural revolution led human societies to begin changing their surroundings in order to accommodate their needs for shelter and room to cultivate food and to provide for domestic animals. Clearing ground for crops, redirecting waterways for irrigation purposes, and building permanent settlements all create major changes in the environment. Large-scale agriculture can lead to loose topsoil and damaging erosion. Building large cities leads to degraded air quality, water pollution from energy consumption, and many other side effects that can severely damage the environment. Recently, many countries have taken action by passing laws to reduce human impact on the environment and reduce the potentially damaging side effects. This is called environmental policy.

Ecology

Ecology is the study of the way living creatures interact with their environment. Biogeography explores the way physical features of the earth affect living creatures. Ecology bases its studies on three different levels of the environment:

- Ecosystem—this is a specific physical environment and all the organisms that live there.
- Biome—this is a group of ecosystems, usually consisting of a large area with similar flora and fauna as well as similar climate and soil. Examples of biomes include deserts, tropical rain forests, taigas, and tundra.
- Habitat—this is an area in which a specific species usually lives. The habitat includes the necessary soil, water, and resources for that particular species, as well as predators and other species that compete for the same resources.

Interactions between species

Different interactions occur among species and members of single species within a habitat. These interactions fall into three categories:

- Competition — competition occurs when different animals, either of the same species or of different species, compete for the same resources. Robins can compete with other robins for available food, but other insectivores also compete for these same resources.
- Predation— predation occurs when one species depends on the other species for food, such as a fox who subsists on small mammals.
- Symbiosis — symbiosis occurs when two different species exist in the same environment without negatively affecting each other. Some symbiotic relationships are beneficial to one or both organisms without harm occurring to either.

Ability to adapt

If a species is relocated from one habitat to another, it must adapt in order to survive. Some species are more capable of adapting than others. Those that cannot adapt will not survive. There are different ways a creature can adapt, including behavior modification as well as structure or physiological changes. Adaptation is also vital if an organism's environment changes around it. Although the creature has not been relocated, it finds itself in a new environment that requires changes in order to survive. The more readily an organism can adapt, the more likely it is to survive. The almost infinite ability of humans to adapt is a major reason why they are able to survive in almost any habitat in any area of the world.

Biodiversity

Biodiversity refers to the variety of habitats that exist on the planet, as well as the variety of organisms that can exist within these habitats. A greater level of biodiversity makes it more likely that an individual habitat will flourish along with the species that depend upon it. Changes in habitat, including climate change, human intervention, or other factors, can reduce biodiversity by causing the extinction of certain species.

Ottoman Empire

By 1400, the Ottomans had grown in power in Anatolia and had begun attempts to take Constantinople. In 1453 they finally conquered the Byzantine capital and renamed it Istanbul. The Ottoman Empire's major strength, much like Rome before it, lay in its ability to unite widely disparate people through religious tolerance. This tolerance, which stemmed from the idea that Muslims, Christians, and Jews were fundamentally related and could coexist, enabled the Ottomans to develop a widely varied culture. They also believed in just laws and just government, with government centered in a monarch, known as the sultan.

Renaissance

Renaissance literally means "rebirth." After the darkness of the Dark Ages and the Black Plague, interest rose again in the beliefs and politics of ancient Greece and Rome. Art, literature, music, science, and philosophy all burgeoned during the Renaissance.

Many of the ideas of the Renaissance began in Florence, Italy, in the fourteenth century, spurred by the Medici family. Education for the upper classes expanded to include law, math, reading, writing, and classical Greek and Roman works. As the Renaissance progressed, the world was presented through art and literature in a realistic way that had never been explored before. This realism drove culture to new heights.

Artists, authors and scientists
Artists of the Renaissance included Leonardo da Vinci, also an inventor, Michelangelo, also an architect, and others who focused on realism in their work. In literature, major contributions came from humanist authors like Petrarch, Erasmus, Sir Thomas More, and Boccaccio, who believed man should focus on reality rather than on the ethereal. Shakespeare, Cervantes and Dante followed in their footsteps, and their works found a wide audience thanks to Gutenberg's development of the printing press.
Scientific developments of the Renaissance included the work of Copernicus, Galileo and Kepler, who challenged the geocentric philosophies of the day by proving that the earth was not the center of the solar system.

> ➢ **Review Video:** Renaissance
> *Visit* ***mometrix.com/academy*** *and enter* ***Code*: 123100**

Reformation

The Reformation consisted of both the Protestant and the Catholic Reformation. The Protestant Reformation rose in Germany when Martin Luther protested abuses of the Catholic Church. John Calvin led the movement in Switzerland, while in England King Henry VIII made use of the Reformation's ideas to further his own political goals. The Catholic Reformation, or Counter-Reformation, occurred in response to the Protestant movement, leading to various changes in the Catholic Church. Some provided wider tolerance of different religious viewpoints, but others actually increased the persecution of those deemed to be heretics.

From a religious standpoint, the Reformation occurred due to abuses by the Catholic Church such as indulgences and dispensations, religious offices being offered up for sale, and an increasingly dissolute clergy. Politically, the Reformation was driven by increased power of various ruling monarchs, who wished to take all power to themselves rather than allowing power to remain with the church. They also had begun to chafe at papal taxes and the church's increasing wealth. The ideas of the Protestant Revolution removed power from the Catholic Church and the Pope himself, playing nicely into the hands of those monarchs, such as Henry VIII, who wanted out from under the church's control.

> ➢ **Review Video:** The Reformation: The Protestants
> *Visit* ***mometrix.com/academy*** *and enter* ***Code*: 583582**

Scientific Revolution

In addition to holding power in the political realm, church doctrine also governed scientific belief. During the Scientific Revolution, astronomers and other scientists began to amass evidence that challenged the church's scientific doctrines. Major figures of the Scientific Revolution included:

- Nicolaus Copernicus—wrote *On the Revolutions of the Celestial Spheres*, arguing that the earth revolved around the sun
- Tycho Brahe—catalogued astronomical observations
- Johannes Kepler—developed laws of planetary motion

- Galileo Galilei—defended the heliocentric theories of Copernicus and Kepler, discovered four moons of Jupiter, and died under house arrest by the church, charged with heresy
- Isaac Newton—discovered gravity, studied optics, calculus and physics, and believed the workings of nature could be studied and proven through observation

> ➢ **Review Video:** The Scientific Revolution
> *Visit **mometrix.com/academy** and enter **Code**:* **974600**

Enlightenment

During the Enlightenment, philosophers and scientists began to rely more and more on observation to support their ideas, rather than building on past beliefs, particularly those held by the church. A focus on ethics and logic drove their work. Major philosophers of the Enlightenment included:

- Rene Descartes—he famously wrote, "I think, therefore I am." He believed strongly in logic and rules of observation.
- David Hume—he pioneered empiricism and skepticism, believing that truth could only be found through direct experience, and that what others said to be true was always suspect.
- Immanuel Kant—he believed in self-examination and observation, and that the root of morality lay within human beings.
- Jean-Jacques Rousseau—he developed the idea of the social contract, that government existed by the agreement of the people, and that the government was obligated to protect the people and their basic rights. His ideas influenced John Locke and Thomas Jefferson.

> ➢ **Review Video:** The Enlightenment
> *Visit **mometrix.com/academy** and enter **Code**:* **540039**

American Revolution and French Revolution

Both the American and French Revolution came about as a protest against the excesses and overly controlling nature of their respective monarchs. In America, the British colonies had been left mostly to self-govern until the British monarchs began to increase control, spurring the colonies to revolt. In France, the nobility's excesses had led to increasingly difficult economic conditions, with inflation, heavy taxation and food shortages creating great burdens on the lower classes. Both revolutions led to the development of republics to replace the monarchies that were displaced. However, the French Revolution eventually led to the rise of the dictator Napoleon Bonaparte, while the American Revolution produced a working republic from the beginning.

In 1789, King Louis XVI, faced with a huge national debt, convened parliament. The Third Estate, or Commons, a division of the French parliament, then claimed power, and the king's resistance led to the storming of the Bastille, the royal prison. The people established a constitutional monarchy. When King Louis XVI and Marie Antoinette attempted to leave the country, they were executed on the guillotine. From 1793 to 1794, Robespierre and extreme radicals, the Jacobins, instituted a Reign of Terror, executing tens of thousands of nobles as well as anyone considered an enemy of the Revolution. Robespierre was then executed, as well, and the Directory came into power, leading to a temporary return to bourgeois values. This governing body proved incompetent and corrupt, allowing Napoleon Bonaparte to come to power in 1799, first as a dictator, then as emperor. While the French Revolution threw off the power of a corrupt monarchy, its immediate results were likely not what the original perpetrators of the revolt had intended.

> ➢ **Review Video:** The Revolutionary War
> *Visit* ***mometrix.com/academy*** *and enter* ***Code*: 935282**

> ➢ **Review Video:** The French Revolution: Napoleon Bonaparte
> *Visit* ***mometrix.com/academy*** *and enter* ***Code*: 876330**

Russian Revolution of 1905

In Russia, rule lay in the hands of the Czars, and the overall structure was feudalistic. Beneath the Czars was a group of rich nobles, landowners whose lands were worked by peasants and serfs. The Russo-Japanese War (1904-1905) made conditions much worse for the lower classes. When peasants demonstrated outside the Czar's Winter Palace, the palace guard fired upon the crowd. The demonstration had been organized by a trade union leader, and after the violent response, many unions as well as political parties blossomed and began to lead numerous strikes. When the economy ground to a halt, Czar Nicholas II signed a document known as the October Manifesto, which established a constitutional monarchy and gave legislative power to parliament. However, he violated the Manifesto shortly thereafter, disbanding parliament and ignoring the civil liberties granted by the Manifesto. This eventually led to the Bolshevik Revolution.

Bolshevik Revolution of 1917

Throughout its modern history, Russia had lagged behind other countries in development. The continued existence of a feudal system, combined with harsh conditions and the overall size of the country, led to massive food shortages and increasingly harsh conditions for the majority of the population. The tyrannical rule of the Czars only made this worse, as did repeated losses in various military conflicts. Increasing poverty, decreasing supplies, and the Czar's violation of the October Manifesto which had given some political power and civil rights to the people finally came to a head with the Bolshevik Revolution. A workers' strike in Petrograd in 1917 set the revolutionary wheels in motion when the army sided with the workers. While parliament set up a provisional government made up of nobles, the workers and military joined to form their own governmental system known as soviets, which consisted of local councils elected by the people. The ensuing chaos opened the doors for formerly exiled leaders Vladimir Lenin, Joseph Stalin and Leon Trotsky to move in and gain popular support as well as the support of the Red Guard. Overthrowing parliament, they took power, creating a communist state in Russia. This development led to the spread of communism throughout Eastern Europe and elsewhere, greatly affecting diplomatic policies throughout the world for several decades.

Industrial Revolution

The Industrial Revolution began in Great Britain, bringing coal- and steam-powered machinery into widespread use. Industry began a period of rapid growth with these developments. Goods that had previously been produced in small workshops or even in homes were produced more efficiently and in much larger quantities in factories. Where society had been largely agrarian-based, the focus swiftly shifted to an industrial outlook. As electricity and internal combustion engines replaced coal and steam as energy sources, even more drastic and rapid changes occurred. Western European countries in particular turned to colonialism, taking control of portions of Africa and Asia to ensure access to the raw materials needed to produce factory goods. Specialized labor became very much in demand, and businesses grew rapidly, creating monopolies, increasing world trade, and developing large urban centers. Even agriculture changed fundamentally as the Industrial Revolution led to a second Agricultural Revolution with the addition of new technology to advance agricultural production.

The first phase of the Industrial Revolution took place from roughly 1750 to 1830. The textile industry experienced major changes as more and more elements of the process became mechanized. Mining benefited from the steam engine. Transportation became easier and more widely available as waterways were improved and the railroad came into prominence. In the second phase, from 1830 to 1910, industries further improved in efficiency and new industries were introduced as photography, various chemical processes, and electricity became more widely available to produce new goods or new, improved versions of old goods. Petroleum and hydroelectricity became major sources of power. During this time, the Industrial Revolution spread out of Western Europe and into the US and Japan. The Industrial Revolution led to widespread education, a wider franchise, and the development of mass communication in the political arena. Economically, conflicts arose between companies and their employees, as struggles for fair treatment and fair wages increased. Unions gained power and became more active. Government regulation over industries increased, but at the same time, growing businesses fought for the right to free enterprise. In the social sphere, populations increased and began to concentrate around centers of industry. Cities became larger and more densely populated. Scientific advancements led to more efficient agriculture, greater supply of goods, and increased knowledge of medicine and sanitation, leading to better overall health.

➢ **Review Video:** The Industrial Revolution
Visit ***mometrix.com/academy*** *and enter* ***Code*****: 372796**

Nationalism in the eighteenth and nineteenth centuries

Nationalism, put simply, is a strong belief in, identification with, and allegiance to a particular nation and people. Nationalistic belief unified various areas that had previously seen themselves as fragmented, which led to patriotism and, in some cases, imperialism. As nationalism grew, individual nations sought to grow, bringing in other, smaller states that shared similar characteristics such as language and cultural beliefs. Unfortunately, a major side effect of these growing nationalistic beliefs was often conflict and outright war. In Europe, imperialism led countries to spread their influence into Africa and Asia. Africa was eventually divided among several European countries that wanted the raw materials. Asia also came under European control, with the exception of China, Japan and Siam (now Thailand). In the US, Manifest Destiny became the rallying cry as the country expanded west. Italy and Germany formed larger nations from a variety of smaller states.

➢ **Review Video:** Nationalism

Visit ***mometrix.com/academy*** *and enter* ***Code*****: 865693**

World War I

Europe

WWI began in 1914 with the assassination of Archduke Franz Ferdinand, heir to the throne of Austria-Hungary, by a Serbian national. This led to a conflict between Austria-Hungary and Serbia that quickly escalated into the First World War. Europe split into the Allies—Britain, France, and Russia, and later Italy, Japan, and the US, against the Central Powers—Austria-Hungary, Germany, the Ottoman Empire, and Bulgaria. As the war spread, countries beyond Europe became involved. The war left Europe deeply in debt, and particularly devastated the German economy. The ensuing Great Depression made matters worse, and economic devastation opened the door for communist, fascist, and socialist governments to gain power.

Trench warfare

Fighting during WWI largely took place in a series of trenches built along the Eastern and Western Fronts. These trenches added up to more than 24,000 miles. This produced fronts that stretched over 400 miles, from the coast of Belgium to the border of Switzerland. The Allies made use of straightforward open-air trenches with a front line, supporting lines, and communications lines. By contrast, the German trenches sometimes included well-equipped underground living quarters.

> **Review Video:** World War I
> *Visit* ***mometrix.com/academy*** *and enter* ***Code*****: 659767**

Communism and Socialism

At their roots, socialism and communism both focus on public ownership and distribution of goods and services. However, communism works toward revolution by drawing on what it sees to be inevitable class antagonism, eventually overthrowing the upper classes and the systems of capitalism. Socialism makes use of democratic procedures, building on the existing order. This was particularly true of the utopian socialists, who saw industrial capitalism as oppressive, not allowing workers to prosper.

While socialism struggled between the World Wars, communism took hold, especially in Eastern Europe. After WWII, democratic socialism became more common. Later, capitalism took a stronger hold again, and today most industrialized countries in the western world function under an economy that mixes elements of capitalism and socialism.

> **Review Video:** Socialism
> *Visit* ***mometrix.com/academy*** *and enter* ***Code*****: 917677**

Rise of the Nazi party

The Great Depression had a particularly devastating effect on Germany's economy, especially after the US was no longer able to supply reconstruction loans to help the country regain its footing. With unemployment rising rapidly, dissatisfaction with the government grew. Fascist and Communist parties rose, promising change and improvement.

Led by Adolf Hitler, the fascist Nazi Party eventually gained power in Parliament based on these promises and the votes of desperate German workers. When Hitler became Chancellor, he launched numerous expansionist policies, violating the peace treaties that had ended WWI. His military buildup and conquering of neighboring countries sparked the aggression that soon led to WWII.

Blitzkrieg

The blitzkrieg, or "lightning war," consisted of fast, powerful surprise attacks that disrupted communications, made it difficult if not impossible for the victims to retaliate, and demoralized Germany's foes. The "blitz," or the aerial bombing of England in 1940, was one example, with bombings occurring in London and other cities 57 nights in a row. The Battle of Britain in 1940 also brought intense raids by Germany's air force, the Luftwaffe, mostly targeting ports and British air force bases. Eventually, Britain's Royal Air Force blocked the Luftwaffe, ending Germany's hopes for conquering Britain.

Battle of the Bulge

Following the D-Day Invasion, Allied forces gained considerable ground and began a major campaign to push through Europe. In December of 1944, Hitler launched a counteroffensive, attempting to retake Antwerp, an important port. The ensuing battle became the largest land battle on the war's Western Front, and was known as the Battle of the Ardennes, or the Battle of the Bulge. The battle lasted from December 16, 1944 to January 25, 1945. The Germans pushed forward, making inroads into Allied lines, but in the end the Allies brought the advance to a halt. The Germans were pushed back, with massive losses on both sides. However, those losses proved crippling to the German army.

Holocaust

As Germany sank deeper and deeper into dire economic straits, the tendency was to look for a person or group of people to blame for the problems of the country. With distrust of the Jewish people already ingrained, it was easy for German authorities to set up the Jews as scapegoats for Germany's problems. Under the rule of Hitler and the Nazi party, the "Final Solution" for the supposed Jewish problem was devised. Millions of Jews, as well as Gypsies, homosexuals, communists, Catholics, the mentally ill and others, simply named as criminals, were transported to concentration camps during the course of the war. At least six million were slaughtered in death camps such as Auschwitz, where horrible conditions and torture of prisoners were commonplace. The Allies were aware of rumors of mass slaughter throughout the war, but many discounted the reports. Only when troops went in to liberate the prisoners was the true horror of the concentration camps brought to light.

The Holocaust resulted in massive loss of human life, but also in the loss and destruction of cultures. Because the genocide focused on specific ethnic groups, many traditions, histories, knowledge, and other cultural elements were lost, particularly among the Jewish and Gypsy populations. After World War II, the United Nations recognized genocide as a "crime against humanity." The UN passed the Universal Declaration of Human Rights in 1948 in order to further specify what rights the organization protected. Nazi war criminals faced justice during the Nuremberg Trials. There individuals, rather than their governments, were held accountable for war crimes.

➢ **Review Video:** The Holocaust
*Visit **mometrix.com/academy** and enter **Code**:* **350695**

Cold War

With millions of military and civilian deaths and over 12 million persons displaced, WWII left large regions of Europe and Asia in disarray. Communist governments moved in with promises of renewed prosperity and economic stability. The Soviet Union backed communist regimes in much of Eastern Europe. In China, Mao Zedong led communist forces in the overthrow of the Chinese Nationalist Party and instituted a communist government in 1949. While the new communist governments restored a measure of stability to much of Eastern Europe, it brought its own problems, with dictatorial governments and an oppressive police force. The spread of communism also led to several years of tension between communist countries and the democratic west, as the west fought to slow the spread of oppressive regimes throughout the world. With both sides in possession of nuclear weapons, tensions rose. Each side feared the other would resort to nuclear attack. This standoff lasted until 1989, when the Berlin Wall fell. The Soviet Union was dissolved two years later.

United Nations

The United Nations (UN) came into being toward the end of World War II. A successor to the less-than-successful League of Nations formed after World War I, the UN built and improved on those ideas. Since its inception, the UN has worked to bring the countries of the world together for diplomatic solutions to international problems, including sanctions and other restrictions. It has also initiated military action, calling for peacekeeping troops from member countries to move against countries violating UN policies. The Korean War was the first example of UN involvement in an international conflict.

Decolonization

A rise of nationalism among European colonies led to many of them declaring independence. India and Pakistan became independent of Britain in 1947, and numerous African and Asian colonies declared independence as well. This period of decolonization lasted into the 1960s. Some colonies moved successfully into independence but many, especially in Africa and Asia, struggled to create stable governments and economies, and suffered from ethnic and religious conflicts, some of which continue today.

Korean War

In 1910, Japan annexed Korea and maintained this control until 1945. After WWII, Soviet and US troops occupied Korea, with the Soviet Union controlling North Korea and the US controlling South Korea. In 1947, the UN ordered elections in Korea to unify the country but the Soviet Union refused to allow them to take place in North Korea, instead setting up a communist government. In 1950, the US withdrew troops, and the North Korean troops moved to invade South Korea. The Korean War was the first war in which the UN—or any international organization—played a major role. The US, Australia, Canada, France, Netherlands, Great Britain, Turkey, China, USSR and other countries sent troops at various times, for both sides, throughout the war. In 1953, the war ended in a truce, but no peace agreement was ever achieved, and Korea remains divided.

Vietnam War and involvement of France

Vietnam had previously been part of a French colony called French Indochina. The Vietnam War began with the First Indochina War from 1946-1954, in which France battled with the Democratic Republic of Vietnam, ruled by Ho Chi Minh. In 1954, a siege at Dien Bien Phu ended in a Vietnamese victory. Vietnam was then divided into North and South, much like Korea. Communist forces controlled the North and the South was controlled by South Vietnamese forces, supported by the US. Conflict ensued, leading to another war. US troops eventually led the fight, in support of South Vietnam. The war became a major political issue in the US, with many citizens protesting American involvement. In 1975, South Vietnam surrendered, and Vietnam became the Socialist Republic of Vietnam.

Globalism

In the modern era, globalism has emerged as a popular political ideology. Globalism is based in the idea that all people and all nations are interdependent. Each nation is dependent on one or more other nations for production of and markets for goods, and for income generation. Today's ease of international travel and communication, including technological advances such as the airplane, has heightened this sense of interdependence. The global economy, and the general idea of globalism, has shaped many economic and political choices since the beginning of the twentieth century. Many of today's issues, including environmental awareness, economic struggles, and continued warfare, often require the cooperation of many countries if they are to be dealt with effectively.

Effects of globalization

Countries worldwide often seek the same resources, leading to high demand, particularly for nonrenewable resources. This can result in heavy fluctuations in price. One major example is the demand for petroleum products such as oil and natural gas. Increased travel and communication make it possible to deal with diseases in remote locations; however, this also allows diseases to be spread via travelers.

A major factor contributing to increased globalization over the past few decades has been the Internet. By allowing instantaneous communication with anyone nearly anywhere on the globe, the Internet has led to interaction between far-flung individuals and countries, and an ever increasing awareness of events all over the world.

Middle East in international relations and economics

The location on the globe, with ease of access to Europe and Asia, and its preponderance of oil deposits, makes the Middle Eastern countries crucial in many international issues, both diplomatic and economic. Because of its central location, the Middle East has been a hotbed for violence since before the beginning of recorded history. Conflicts over land, resources, and religious and political power continue in the area today, spurred by conflict over control of the area's vast oil fields as well as over territories that have been disputed for thousands of years.

> **Review Video:** Globalization: The Middle East
> *Visit **mometrix.com/academy** and enter **Code**:* **655231**

Genocide

The three major occurrences of genocide in modern history other than the Holocaust are:

- Armenian genocide—from 1914 to 1918, the Young Turks, heirs to the Ottoman Empire, slaughtered between 800,000 and 1.5 million Armenians. This constituted approximately half of the Armenian population at the time.
- Russian purges under Stalin—scholars have attributed deaths between 3 and 60 million, both directly and indirectly, to the policies and edicts of Joseph Stalin's regime. The deaths took place from 1921 to 1953, when Stalin died. In recent years, many scholars have settled on a number of deaths near 20 million but this is still disputed today.
- Rwandan genocide—in 1994, hundreds of thousands of Tutsi, as well as Hutu who sympathized with them, were slaughtered during the Rwandan Civil War. The UN did not act or authorize intervention during these atrocities.

Social Studies Practice Test

Multiple Choice Questions

1. Some countries in the Americas still have large populations of indigenous or partly indigenous peoples. Of the following, which pair of countries does not have comparatively as large of an indigenous population as the other countries?
   a. Guatemala and Peru
   b. Ecuador and Bolivia
   c. Paraguay and Mexico
   d. Argentina and Uruguay

2. Which of the following statements is not true regarding English expansionism in the 16th century?
   a. England's defeat of the Spanish Armada in 1588 brought a decisive end to their war with Spain.
   b. King Henry VIII's desire to divorce Catherine of Aragon strengthened English expansionism.
   c. Queen Elizabeth's support for the Protestant Reformation strengthened English expansionism.
   d. Sir Francis Drake and other English sea captains plundered the Spaniards' plunders of Indians.

3. Which of the following is not true regarding the Virginia Companies?
   a. One of these companies, the Virginia Company of Plymouth, made its base in North America.
   b. One of these companies, the Virginia Company of London, made its base in Massachusetts.
   c. One company had a charter to colonize America between the Hudson and Cape Fear rivers.
   d. One company had a charter to colonize America from the Potomac River to north Maine.

4. Which of the following statements is not true regarding the colony of Jamestown?
   a. The colony of Jamestown was established by the Virginia Company of London in 1607.
   b. The colony of Jamestown became the first permanent English colony in North America.
   c. The majority of settlers in early Jamestown died of starvation, disease, or Indian attacks.
   d. John Smith's governance helped Jamestown more than John Rolfe's tobacco discovery.

5. Which of the following conquistadores unwittingly gave smallpox to the Indians and destroyed the Aztec empire in Mexico?
   a. Balboa
   b. Ponce de Leon
   c. Cortes
   d. De Vaca

6. Which of these factors was not a direct contributor to the beginning of the American Revolution?
  a. The attitudes of American colonists toward Great Britain following the French and Indian War
  b. The attitudes of leaders in Great Britain toward the American colonies and imperialism
  c. James Otis's court argument against Great Britain's Writs of Assistance as breaking natural law
  d. Lord Grenville's Proclamation of 1763, Sugar Act, Currency Act, and especially Stamp Act

7. Which of the following statements is not true regarding the Tea Act of 1773?
  a. The British East India Company was suffering financially because Americans were buying tea smuggled from Holland.
  b. Parliament granted concessions to the British East India Company to ship tea straight to America, bypassing England.
  c. Colonists found that even with added taxes, tea directly shipped by the British East India Company cost less, and they bought it.
  d. American colonists refused to buy less expensive tea from the British East India Company on the principle of taxation.

8. Which of the following were dispatch riders notifying Americans of British troop movements reported by American surveillance in 1775?
  a. Paul Revere
  b. William Dawes
  c. John Parker
  d. (a) and (b)

9. Which of the following is true concerning the formation of new state governments in the new United States of America following freedom from British rule?
  a. By the end of 1777, new constitutions had been created for twelve of the American states.
  b. The states of Connecticut and Massachusetts retained their colonial charters, minus the British parts.
  c. The state of Massachusetts required a special convention for its constitution, setting a good example.
  d. The state of Massachusetts did not formally begin to use its new constitution until 1778.

10. Which of the following is not a true statement regarding the Louisiana Purchase?
  a. Jefferson sent a delegation to Paris to endeavor to purchase only the city of New Orleans from Napoleon.
  b. Napoleon, anticipating U.S. intrusions into Louisiana, offered to sell the U.S. the entire Louisiana territory.
  c. The American delegation accepted Napoleon's offer, though they were only authorized to buy New Orleans.
  d. The Louisiana Purchase, once it was completed, increased the territory of the U.S. by 50% overnight.

11. Which of the following is not correct about the growth of America in the first half of the 19th century?
a. By 1840, two thirds of all Americans resided west of the Allegheny Mountains.
b. The population of America doubled every 25 years during this time period.
c. The trend of westward expansion increased as more people migrated west.
d. Immigration to America from other countries was not substantial prior to 1820.

12. Which of the following did not occur during the War of 1812?
a. Early in the war, the U.S. executed a three-pronged invasion of Canada and succeeded on two of three fronts.
b. Early in the war, Americans won naval battles against the British, but were soon beaten back by the British.
c. Admiral Oliver Hazard Perry's fleet defeated the British navy on Lake Erie in September, 1813.
d. William Henry Harrison invaded Canada and defeated the British and the Indians in the Battle of the Thames.

13. Which of the following is not correct concerning the growth of American labor unions?
a. The new factory system separated workers from owners, which tended to depersonalize workplaces.
b. The goal of attaining an 8-hour work day stimulated growth in labor organizing in the early 1800s.
c. The first organized workers' strike was in Paterson, New Jersey in 1828, and was by child laborers.
d. Recurring downturns in the economy tended to limit workers' demands for rights until the 1850s.

14. Which of the following is not true regarding public schools in the early 19th century?
a. Virtually no public schools existed in America prior to around 1815.
b. Schools were mainly financed by private corporate or religious groups.
c. Thomas Jefferson's plan of a free school in Virginia was realized.
d. American schools were elitist, catering to the rich and to males in academics.

15. Which of the following was not an immediate effect of rapid urban growth in the 1800s?
a. Poor sanitation conditions in the cities
b. Epidemics of diseases in the cities
c. Inadequate police and fire protection
d. Widespread urban political corruption

16. Which of the following laws was instrumental in spurring westward migration to the Great Plains between 1860 and 1880?
a. The Homestead Act
b. The Timber Culture Act
c. The Desert Land Act
d. All of these laws were instrumental in spurring westward migration to the Great Plains during that period.

17. Which of the following did not contribute to ending America's neutrality in World War I?
  a. Germany's declaration of a war zone surrounding the British Isles in February, 1913
  b. Germany's declaration of a war on Russia after Archduke Ferdinand's assassination
  c. Germany's sinking the British ship Lusitania, which killed 128 American passengers
  d. Germany's declaration of unrestricted submarine warfare on all ships in the war zone

18. Of the following international diplomatic conferences, which one made US-Soviet differences apparent?
  a. The Potsdam conference
  b. The conference at Yalta
  c. Dumbarton Oaks conference
  d. The Tehran conference

19. Which statement about relations between the Middle East and the US and Europe in the 1950s is incorrect?
  a. President Nasser of Egypt refused to align with the US in the Cold War.
  b. President Eisenhower removed US funding from the Aswan Dam in 1956.
  c. President Nasser nationalized the Suez Canal, which was owned by England.
  d. In 1956, Egypt attacked Israel, and England and France joined in the war.

20. Which of the following statements regarding events in the Middle East that took place during the Reagan administration is not correct?
  a. Israel invaded Lebanon to get rid of the Palestine Liberation Organization's camps there.
  b. When a terrorist bombing killed 240 US Marines, Reagan escalated military action.
  c. Lebanon was already in the midst of a civil war when Israeli troops invaded the country.
  d. President Reagan deployed US Marines to Lebanon in 1982 on a peacekeeping mission.

21. Of the following, which person or group was not instrumental in advancement of civil rights and desegregation during the 1940s and 1950s?
  a. The President
  b. The Supreme Court
  c. The Congress
  d. The NAACP

22. Of the programs enacted by President Lyndon B. Johnson's administration, which was most closely related to John F. Kennedy's legacy?
  a. The Economic Opportunity Act
  b. The Civil Rights Act
  c. The Great Society program
  d. All of these were equally related to JFK's legacy.

23. Which statement regarding US international trade policy in the 1990s is incorrect?
a. In 1994, the General Agreement on Tariffs and Trade (GATT) was approved by Congress.
b. The GATT included 57 countries who agreed they would remove or reduce many of their tariffs.
c. The GATT created the World Trade Organization (WTO) to settle international trade differences.
d. The NAFTA (North American Free Trade Agreement), ratified in 1994, had originally been set up by George H.W. Bush's administration.

24. Which of the following statements regarding the Branch Davidians in 1993 is not true?
a. The Branch Davidians were a Seventh Day Adventist sect living on a compound located near Waco, Texas.
b. The Bureau of Alcohol, Tobacco, and Firearms got a search warrant for the Branch Davidian compound.
c. When attempts to look for weapon stockpiles led to gunfire and deaths, the FBI attacked the compound.
d. The incident at the Branch Davidian compound in Waco developed into a siege that lasted for six months.

25. Which statement about factors related to the growth of the US economy between 1945 and 1970 is incorrect?
a. The Baby Boom's greatly increased birth rates contributed to economic growth during this time.
b. The reduction in military spending after World War II contributed to the stronger US economy.
c. Government programs and growing affluence nearly quadrupled college enrollments in 20 years.
d. Increased mobility and bigger families caused fast suburban expansion, especially in the Sunbelt.

26. Which of the following statements regarding immigration to America during the 1980s is not true?
a. Twice as many immigrants came to America during the 1980s than during the 1970s.
b. Latin Americans comprised the largest proportion of immigrants to America in the 1980s.
c. Most immigrants to the US in the 1980s were Latin American, Asian, and Caribbean.
d. The 1986 Immigration Reform and Control Act impeded illegal Mexican immigration.

27. Which is not correct regarding black activism during the 1960s?
a. There was a riot in the Los Angeles ghetto of Watts in 1965.
b. There was a riot involving black activists in Newark, New Jersey, after the Watts riot.
c. The Mississippi Freedom Democrats unseated that state's delegation at the convention.
d. There was a riot involving black activists in Detroit, Michigan, after the riot in Watts.

28. What was the earliest written language in Mesopotamia?
  a. Sumerian
  b. Elamite
  c. Akkadian
  d. Aramaic

29. During which of these periods were pyramids not built in Egypt?
  a. The Old Kingdom
  b. The Middle Kingdom
  c. The New Kingdom
  d. The Third Dynasty

30. The Indus Valley or Harappan civilization existed in what is now:
  a. Iran
  b. India
  c. Pakistan
  d. All of these

31. The Yellow River Valley began to emerge as a cultural center during the:
  a. Shang Dynasty
  b. Neolithic Era
  c. Xia Dynasty
  d. Paleolithic Era

32. Which statement is not true regarding ancient Greek democracy?
  a. Democracy began to develop approximately 500 B.C.E.
  b. One of the first, best-known democracies was in Athens
  c. It was a direct democracy, not using any representatives
  d. It was a democracy completely open to all of the public

33. Which of the following statements is incorrect regarding these religions under the Roman Empire?
  a. The Romans generally protected the Jews until the rebellion in Judea (66 C.E.)
  b. Julius Caesar circumvented Roman law to help Jews have freedom of worship
  c. The Druids were a religious group that the Romans ignored but also tolerated
  d. Romans viewed Christianity as a Jewish sect for its first two centuries

34. Which of the following came chronologically the earliest in what is now the Republic of Ghana?
  a. The Kingdom of Ghana
  b. The Akan state of Bono
  c. The Ashanti federation
  d. The states of the Fante

35. Which of the following is not true about the Crusades?
  a. Their purpose was for European rulers to retake the Middle East from Muslims
  b. The Crusades succeeded at European kings' goal of reclaiming the "holy land"
  c. The Crusades accelerated the already incipient decline of the Byzantine Empire
  d. Egypt saw a return as a major Middle Eastern power as a result of the Crusades

36. Which of the following events did not contribute to the growth of the Italian Renaissance?
   a. The Black Death killed 1/3 of the population of Europe
   b. The lower classes benefited from the need for laborers
   c. The middle classes developed from a need for services
   d. All these events contributed to the Italian Renaissance

37. Which of the following was not a characteristic of the Renaissance in 14th-16th century Europe?
   a. The development of linear perspective in the art of painting
   b. The rejection of classical antiquity as a source of education
   c. The educational reform that grew slowly but spread widely
   d. The innovation of using the Scientific Method for learning

38. Which of the following is not correct regarding assumptions of mercantilism?
   a. The money and the wealth of a nation are identical properties
   b. In order to prosper, a nation should try to increase its imports
   c. In order to prosper, a nation should try to increase its exports
   d. Economic protectionism by national governments is advisable

39. Which of the following choices is/are not considered among causes of the French Revolution?
   a. Famines causing malnutrition and starvation
   b. War debt, Court spending, bad monetary system
   c. Resentment against the Catholic Church's rule
   d. Resentment against the Protestant Reformation

40. Of the following statements, which is true about the March on Versailles during the French Revolution?
   a. The March on Versailles was an action undertaken by equal numbers of both men and women
   b. The March on Versailles was an action undertaken primarily by women
   c. The March on Versailles happened prior to the storming of the Bastille
   d. The March on Versailles was not effective in accomplishing its purpose

41. Which of the following statements is accurate regarding the end of the First World War?
   a. The Treaty of Versailles brought peace among all countries involved in the war
   b. The Treaty of Versailles contained a clause for establishing the United Nations
   c. President Woodrow Wilson had proposed forming a coalition of world nations
   d. President Wilson succeeded in getting the USA to ratify the League of Nations

42. Which of the following empire(s) no longer existed following the armistice ending World War I?
   a. The Austro-Hungarian Empire
   b. The Ottoman Empire
   c. The German Empire
   d. All of these empires

43. Which of the following events of Communism occurred the earliest?
 a. Chairman Mao's Communist Party of China formed the People's Republic
 b. Joseph Stalin became party leader in Russia and made his first 5-year plan
 c. Lenin created the New Economic Policy allowing capitalism within limits
 d. Bolsheviks instituted a policy of "war communism" nationalizing property

44. During the decolonization of the Cold War years, which of the following events occurred chronologically latest?
 a. The Eastern Bloc and Satellite states became independent from the Soviet Union
 b. Canada became totally independent from British Parliament via the Canada Act
 c. The Bahamas, in the Caribbean, became independent from the United Kingdom
 d. The Algerian War ended, and Algeria became independent from France

45. Why was U.S. industrialization confined to the Northeast until after the Civil War?
 a. Because the Civil War delayed the development of water-powered manufacturing
 b. Because the Northeast had faster-running rivers than the rivers found in the South
 c. Because Slater's first cotton mill with horse-drawn production lost so much money
 d. Because the technical innovations for milling textiles had not as yet been invented

46. Which of the following statements is not an accurate statement about the Puritans in England?
 a. The Puritans unconditionally gave all their support to the English Reformation
 b. The Puritans saw the Church of England as too much like the Catholic Church
 c. The Puritans became a chief political power because of the English Civil War
 d. The Puritans' clergy mainly departed from the Church of England after 1662

47. Which of the following statements is true regarding the Puritans?
 a. In terms of their theology, the Puritans were considered Calvinists
 b. Many Puritans agreed with the radical criticisms of the Swiss Calvinists
 c. Many of those identified as Calvinists opposed the Puritans
 d. All these statements are true regarding the Puritan movement

48. A monotheistic religious practice was central to which of the following cultures?
 a. Egyptians.
 b. Hebrews.
 c. Sumerians.
 d. Babylonians.

49. Which of the following statements is not true about the Gilded Age in America?
 a. The Gilded Age was the era of the "robber barons" in the business world
 b. The Gilded Age got its name from the excesses of the wealthy upper class
 c. The Gilded Age had philanthropy Carnegie called the "Gospel of Wealth"
 d. The Gilded Age is a term whose origins have not been identified clearly

50. Which of the following is not true about Democracy and the formation of the United States?
 a. The founding fathers stated in the Constitution that the USA would be a democracy
 b. The Declaration of Independence did not dictate democracy but stated its principles
 c. The United States Constitution stipulated that government be elected by the people
 d. The United States Constitution had terms to protect some, but not all, of the people

51. Who wrote about the concept of the Social Contract, which was incorporated into the Declaration of Independence?
a. Thomas Hobbes
b. John Locke
c. Neither of these
d. Both of these

52. Which of the following statements does not describe the average European diet before the expansion of trade routes?
a. Europeans ate for survival, not enjoyment.
b. They had an abundance of preservatives such as salt that could make food last longer.
c. Grain-based foods such as porridge and bread were staple meals.
d. Spices were unavailable.

53. Which of the following statements is not true of daily life for the average European in the 1500s?
a. Life was not significantly different from the medieval era.
b. The majority of people worked in agriculture.
c. Life expectancy was short.
d. Most people were literate, due to well-financed public education programs.

54. Which of these is true concerning the French Revolution, America, and Europe?
a. When France's revolution spread and they went to war with other European countries, George Washington allied with the French.
b. During the time period around 1792, American merchants were trading with countries on both sides of the war.
c. American traders conducted business with various countries, profiting the most from the British West Indies.
d. The Spanish navy retaliated against America for trading with the French by capturing American trading ships.

55. Which group overtook Rome in the mid-600s B.C. and established much of its infrastructure, including sewers, roads, and fortifications, only to be driven out of the city in 509 B.C.?
a. Latins.
b. Etruscans.
c. Greeks.
d. Persians.

56. The writers of The Federalist Papers published under the pen name "Publius." Who were the authors?
a. James Madison, John Jay, and Alexander Hamilton
b. George Washington, Thomas Jefferson, and James Madison
c. Alexander Hamilton, Benjamin Franklin, and Thomas Jefferson
d. Benjamin Franklin, John Jay, and Thomas Jefferson

57. What demographics have recently shown support for Democratic candidates?
   a. Men and young voters
   b. Women and young voters
   c. Women and gun owners
   d. Men and gun owners

58. One reason the Articles of Confederation created a weak government was because it limited Congress's ability to do what?
   a. Declare war
   b. Conduct a census
   c. Vote
   d. Tax

59. The philosophy of the late 17th-18th centuries that influenced the Constitution was from the Age of:
   a. Enlightenment
   b. Empire
   c. Discovery
   d. Industry

60. The votes of how many states were needed to ratify the Constitution?
   a. Five
   b. Ten
   c. Nine
   d. Seven

61. Power divided between local and central branches of government is a definition of what term?
   a. Bicameralism
   b. Checks and balances
   c. Legislative oversight
   d. Federalism

62. The Senate and the House of Representatives are an example of:
   a. Bicameralism
   b. Checks and balances
   c. Legislative oversight
   d. Federalism

63. When the Senate held an impeachment hearing against Andrew Johnson for overstepping his authority, what did they invoke?
   a. Checks and balances
   b. Bicameralism
   c. Legislative oversight
   d. Supremacy

64. Which statement describes the authority of most local officials?
a. Members of local government are generally elected by the people, but their authority is granted by the state
b. Members of local government are given their authority directly from the people
c. Members of local government have constitutionally-granted authority
d. Members of local government are elected by the people, but the state Supreme Court determines their authority

65. The Animal and Plant Health Inspection Service, the Food and Nutrition Service, and the Forest Service are members of which department?
a. The Department of Health and Human Services
b. The Department of Agriculture
c. The Department of the Interior
d. The Department of Transportation

66. A filibuster is used to delay a bill. Where can a filibuster take place?
I. The House
II. The Senate
III. Committees
a. I only
b. II only
c. I and II
d. I, II, and III

67. Which organization is maintained by Congress to oversee the effectiveness of government spending?
a. The House Committee on Oversight and Government Reform
b. The Office of Management and Budget
c. Government Accountability Office
d. The Department of the Interior

68. The civil rights act that outlawed segregation in schools and public places also:
a. Gave minorities the right to vote
b. Established women's right to vote
c. Outlawed unequal voter registration
d. Provided protection for children

69. How many Southern states originally ratified the 14th Amendment?
a. Three
b. Five
c. One
d. Ten

70. Senators were originally chosen by state legislatures. In what year was the constitution amended to allow for them to be elected by popular vote?
a. 1826
b. 1891
c. 1913
d. 1935

71. How many judges are on a panel that decides federal appeals?
a. Five
b. Three
c. Nine
d. Six

72. What petition needs to be filed to request that the Supreme Court hear a case?
a. Writ of certiorari
b. Writ of habeas corpus
c. Writ of mandamus
d. Writ of attachment

73. Every citizen 18 years of age and older has the constitutional right to vote. What do states govern in the voting process?
a. The registration for elections
b. The administration of elections
c. Both A and B
d. State governments are not involved in federal elections

74. The Supreme Court has nine members. How is this number determined?
a. It is outlined in the Constitution
b. Congress determines the number
c. The President determines the number
d. The Court decides on the number

75. What are campaign funds given directly to a candidate called?
a. Soft money
b. Hard money
c. Bundling
d. Independent expenditure

76. Presidential candidates are eligible for public funding if they raise $5,000 per state in how many states?
a. Twenty
b. Ten
c. Twenty-five
d. Seventeen

77. What judicial system did America borrow from England?
a. Due process
b. Federal law
c. Commerce law
d. Common law

78. Most state governments have a bicameral legislature. Which one of the following states does not?
a. Utah
b. Nebraska
c. Washington
d. Louisiana

79. What is the main difference between a primary election and a caucus?
   a. A primary election is privately run by political parties, and a caucus is held by local governments
   b. Caucuses are always held on the same day, but the dates of state primaries vary
   c. A caucus is privately run by political parties, and a primary is an indirect election run by state and local governments
   d. Primary elections are all held on the same date, but the dates of caucuses vary

80. Who negotiates treaties?
   a. The President
   b. The House of Representatives
   c. Ambassadors
   d. The Senate

81. Delegates awarded to Puerto Rico, Guam, and American Samoa in the Democratic National Convention are:
   a. PLEO delegates
   b. Base delegates
   c. District delegates
   d. Bonus delegates

82. The shortest distance between New York and Paris goes
   a. over Florida and Spain.
   b. along the 42nd parallel.
   c. over Labrador and Greenland.
   d. over Philadelphia and London.

83. On which type of map are different countries represented in different colors, with no two adjacent countries sharing a color?
   a. Physical map
   b. Political map
   c. Climate map
   d. Contour map

84. On a map of Africa, there is a small box around Nairobi. This city is depicted in greater detail in a box at the bottom of the map. What is the name for this box at the bottom of the map?
   a. Inset
   b. Legend
   c. Compass Rose
   d. Key

85. Which of the following gives the clearest relative location of Milwaukee?
   a. in Wisconsin
   b. on Lake Michigan
   c. 44° N, 88° W
   d. 100 miles north of Chicago

86. On which type of map would Nigeria be bigger than Australia?
    a. Contour map of elevation
    b. Flow-line map of the spice trade
    c. Mercator projection
    d. Cartogram of population

87. Which of the following are not included in a geographical definition of Southeast Asia?
    a. Myanmar, Laos, Cambodia, and Thailand
    b. Vietnam, the Malay Peninsula, and Brunei
    c. East Malaysia, Indonesia, and the Philippines
    d. These are all geographical parts of Southeast Asia

88. How many intermediate directions are there?
    a. 2
    b. 4
    c. 8
    d. 16

89. What is the name for a line that connects points with equal total rainfall?
    a. Isotherm
    b. Isoline
    c. Isobar
    d. Isohyet

90. Which part of a hurricane features the strongest winds and greatest rainfall?
    a. Eye wall
    b. Front
    c. Eye
    d. Outward spiral

91. What is the most common type of volcano on earth?
    a. Lava dome
    b. Composite volcano
    c. Shield volcano
    d. Cinder cone

92. Which map describes the movement of people, trends, or materials across a physical area?
    a. Political Map
    b. Cartogram
    c. Qualitative Map
    d. Flow-line Map

93. Which of the following exemplifies the multiplier effect of large cities?
    a. The presence of specialized equipment for an industry attracts even more business.
    b. The large population lowers the price of goods.
    c. Public transportation means more people can commute to work.
    d. A local newspaper can afford to give away the Sunday edition.

94. Where is the area of greatest corn production?
   a. South Africa
   b. Kazakhstan
   c. United States
   d. Mexico

95. Thai food has become increasingly popular in the United States, though it is prepared in slightly different ways here. This is an example of
   a. Cultural divergence.
   b. Assimilation.
   c. Cultural convergence.
   d. Acculturation.

96. Which type of chart is best at representing the cycle of demographic transition?
   a. Pie chart
   b. Political map
   c. Line graph
   d. Flow-line map

97. Last year, 4 residents of Henrytown died. The population of Henrytown is 500. What is the death rate of Henrytown?
   a. 1
   b. 4
   c. 8
   d. 12

98. In which stage of demographic transition does fertility remain high while mortality declines?
   a. High stationary stage
   b. Early expanding stage
   c. Late expanding stage
   d. Low stationary stage

99. Which of the following countries are separated by a geometric border?
   a. Turkish Cyprus and Greek Cyprus
   b. North Korea and South Korea
   c. France and Spain
   d. England and Ireland

100. On a political map of India, the northernmost part of the border with Pakistan is represented as a dotted line. Why is this so?
   a. Pakistan does not have control of this border.
   b. This area has never been comprehensively mapped.
   c. Indian Sikhs are threatening to secede.
   d. The borders of the Kashmir region remain in dispute.

101. The price of oil drops dramatically, saving soda pop manufacturers great amounts of money spent on making soda pop and delivering their product to market. Prices for soda pop, however, stay the same. This is an example of what?

a. Sticky prices
b. Sticky wages
c. The multiplier effect
d. Aggregate expenditure

102. John Maynard Keynes advocated what?

a. Supply-side economics
b. Demand-side economics
c. Laissez faire economics
d. The Laffer Curve

103. Assume a society has a given production possibilities frontier (PPF) representing the production of guns and butter. Which of the following would cause the PPF to move outward?

a. The invention of a new machine that makes guns more efficiently
b. An increase in the production of butter
c. An increase in the production of guns
d. A decrease in the production of guns and butter

104. Which of the following is a supply shock likely to produce?

I. An increase in input prices
II. An increase in price levels
III. A decrease in employment
IV. A decrease in GDP
a. I and III only
b. II and IV only
c. I, II, and III only
d. I, II, III, and IV

105. Which of the following would not cause aggregate supply (AS) to change?

a. An increase or decrease in land availability
b. The labor force suddenly increases dramatically
c. A new oil discovery causes dramatic decreases in power production
d. Worker productivity remains the same

106. Assume that aggregate demand (AD) decreases. How will this decrease affect real GDP if there is a lot of unemployment as opposed to full employment?

a. If there is a lot of unemployment, prices will rise dramatically
b. If there is a lot of unemployment, GDP will stay the same
c. If there is full employment, GDP will increase dramatically
d. None of the above

107. Assume that aggregate demand is at AD1 and the government borrows money and then spends that money in order to attempt to move aggregate demand to AD3. According to the theory of "crowding out," where is AD likely to wind up?

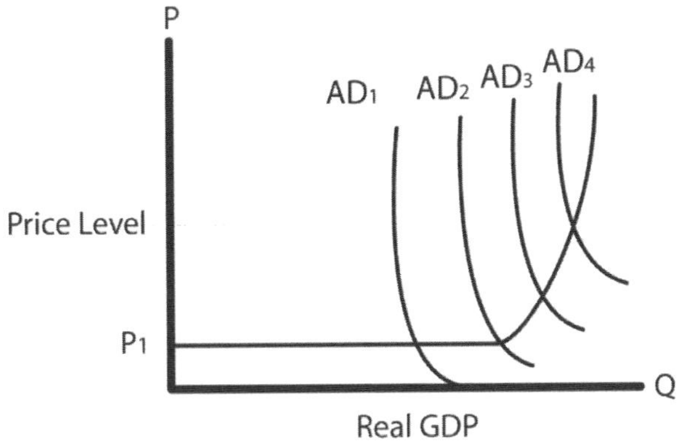

a. AD1
b. AD2
c. AD3
d. AD4

108. Which of the following will bring about greater income equity in a society?
a. imposing a progressive income tax.
b. imposing high estate taxes.
c. imposing a gift tax.
d. All of the above

Consider the following table to answer Question 109:

Inputs	1	2	3	4
Output	20	50	80	100

109. What does the data in this table most directly describe?
a. The Law of Diminishing Marginal Returns
b. Law of Increasing Opportunity Cost
c. Law of Demand
d. Consumer surplus

110. Ivy loses her job because her skills as a seamstress are no longer required due to a new piece of machinery that does the work of a seamstress more quickly and for less money. Which type of unemployment is this?
a. Frictional
b. Structural
c. Cyclical
d. Careless

111. Which is considered part of the natural rate of unemployment?
I. Structural unemployment
II. Frictional unemployment
III. Cyclical unemployment
a. I only
b. II only
c. III only
d. I and II only

112. Inflation has what effects?
a. Harms all members of an economy
b. Helps all members of an economy
c. Harms no members of an economy
d. Harms some members of an economy, helps others

113. Hyperinflation is most likely to be associated with:
I. Demand-pull inflation
II. Cost-push inflation
a. I
b. II
c. I and II
d. I or II

114. Which of the following is not a part of the business cycle?
a. Expansion
b. Contraction
c. Recovery
d. Stagflation

115. Assume a nation's economy is in recession. The nation has an MPC of 0.9 and the government wants to enact fiscal policy to shift the AD curve by $10 billion dollars. What must the government do to its current spending rate?
a. Decrease spending by $10 billion
b. Increase spending by $10 billion
c. Decrease spending by $1 billion
d. Increase spending by $1 billion

116. How do banks create money?
a. By printing it
b. By taking it out of the Federal Reserve
c. By loaning it out
d. By putting it into the Federal Reserve

117. Which of the following might happen if the FOMC uses Treasury Bills to pursue a contractionary monetary policy?
a. The money supply decreases
b. The international value of the American dollar increases
c. The price of US goods to foreigners increases
d. All of the above

118. Which of the following correctly states the equation of exchange?
a. MV = PQ
b. MP x VQ
c. MP / VQ
d. VP = MQ

119. Which of the following best defines American GDP?
a. The value, in American dollars, of all goods and services produced within American borders during one calendar year
b. The value, in American dollars, of all goods and services produced by American companies during one calendar year
c. The total value, in American dollars, of all American household incomes during one calendar year
d. The value, in American dollars, of a "market basket" of goods and services in one year divided by the value of the same market basket in a previous year multiplied by 100

120. "Self-actualization" is a term associated with the ____________ approach to understanding human behavior
a. Behaviorist
b. Humanistic
c. Psychodynamic
d. All of the above

121. Which of the following is *not* one of the Big Five personality traits?
a. Aggression
b. Conscientiousness
c. Extroversion
d. Neuroticism

122. Sigmund Freud is associated with which of the following approaches?
a. Behaviorist
b. Humanistic
c. Psychodynamic
d. None of the above

123. The train tracks seemed to be moving as I drove by the stationary train. Which of the following terms would explain this?
a. Difference threshold
b. Interposition
c. Linear perspective
d. Motion parallax

124. According to George Murdock, which of the following is *not* a general characteristic of all cultural practices?
a. Religion
b. Folklore
c. Property disputes
d. Laws

125. A father from a patriarchal society who passes on his property to his youngest son is practicing:

a. Ultimogeniture
b. Primogeniture
c. Neolocality
d. Patrilocality

126. Of the factors listed below, which one is *not* among Max Weber's independent factors associated with his theory of social stratification?

a. Social class
b. Personal power
c. Social status
d. Race

127. The sociologist who is credited with developing the action theory of society is:

a. Talcott Parsons
b. Robert Merton
c. C. Wright Mills
d. Dennis Wong.

128. Which of the following questions would most likely be asked by a historian concerned with the philosophy of history?

a. What issues shaped the writing of Plato's Republic?
b. Should history be measured by changes in individual lives or by larger political trends?
c. Why were the religions of Shinto and Buddhism able to merge in Japan?
d. Should historians study modern primitive cultures as a means of learning about past civilizations?

129. Which of the following is *not* necessarily an example of an educator introducing his own bias into the educational process?

a. A teacher only using materials and sources that he knows are reputable and declining to use unverified material in his lessons.
b. A textbook author choosing to only use sources that place his favorite U.S. president in a good light and his least favorite U.S. president in a bad light.
c. A teacher only using primary sources that he agrees with and ridiculing a student who provides a verifiable primary source that offers a conflicting opinion.
d. All of the above are examples of bias

Use the following statistical table to answer Question 130

Median U.S. income by amount of schooling, in dollars
Source: U.S. Census Bureau, Current Population Survey, Annual Social and Economic Supplements.

Year	9-12th grade, no diploma	High School graduate	Some College, no degree	Associates Degree	Bachelors Degree or higher
2007	24,492	40,456	50,419	60,132	84,508
2002	23,267	35,646	45,333	51,058	73,600
1997	19,851	33,779	40,015	45,258	63,292

130. Which of the following could you infer from the data presented above?
   a. Persons without a high school diploma receive smaller monetary increases in their income than persons with a high school diploma.
   b. Increased education increases a person's earning potential
   c. Income generally increases over time.
   d. All of the above

Answers and Explanations

1. D: Of those countries listed here, the two countries whose respective indigenous populations are not as large as the populations of the other countries are Argentina and Uruguay. Argentina's population is approximately 86.4% of European descent, roughly 8% of mestizo (of mixed European and Amerindian heritage), and an estimated 4% of Arab or East Asian ancestry. Uruguay's population is estimated to be 88% of European descent, 4% of African, and 2% of Asian, with 6% of mestizo ancestry in its rural northwest region. Guatemala and Peru (a) have larger indigenous populations. Guatemala, in Central America, has approximately over 40% of its population as indigenous peoples. Peru, in South America, is estimated to have 45% indigenous peoples and 37% partly indigenous peoples for a total of 82%. Ecuador and Bolivia (b) in South America still have indigenous peoples. The population of Ecuador has an estimated 25% indigenous and 65% partly indigenous peoples, for a total of 90%. Paraguay in South America and Mexico in North America (c) both have sizeable indigenous populations. Paraguay's population is estimated to include 95% partly indigenous peoples. Mexico is estimated to have 30% indigenous and 60% partly indigenous peoples in its population for a total of 90%. El Salvador and Honduras in Central America also still have numbers of indigenous peoples. The population of El Salvador is estimated to include 90% partly indigenous peoples and 8% purely indigenous peoples for a total of 98%. Honduras is estimated to have 90% partly indigenous and 7% purely indigenous peoples for a total of 97% of its population.

2. A: It is not true that England's defeat of the Spanish Armada in 1588 ended their war with Spain. It did establish England's naval dominance and strengthened England's future colonization of the New World, but the actual war between England and Spain did not end until 1604. It is true that Henry VIII's desire to divorce Catherine of Aragon strengthened English expansionism (b). Catherine was Spanish, and Henry split from the Catholic Church because it prohibited divorce. Henry's rejection of his Spanish wife and his subsequent support of the Protestant movement angered King Philip II of Spain and destroyed the formerly close ties between the two countries. When Elizabeth became Queen of England, she supported the Reformation as a Protestant, which also contributed to English colonization (c). Sir Francis Drake, one of the best known English sea captains during this time period, would attack and plunder Spanish ships that had plundered American Indians (d), adding to the enmity between Spain and England. Queen Elizabeth invested in Drake's voyages and gave him her support in claiming territories for England.

3. B: The Virginia Company of London was based in London, not Massachusetts. It had a charter to colonize American land between the Hudson and Cape Fear rivers (c). The other Virginia Company was the Virginia Company of Plymouth, which was based in the American colony of Plymouth, Massachusetts (a). It had a charter to colonize North America between the Potomac River and the northern boundary of Maine (d). Both Virginia Companies were joint-stock companies, which had often been used by England for trading with other countries.

4. D: It is not true that John Smith's governance helped Jamestown more than John Rolfe's discovery that a certain type of East Indian tobacco could be grown in Virginia. Smith's strong leadership from 1608-1609 gave great support to the struggling colony. However, when Smith's return to England left Jamestown without this support, the future of the colony was again in question. In 1612, however, when John Rolfe found that an East Indian

tobacco strain popular in Europe could be farmed in Virginia, the discovery gave Jamestown and Virginia a lucrative crop. Therefore, both Smith's time in office and Rolfe's discovery were beneficial to Jamestown. Jamestown was established by the Virginia Company of London in 1607 (a), and it became the first permanent settlement by the English in North America (b). It is also true that Jamestown survived in spite of the fact that most of its early settlers died from starvation, disease, and Indian attacks (c). It is also true that many of Jamestown's settlers came from the English upper class and were unwilling to farm the land, while others came hoping to find gold or other treasures, and persisted in their search for these instead of working to make the land sustainable.

5. C: Hernando Cortes conquered the Mexican Aztecs in 1519. He had several advantages over the Indians, including horses, armor for his soldiers, and guns. In addition, Cortes' troops unknowingly transmitted smallpox to the Aztecs, which devastated their population as they had no immunity to this foreign illness. Vasco Nunez de Balboa (a) was the first European explorer to view the Pacific Ocean when he crossed the Isthmus of Panama in 1513. Juan Ponce de Leon (b) also visited and claimed Florida in Spain's name in 1513. Cabeza de Vaca (d) was one of only four men out of 400 to return from an expedition led by Panfilio de Narvaez in 1528, and was responsible for spreading the story of the Seven Cities of Cibola (the "cities of gold"). Hernando de Soto led an expedition from 1539-1541 to the southeastern part of America.

6. A: The attitudes of American colonists after the 1763 Treaty of Paris ended the French and Indian War was not a direct contributor to the American Revolution. American colonists had a supportive attitude toward Great Britain then, and were proud of the part they played in winning the war. Their good will was not returned by British leaders (b), who looked down on American colonials and sought to increase their imperial power over them. Even in 1761, a sign of Americans' objections to having their liberty curtailed by the British was seen when Boston attorney James Otis argued in court against the Writs of Assistance (c), search warrants to enforce England's mercantilist trade restrictions, as violating the kinds of natural laws espoused during the Enlightenment. Lord George Grenville's aggressive program to defend the North American frontier in the wake of Chief Pontiac's attacks included stricter enforcement of the Navigation Acts, the Proclamation of 1763, the Sugar Act (or Revenue Act), the Currency Act, and most of all the Stamp Act (d). Colonists objected to these as taxation without representation. Other events followed in this taxation dispute, which further eroded Americans' relationship with British government, including the Townshend Acts, the Massachusetts Circular Letter, the Boston Massacre, the Tea Act, and the resulting Boston Tea Party. Finally, with Britain's passage of the Intolerable Acts and the Americans' First Continental Congress, which was followed by Britain's military aggression against American resistance, actual warfare began in 1775. While not all of the colonies wanted war or independence by then, things changed by 1776, and Jefferson's Declaration of Independence was formalized. James Otis, Samuel Adams, Patrick Henry, the Sons of Liberty, and the Stamp Act Congress also contributed to the beginning of the American Revolution.

7. C: Colonists did find that tea shipped directly by the British East India Company cost less than smuggled Dutch tea, even with tax. The colonists, however, did not buy it. They refused, despite its lower cost, on the principle that the British were taxing colonists without representation (d). It is true that the British East India Company lost money as a result of colonists buying tea smuggled from Holland (a). They sought to remedy this problem by getting concessions from Parliament to ship tea directly to the colonies instead

of going through England (b) as the Navigation Acts normally required. Boston Governor Thomas Hutchinson, who sided with Britain, stopped tea ships from leaving the harbor, which after 20 days would cause the tea to be sold at auction. At that time, British taxes on the tea would be paid. On the 19th night after Hutchinson's action, American protestors held the Boston Tea Party, dressing as Indians and dumping all the tea into the harbor to destroy it so it could not be taxed and sold. Many American colonists disagreed with the Boston Tea Party because it involved destroying private property. When Lord North and the British Parliament responded by passing the Coercive Acts and the Quebec Act, known collectively in America as the Intolerable Acts, Americans changed their minds, siding with the Bostonians against the British.

8. D: Paul Revere (a) and William Dawes (b) were both dispatch riders who set out on horseback from Massachusetts to spread news of British troop movements across the American countryside around the beginning of the War of Independence. John Parker (c) was the captain of the Minutemen militia, who were waiting for the British at Lexington, Massachusetts.

9. C: Massachusetts did set a valuable example for other states by stipulating that its constitution should be created via a special convention rather than via the legislature. This way, the constitution would take precedence over the legislature, which would be subject to the rules of the constitution. It is not true that twelve states had new constitutions by the end of 1777 (a). By this time, ten of the states had new constitutions. It is not true that Connecticut and Massachusetts retained their colonial charters minus the British parts (b). Connecticut and Rhode Island were the states that preserved their colonial charters. They simply removed any parts referring to British rule. Massachusetts did not formalize its new constitution in 1778 (d). This state did not actually finish the process of adopting its new constitution until 1780. Finally, it is not true that Pennsylvania began with a viable constitution featuring checks and balances. It is true that Maryland and Virginia did initially provide such workable constitutions. Pennsylvania, however, began with such a hyper-democratic document with so little in the way of checks and balances that officials found it impossible to manage and quickly got rid of it, eventually coming up with a more reasonable constitution.

10. D: The Louisiana Purchase actually increased the U.S.'s territory by 100% overnight, not 50%. The Louisiana territory doubled the size of the nation. It is true that Jefferson initially sent a delegation to Paris to see if Napoleon would agree to sell only New Orleans to the United States (a). It is also true that Napoleon, who expected America to encroach on Louisiana, decided to avoid this by offering to sell the entire territory to the U.S. (b). It is likewise true that America only had authority to buy New Orleans. Nevertheless, the delegation accepted Napoleon's offer of all of Louisiana (c). Due to his belief in strict interpretation of the Constitution, Jefferson did require approval from Congress to make the purchase. When his advisors characterized the purchase as being within his purview based on the presidential power to make treaties, Congress agreed.

11. A: By 1840, more than one third of all Americans lived west of the Alleghenies, but not two thirds. It is correct that in the first half of the 19th century, the American population doubled every 25 years (b). It is also correct that westward expansion increased as more people moved west (c) during these years. It is correct that there was not a lot of immigration to the U.S. from other countries before 1820 (d). It is also true that foreign

immigration to America increased quickly around that time, with most immigrants coming from the British Isles.

12. A: The U.S. did carry out a three-pronged invasion of Canada early in the war, but they did not succeed on two fronts. Instead, they lost on all three. Americans did win sea battles against the British early in the war, but were soon beaten back to their homeports and then blockaded by powerful British warships (b). Admiral Perry did defeat the British on Lake Erie on September 10, 1813 (c). Perry's victory allowed William Henry Harrison to invade Canada (d) in October of 1813, where he defeated British and Indians in the Battle of the Thames. *Old Ironsides* was one of the ships that won early naval battles during the war before Britain drove American ships to retreat.

13. B: Growth in labor organizing was stimulated by organizers wanting to achieve the goal of a shorter workday. However, what they were aiming for in the 1800s was a 10-hour day, not an 8-hour day, which was not realized until 1936. It is true that when the factory system supplanted the cottage industry, owners and workers became separate, and this depersonalized workplaces (a). Child laborers did conduct the first organized workers' strike in Paterson, N.J., in 1828 (c). Although the first strike did occur this early, there were not a lot of strikes or labor negotiations during this time period due to periodic downturns in the economy (d), which had the effect of keeping workers dependent and less likely to take action against management. The campaign to attain a 10-hour work day did stimulate a period of growth in labor organizing, but this growth period ended with the depression of 1837.

14. C: Thomas Jefferson did describe a plan for Virginia to have a free school, but it was not realized. Jefferson's plan was never implemented. It is true that there were really no public schools worth mentioning in America before around 1815 (a). Once there were schools, they were mainly paid for by private organizations – corporate ones in the Northeastern states and religious ones in the Southern and Mid-Atlantic states (b). America's early schools did cater to rich people, and specialized in providing academic instruction to males (d). The few schools for females in existence taught homemaking and fine arts rather than academic subjects. The New York Free School was a very unusual instance of an early American school that provided education for the poor. This school tried out the Lancastrian system, wherein older students tutor younger students, which not only employed a sound educational principle, but also helped the school to operate within its limited budget.

15. D: Political corruption was not an immediate effect of the rapid urban growth during this time. The accelerated growth of cities in America did soon result in services being unable to keep up with that growth. The results of this included deficiencies in clean water delivery and garbage collection, causing poor sanitation (a). That poor sanitation led to outbreaks of cholera and typhus, as well as typhoid fever epidemics (b). Police and fire fighting services could not keep up with the population increases, and were often inadequate (c). With people moving to the cities at such a fast rate, there were also deficits in housing and public transportation.

16. D: All the laws named were instrumental in spurring westward migration to the Great Plains. The Homestead Act (a), passed in 1862, gave settlers 160 acres of land at no monetary cost in exchange for a commitment to cultivating the land for five years. The Timber Culture Act (b), passed in 1873, gave the settlers 160 acres more of land in exchange for planting trees on one quarter of the acreage. The Desert Land Act (c), passed in 1877, allowed buyers who would irrigate the land to buy 640

acres for only 25 cents an acre. Thus,, all of these laws were instrumental to spurring westward migration to the Great Plains during that period, is correct.

17. B: Germany's declaration of war on Russia in 1914, following the assassination of Archduke Ferdinand (b), did not contribute to ending American neutrality in World War I. Once Germany declared war, England, France, Italy, Russia, and Japan joined as the Allied Powers against the Central Powers of Germany and Austria-Hungary, and US President Woodrow Wilson declared America's neutrality. When Germany designated the area surrounding the British Isles as a war zone in February 1913 (a), and warned all ships from neutral countries to stay out of the zone, an end to American neutrality was prompted. President Wilson's responded to Germany's declaration by proclaiming that America would hold Germany responsible for any American losses of life or property. When Germany sank the British passenger vessel *Lusitania,* 128 American passengers were killed (c). This further eroded Wilson's resolve to remain neutral. In February 1917, Germany declared unrestricted submarine warfare on any ship in the war zone (d); this signified that ships from any country would face German attack. President Wilson's reaction to this declaration was to cease diplomatic relations with Germany. Meanwhile, England intercepted a telegram from Germany to Mexico asking Mexico to join forces with Germany.. This infuriated the American public. President Wilson then asked for a declaration of war on Germany on April 2, 1917, which Congress approved.

18. A: The postwar conference that brought US-Soviet differences to light was (a) the Potsdam conference in July of 1945. The conference at Yalta (b), in February of 1945, resulted in the division of Germany into Allied-controlled zones. The Dumbarton Oaks conference (c) (1944) established a Security Council, on which with the US, England, Soviet Union, France, and China served as the five permanent members. Each of the permanent members had veto power, and a General Assembly, with limited power, was also established. The Tehran conference (d) included FDR's proposal for a new international organization to take the place of the League of Nations. This idea would later be realized in the form of the United Nations. Earlier in 1943, at the Casablanca Conference, President Roosevelt and Prime Minister Churchill agreed to a policy of unconditional surrender for all enemies of the Allied powers .

19. D: In 1956, Egypt did not attack Israel. On October 29, 1956, Israel attacked Egypt. England and France did join this war within two days. It is true that Egyptian President Gamal Abdul Nasser refused to take America's side in the Cold War (a). In reaction to his refusal, President Eisenhower's administration pulled its funding from the Aswan Dam project in Egypt (b). Nasser then nationalized the British-owned Suez Canal (c). Eisenhower further declared in 1957 that America would provide aid to any country in the Middle East facing Communist control. Pursuant to Eisenhower's declaration, the US invaded Lebanon in 1958 to resolve a conflict in government.

20. B: Reagan escalated military action in response to a terrorist bombing that killed 240 US Marines, is not true. Reagan sent the Marines to Lebanon in 1982 as part of a peacekeeping effort (d) after Israel invaded Lebanon on a mission to eradicate its PLO camps (a). At the time, Lebanon was already engaged in a civil war (c). When the terrorist attack killed 240 Marines, Reagan withdrew the rest of the troops rather than escalate the action. In 1988, an uprising of Palestinians known as the First Intifada started on the Jordan River's much-contested West Bank. In response to this uprising, Reagan initiated peace talks with the PLO's leader, Yasser Arafat. However, the goal of peace in the Middle East never materialized.

21. C: The person or group *not* instrumental in advancing civil rights and desegregation immediately after WWII was (c), Congress. As African American soldiers came home from the war, racial discord increased. President Harry Truman (a) appointed a Presidential Committee on Civil Rights in 1946. This committee published a report recommending that segregation and lynching be outlawed by the federal government. However, Congress ignored this report and took no action. Truman then used his presidential powers to enforce desegregation of the military and policies of "fair employment" in federal civil service jobs. The National Association for the Advancement of Colored People (NAACP) (d) brought lawsuits against racist and discriminatory practices, and in resolving these suits, the

Supreme Court (b) further eroded segregation. For example, the Supreme Court ruled that primaries allowing only whites would be illegal, and it ended the segregation of interstate bus lines. The landmark civil rights laws were not passed by Congress until the 1960s

22. B: Of the programs enacted by Johnson, the one most closely related to JFK's legacy was (b), the Civil Rights Act, which Johnson pushed through Congress using allusions to Kennedy's and his goals. While Kennedy received congressional backing for a raise in minimum wage and public housing improvements, his efforts regarding civil rights were thwarted by conservative Republicans and Southern Democrats in Congress. However, as the Civil Rights movement progressed through the campaigns of the Freedom Riders, Kennedy developed a strong commitment to the cause.
The Economic Opportunity Act gave almost $1 billion to wage Johnson's War on Poverty. The Great Society (c) was Johnson's name for his comprehensive reform program which included a variety of legislation.

23. B: The GATT countries did agree to abolish or decrease many of their tariffs, but this agreement did not include only 57 countries. Then number of signatories was much larger, totaling 117 countries. The GATT was approved by Congress in 1994 (a). In addition to having 117 countries agree to increase free trade, the GATT also set up the World Trade Organization (WTO) for the purpose of settling any differences among nations related to trade (c). Another instance of free trade policy established in the 1990s was the Senate's ratification of NAFTA. The negotiation of this agreement was originally made by the first Bush administration, with President Bush and the leaders of Canada and Mexico signing it in 1992 (d), but it still needed to be ratified. When he was elected President following the senior Bush's second term, Bill Clinton also supported NAFTA, and the Senate ratified it in 1994.

24. D: It is not true that (d) the Waco siege at the Branch Davidian compound lasted for six months. In fact, once the FBI attacked the compound, the resulting siege lasted for 51 days. It is true that the Branch Davidians were a Protestant sect that had split off from the Seventh Day Adventists and lived on a compound near Waco, Texas (a). Following reports of gunfire and weapons caches there, the Bureau of Alcohol, Tobacco and Firearms (ATF) conducted surveillance and obtained a search warrant (b). When ATF attempted to execute the warrant, gunfire was exchanged between the compound and ATF agents, and four agents were killed, whereupon the FBI became involved and attacked the compound (c). Following the 51-day siege, the FBI gassed the main building as Davidians set several fires in the building. Various sources claim the deaths totaled 76-86. One of the fatalities was Branch Davidian leader David Koresh, whose original name was Vernon Wayne Howell. Note: Despite videotaped records, there is still much controversy surrounding this event.

25. B: There was not a reduction in military spending after the war. Although the manufacturing demand for war supplies and the size of the military decreased, the government had increased military spending from $10 billion in 1947 to more than $50 billion by 1953—a more than fivefold increase. This increase strengthened the American economy. Other factors contributing to the strengthened economy included the significantly higher birth rates during the Baby Boom (a) from 1946 to 1957, which stimulated the growth of the building and automotive industries by increased demand. Government programs, such as the GI Bill (the Servicemen's Readjustment Act of 1944), other veterans' benefits, and the National Defense Education Act all encouraged college enrollments, which increased by nearly four times (c). Additionally, larger families, increased mobility and low-interest loans offered to veterans led to suburban development and growth (d) as well as an increased home construction. Improvements in public health were also results of the new affluence; the rate of infant deaths decreased significantly, and as a result, from 1946-1957, the American life span rose from 67 to 71 years. Moreover, Dr. Jonas Salk developed the polio vaccine in 1955, which virtually wiped out poliomyelitis, preventing many deaths and disabilities in children.

26. D: The statement that the 1986 Immigration Reform and Control Act impeded illegal Mexican immigration is not true. This legislation punished employers with sanctions for hiring undocumented employees, but despite this the illegal immigration of Mexicans to America was largely unaffected by

the law. It is true that twice as many people immigrated to America in the 1980s than in the 1970s (a): the number reached over nine million in the 80s. It is true that the majority of immigrants were Latin American (b). In addition to Latin Americans, other large groups of immigrants in the 1980s were Asians and Caribbean inhabitants (c).

27. C: T he Mississippi Freedom Democratic Party did attend the 1964 Democratic convention; however, they were unable garner Lyndon Johnson's support to unseat the regular delegation from Mississippi. A riot did break out in Watts in 1965 (a), and in the following three years, more riots occurred in Newark, N.J. (b) and in Detroit, Michigan (d). These riots were manifestations of the frustrations experienced by blacks regarding racial inequities in American society. Another demonstration of black unrest was the increasing activity of the Black Panthers and the Black Muslims in the 1960s. Both were militant organizations demanding civil rights reforms.

28. A: The earliest written language in Mesopotamia was Sumerian. Ancient Sumerians began writing this language around 3500 B.C.E. Elamite (b), from Iran, was the language spoken by the ancient Elamites and was the official language of the Persian Empire from the 6th to 4th centuries B.C.E. Written Linear Elamite was used for a very short time in the late 3rd century B.C.E. The written Elamite cuneiform, used from about 2500 to 331 B.C.E., was an adaptation of the Akkadian (c) cuneiform. Akkadian is the earliest found Semitic language. Written Akkadian cuneiform first appeared in texts by circa 2800 B.C.E., and full Akkadian texts appeared by circa 2500 B.C.E. The Akkadian cuneiform writing system is ultimately a derivative of the ancient Sumerian cuneiform writing system, although these two spoken languages were not related linguistically. Aramaic (d) is another Semitic language, but unlike Akkadian, Aramaic is not now extinct. Old Aramaic, the written language of the Old Testament and the spoken language used by Jesus Christ, was current from c. 1100-200 C.E. Middle Aramaic, used from 200-1200 C.E., included literary Syriac (Christian groups developed the writing system of Syriac in order to be able to write spoken Aramaic) and was the written language of the Jewish books of Biblical commentary (Namely, the Talmud, the Targum, and the Midrash). Modern Aramaic has been used from 1200 to the present. Hurrian was the language spoken and written by the Hurrians or Khurrites, a people who migrated into Northern Mesopotamia, from circa 2300-1000 B.C.E. They are thought to have emigrated from Armenia, settled in Syria, and spread through Southeast Anatolia and Northern Mesopotamia, thereby establishing the Mitanni Kingdom in Northern Mesopotamia during that time period.

29. C: The New Kingdom was the period during which no more pyramids were built in Egypt. The Pyramids were built between the years of 2630 and 1814 B.C.E., and the New Kingdom spanned from circa 1550-1070 B.C. As a result, the last pyramid was built approximately 264 years before the New Kingdom began. 2630 B.C.E. marked the beginning of the reign of the first Pharaoh, Djoser, who had the first pyramid built at Saqqara. 1814 B.C.E. marked the end of the reign of the last Pharaoh, Amenemhat III, who had the last pyramid built at Hawara. In between these years, a succession of pharaohs built many pyramids. The Old Kingdom (a) encompasses both the Third (d) and Fourth Dynasties; therefore, all three of these choices encompass pyramid-building periods. Djoser's had his first pyramid built during the Third Dynasty (d). The Pharaohs Kufu, Khafre, and Menkaure, respectively, build the famous Pyramids of Giza during the Fourth Dynasty during their reigns at different times between circa 2575 and 2467 B.C.E., the period of the Fourth Dynasty. The Middle Kingdom (b) encompassed the 11th through 14th Dynasties, from circa. 2080 to 1640 B.C.E.—also within the time period (2630-1814 B.C.E.) when pyramids were built by the Pharaohs.

30. D: The ancient Indus Valley civilization, also known in its mature phase as the Harappan civilization, existed in what now encompasses all of the listed countries today. This culture flourished from circa 2600-1900 B.C.E., during the Bronze Age. This civilization included the most eastern portion of Balochistan in what is now Iran (a); the most western parts of what is now India (b); the majority of what is now Pakistan (c); and the southeastern part of Afghanistan.

31. B: Historians have determined that the Yellow River Valley in China began to develop into a cultural center during the Neolithic Era between c. 12,000-10,000 B.C.E. The Shang Dynasty (a) occurred between c. 1700-1046 B.C.E.—still part of the Ancient Era, but very long after the Neolithic era. The Xia Dynasty (c) ruled between circa 2100-1600 B.C.E., preceding the Shang Dynasty but still long after the Neolithic Era. The Paleolithic Era (d) came even before the Neolithic Era. Archaeological evidence exists of Homo erectus in China from more than a million years ago, during the Paleolithic Era, but the Yellow River Valley was not an emergent cultural center that long ago. The Zhou Dynasty ruled from circa 1066-221 B.C.E., later than the Neolithic Era, the Xia Dynasty, and overlapping with and then succeeding the Shang Dynasty.

32. D: Ancient Greek democracy was not completely open to all of the public. However, participating persons were not chosen or excluded based on their respective socioeconomic levels. The city-state of Athens had one of the first and most well-known democracies in ancient Greece (b). It began around 500 B.C.E. (a). The experiment of Athenian democracy was unique in that it was a direct democracy, meaning people voted directly for or against proposed legislation without any representation (c) such as the House of Representatives and the Senate, as we have in modern democracies.

33. C: The Druids were neither ignored nor tolerated by the Romans. Conversely, the Druids were viewed as "non-Roman" and therefore were suppressed. Augustus (63 B.C.E.-14 C.E.) forbade Romans to practice Druid rites. According to Pliny, the Senate under Tiberius (42 B.C.E.-37 C.E.) issued a decree suppressing Druids, and in 54 C.E., Claudius outlawed Druid rites entirely. It is correct that the Romans generally protected the Jews up until the rebellion in Judea in 66 C.E. (a). In fact, Julius Caesar circumvented the Roman laws against "secret societies" by designating Jewish synagogues as "colleges," which in essence permitted Jews to have freedom of worship (b). After the rebellion in Judea, according to Suetonius, the Emperor Claudius appeared to have expelled all Jews, probably including early Christians, from Rome. The Roman Empire viewed Christianity as a Jewish sect, which was how Christianity began, for 200 years following its emergence (d). It is also correct that according to Tacitus, when much of the public saw the Emperor Nero as responsible for the Great Fire of Rome in 64 C.E. (the origin of the old saying "Nero fiddled while Rome burned"), Nero blamed the Christians for the fire in order to deflect guilt from himself. Following their persecution of Jews, the Roman Empire would continue to persecute Christians for the next two centuries.

34. A: The earliest existing empire was the Kingdom of Ghana, also known as the Ghana Empire, from circa 790-1076, located north of modern-day Ghana. The Akan peoples formed the first of their states, Bono (b), after the Kingdom of Ghana fell around the turn of the 12th-13th centuries. The Akan peoples also established the Ashanti federation (c) and the states of the Fante people (d), but these existed later than Bono. The Fante repelled Portuguese colonizers in the 15th century. The Fante peoples still exist and never lost their state, despite the Ashanti Empire's expansion. (Kofi Annan, former Secretary General of the

United Nations, is Fante, as is Ghanaian President John Atta Mills.) A number of conflicts have existed between the Fante and the Ashanti. The Empire of Ashanti formed first a loose confederation of city-states, then a centralized kingdom, in the 18th century, uniting much of sub-Saharan Africa until Europeans came to dominate the region.

35. B: It is not true that the Crusades succeeded at Christians' reclaiming the "holy land" (the Middle East) from Muslims. Despite their number (nine not counting the Northern Crusades) and longevity (1095-1291 not counting later similar campaigns), the Crusades never accomplished this purpose (a). While they did not take back the Middle East, the Crusades did succeed in exacerbating the decline of the Byzantine Empire (c), which lost more and more territory to the Ottoman Turks during this period. In addition, the Crusades resulted in Egypt's rise once again to become a major power (d) of the Middle East as it had been in the past. It is also true that during the Crusades, some Christians and Muslims became allies against common enemies. For example, during the Fifth Crusade, in Anatolia, Christian Crusaders with German, Dutch, Flemish, and Frisian soldiers allied themselves with the Sultanate of Rûm, a Seljuk Turk Sultanate that attacked the Ayyubids in Syria, in order to further their aim of attacking and capturing the port of Damietta in Egypt.

36. D: All these events contributed to the Italian Renaissance. After the Black Death killed a third of Europe's population (a), the survivors were mainly upper classes with more money to spend on art, architecture, and other luxuries. The plague deaths also resulted in a labor shortage, thereby creating more work opportunities for the surviving people in lower classes (b). As a result, these survivors' positions in society appreciated. Once plague deaths subsided and population growth in Europe began to reassert itself, a greater demand existed for products and services. At the same time, the number of people available to provide these products and services was still smaller than in the past. Consequently, more merchants, artisans, and bankers emerged in order to provide the services and products people wanted, thereby creating a class of citizens between the lower class laborers and the upper class elite (c). After the two major Italian banks collapsed, wealthy investors who would normally have reinvested their disposable income did not do this, since the economy did not favor it. Instead, they invested their money in artistic and cultural products.

37. B: The rejection of classical antiquity as a source of education was not a characteristic of the European Renaissance. In fact, the opposite was true. The knowledge of the ancient classical civilizations temporarily was lost to Europeans during the middle ages. As a result, this time period often was called the "Dark Ages." After the fall of the Roman Empire, the loss of the unifying Roman rule eliminated the cultural exchange formerly facilitated by trading and other travel. Outside of the Catholic Church, illiteracy became widespread. The European Renaissance saw a revival of interest in classical sources of knowledge. During this period, Renaissance painters developed the use of linear perspective in art (a); reforms in education progressed gradually but spread widely over Europe (c); and scientists first began to use the Scientific Method for discovery (d), which required empirical evidence in order to support scientists' ideas.

38. B: In order to prosper, a nation should not try to increase its imports. Mercantilism is an economic theory including the idea that prosperity comes from a positive balance of international trade. For any one nation to prosper, that nation should increase its exports (c) but decrease its imports. Exporting more to other countries while importing less from them will give a country a positive trade balance. This theory assumes that money and wealth are identical (a) assets of a nation. In addition, this theory also assumes that the

volume of global trade is an unchangeable quantity. Mercantilism dictates that a nation's government should apply a policy of economic protectionism (d) by stimulating more exports and suppressing imports. Some ways to do accomplish this task have included granting subsidies for exports and imposing tariffs on imports. Mercantilism can be regarded as essentially the opposite of the free trade policies that have been encouraged in more recent years.

39. D: Resentment against the Protestant Reformation was not a cause given for the French Revolution. Choices (a), (b), and (c) are just a few among many causes cited for the war. Famines caused malnutrition and even starvation among the poorest people (a). Escalating bread prices contributed greatly to the hunger. Louis XV had amassed a great amount of debt from spending money on many wars in addition to the American Revolution. Military failures as well as a lack of social services for veterans exacerbated these debts. In addition, the Court of Louis XVI and Marie Antoinette spent excessively and obviously on luxuries even while people in the country were starving, and France's monetary system was outdated, inefficient, and thus unable to manage the national debt (b). Much of the populace greatly resented the Catholic Church's control of the country (c). However, there was not great resentment against the Protestant Reformation (d); there were large minorities of Protestants in France, who not only exerted their influence on government institutions, but undoubtedly also contributed to the resentment of the Catholic Church. Because (d) is not a cause of the French Revolution as the other choices are, answer, all of these, is incorrect.

40. B: The only true statement is the March on Versailles was made primarily by women. Therefore, an equal number of both men and women did not undertake the March on Versailles (a). The women took action because of the dire economic conditions from which they suffered, especially the high prices on bread and food shortages. The storming of the Bastille occurred on July 14, 1789; the March on Versailles occurred on October 5, 1789, almost three months later, not prior to it (c). (The date of July 14th is so famous as Bastille Day in France that generally it is familiar in other countries as well.) It is not true that the March on Versailles was not effective in accomplishing its purpose (d). In fact, the marchers did achieve their goal: They stormed the palace and killed several guards. La Fayette, in charge of the National Guard to control the mob, convinced the royals to move from Versailles to Paris and to stop blocking the National Assembly, and the royal family complied with these demands. The women did not march right to Versailles with no preliminaries. First, they assembled in markets around Paris and marched to the Hôtel de Ville. There they made their demands of the Paris city officials. When those officials did not give acceptable responses, the women then joined a march to the palace at Versailles. While the march to Versailles included men and weapons, some 7,000 women made up the majority of the marchers.

41. C: The only accurate statement about the end of WWI is that President Wilson had proposed that the nations of the world form a coalition to prevent future world wars. While he did not give the coalition a name, he clearly expressed his proposal that such a group form in the fourteenth of his Fourteen Points. The Treaty of Versailles (1919) did not bring peace among all countries involved in the war (a); Germany and the United States arrived at a separate peace in 1921. Furthermore, the Treaty of Versailles did not contain a clause for establishing the United Nations (b); it contained a clause for establishing the League of Nations. The League of Nations was created as dictated by the treaty, but when the Second World War proved that this group had failed to prevent future world wars, it was replaced by the United Nations after World War II. President Wilson did not succeed in getting the

USA to ratify the League of Nations (d). Although he advocated vigorously for the League of Nations, the U.S. Senate never ratified the proposal. While the USA signed the League of Nations charter, the Senate never ratified it, and the USA never joined the League of Nations.

42. D: All of these empires no longer existed following the armistice ending WWI. The Austro-Hungarian Empire (a), the Ottoman Empire (b), and the German Empire (c) were all among the Central powers that lost the war. As empires capitulated, armistices and peace treaties were signed and the map of Europe was redrawn as territories formerly occupied by Central powers were partitioned. For example, the former Austro-Hungarian Empire was partitioned into Austria, Hungary, Czechoslovakia, Yugoslavia, Transylvania, and Romania. The Treaty of Lausanne (1923) gave Turkey both independence and recognition as successor to the former Ottoman Empire after Turkey refused the earlier Treaty of Sèvres (1920), and Mustafa Kemal Ataturk led the Turkish Independence War. Greece, Bulgaria, and other former Ottoman possessions became independent. The Lausanne Treaty defined the boundaries of these countries as well as the boundaries of Iraq, Syria, Cyprus, Sudan, and Egypt. The Russian Empire was among the Allied powers. Russia not only sustained losses in WWI, but Russia also lost additional numbers in the Russian Revolution of 1917, which destroyed the Empire. Bolsheviks took power in Russia under Lenin and signed the Treaty of Brest-Litovsk with Germany in 1918, thereby formally ending Russia's part in WWI and ending the Eastern Front theatre of the war. The former Russian Empire territories of Latvia, Lithuania, Estonia, Finland, and Poland became independent. Therefore, by the end of the Second World War, these four multinational empires no longer existed.

43. D: The earliest occurring chronological event was during the Russian Revolution, the Bolsheviks in 1918 instituted a policy of "war communism," nationalizing all productive property, putting railroads and factories under government control, and collecting and rationing food. Lenin created the New Economic Policy (NEP) in 1921 after the Russian Revolution had been going on for three years and the Kronstadt Rebellion had occurred. Lenin stated that the NEP would give "a limited place for a limited time to capitalism" (c). This policy continued until 1928, when Joseph Stalin became party leader and created his first Five-Year Plan (b). Meanwhile, the Russian Revolution had ended in 1922, and once the war was over the Bolsheviks formed the Union of Soviet Socialist Republics (USSR), often called the Soviet Union, in 1922. Chairman Mao's Communist Party of China formed the People's Republic (a) of China in 1949, eleven years later than the latest of the Russian events named here.

44. A: The latest occurring decolonization event was the Eastern Bloc and Soviet Satellite states of Armenia, Azerbaijan, Estonia, Georgia, Kazakhstan, Kyrgyzstan, Latvia, Lithuania, Moldova, Russia, Tajikistan, Turkmenistan, Ukraine, and Uzbekistan all became independent from the Soviet Union in 1991. (Note: This was the last decolonization of the Cold War years, as the end of the Soviet Union marked the end of the Cold War.) Canada completed its independence from British Parliament via the Canada Act (b) in 1982. In the Caribbean, the Bahamas gained independence from the United Kingdom (c) in 1973. Algeria won its independence from France when the Algerian War of Independence, begun in 1954, ended in 1962 (d). In Africa, Libya gained independence from Italy and became an independent kingdom in 1951.

45. B: U.S. industrialization was confined to the Northeast until after the Civil War because the Northeast had faster-running rivers than the South. The earliest American factories

used horse-drawn machines. When waterpower was developed and proved superior, the Northeast's faster rivers were more suited to water-powered mills than the South's slower rivers. The war did not delay the development of water power (a). Waterpower was developed before the Civil War in the late 1790s. Steam power, a more efficient alternative to water power, was developed after the Civil War and eventually replaced waterpower. With steam-powered engines, industry could spread to the South, since steam engines did not depend on rapidly running water like water-powered engines. While British emigré Samuel Slater's first cotton mill using horse-drawn production did lose a lot of money (c), this was not a reason for industrial delay. In fact, Slater's Beverly Cotton Manufactory in Massachusetts, the first American cotton mill, in spite of its financial problems, was successful in both its volume of cotton production and in developing the water-powered technology that ultimately would succeed the horse-drawn method. Slater's second cotton mill in Pawtucket, Rhode Island, was water-powered. Industrial delay was not because milling technology had not yet been invented (d). Slater learned of new textile manufacturing techniques as a youth in England, and he brought this knowledge to America in 1789. Resistance of Southern owners of plantations and slaves did not slow the spread of industrialism. Rather, as seen in (b) above, the South did not have the geographic capability to sustain waterpower. Once steam power was developed, the South joined in industrialization.

46. A: The inaccurate statement is the Puritans unconditionally supported the English Reformation. While they agreed with the Reformation in principle, they felt that it had not pursued those principles far enough and should make greater reforms. Similarly, they felt that the Church of England (or Anglican Church), though it had separated from the Catholic Church in the Protestant Reformation, still allowed many practices they found too much like Catholicism (b). The Puritans did become a chief political power in England because of the first English Civil War (c) between Royalists and Parliamentarians. The Royalists had a profound suspicion of the radical Puritans. Among the Parliament's elements of resistance, the strongest was that of the Puritans. They joined in the battle initially for ostensibly political reasons as others had, but soon they brought more attention to religious issues. Following the Restoration in 1660 and the Uniformity Act of 1662, thereby restoring the Church of England to its pre-English Civil War status, the great majority of Puritan clergy defected from the Church of England (d). It is also accurate that the Puritans in England disagreed about separating from the Church of England. Some Puritans desired complete separation; they were known first as Separatists and after the Restoration as Dissenters. Others did not want complete separation but instead desired further reform in the Church of England. While they remained part of the Church of England, they were called Non-Separating Puritans, and after the Restoration, they were called Nonconformists.

47. D: These are all true. Because the Puritans took on a Reformed theology, they were in this sense Calvinists (a). However, many Puritans endorsed radical views that criticized such Calvinists as founder John (Jean) Calvin and Huldrych (Ulrich) Zwingli in Switzerland. Not only were Puritans critical of Calvinists despite their mutual Reformed approaches, reciprocally many Calvinists were opposed to the Puritans as well (c). The Puritan movement changed less in American colonies than in England during the 1660s. Following the Restoration (1660) and the Uniformity Act (1662) in England, nearly all of the Puritan clergy objected and left the Church of England, thereby creating a dramatic change in the movement in that country. Nevertheless, in America, the Puritans who had emigrated from England continued their original Puritan traditions for a longer time, as they had neither the

same Anglican Church as in England nor the legislation restoring earlier church status against which the English Puritans had reacted.

48. B: is the best answer. Of the cultures listed, only the Hebrews worshipped one God. Egyptians, Sumerians, Babylonians, and Hittites all practiced polytheistic religions that worshipped a host of deities.

49. D: It is not true that the Gilded Age is a term whose origins have not been identified clearly. In 1873, Mark Twain and Charles Dudley Warner co-authored a book entitled The Gilded Age: A Tale of Today. Twain and Warner first coined this term to describe the extravagance and excesses of America's wealthy upper class (b), who became richer than ever due to industrialization. Furthermore, the Gilded Age was the era of the "robber barons" (a) such as John D. Rockefeller, Cornelius Vanderbilt, J.P. Morgan, and others. Because they accumulated enormous wealth through extremely aggressive and occasionally unethical monetary manipulations, critics dubbed them "robber barons" because they seemed to be elite lords of robbery. While these business tycoons grasped huge fortunes, some of them—such as Andrew Carnegie and Andrew Mellon—were also philanthropists, using their wealth to support and further worthy causes such as literacy, education, health care, charities, and the arts. They donated millions of dollars to fund social improvements. Carnegie himself dubbed this large philanthropic movement the "Gospel of Wealth" (c). Another characteristic of the Gilded Age was the Beaux Arts architectural style, a neo-Renaissance style modeled after the great architectural designs of the European Renaissance. The Panic of 1893 ended the Gilded and began a severe four-year economic depression. The Progressive Era followed these events.

50. A: It is not true that the founding fathers specifically stated in the Constitution that the USA would be a democracy. The founding fathers wanted the new United States to be founded on principles of liberty and equality, but they did not specifically describe these principles with the term "Democracy." Thus, the Declaration of Independence, like the Constitution after it, did not stipulate a democracy, although both did state the principles of equality and freedom (b). The Constitution also provided for the election of the new government (c), and for protection of the rights of some, but not all, of the people (d). Notable exceptions at the time were black people and women. Only later were laws passed to protect their rights over the years. Because (b), (c), and (d) are all true, answer, these statements are all untrue, is incorrect.

51. D: Both of these men wrote about the idea of a Social Contract between government and the people that was used in the Declaration of Independence as a democratic principle. Thomas Hobbes (a) wrote about it in his Leviathan (1651), describing it in the context of an authoritarian monarchy. John Locke (b) wrote about it in his Second Treatise of Government (1689), describing it in the context of a liberal monarchy. Jean-Jacques Rousseau wrote about it in his Du Contrat Social, or The Social Contract (1762), in the context of a liberal republic similar to what the new USA would become. These works supplied a theoretical basis for constitutional monarchies, liberal democracies, and republicanism. Since answer (d), all of these, is correct, answer (c), none of these, is incorrect.

52. B: is the answer. Preservatives such as salt were only introduced to the European diet after trade routes opened and these goods could be brought to Europe.

53. D: is the answer. Despite the growing amount of literacy in the 1500s, due principally to the invention of the printing press and the availability of texts, the majority of Europeans remained illiterate.

54. B: In 1792, when the French Revolution turned into European war, American traders conducted business with both sides. It is not true that Washington allied with the French (a) at this time. Washington issued a Proclamation of Neutrality in 1792 when the French went to war with European countries. While they did trade with both sides, American merchants profited the most from the French West Indies, not the British West Indies (c). The Spanish navy did not retaliate against America for trading with the French (d). Though Spain was an ally of Britain, it was the British who most often seized American ships and forced their crews to serve the British navy. Edmond-Charles Genêt, or Citizen Genêt, a French ambassador to the United States during the French Revolution, defied Washington's policy of neutrality by encouraging the American people to support the French. Washington was embarrassed by this violation. He did not agree with it.

55. B: is the best choice. The Etruscans were from a kingdom to the north that seized control of Rome from the Latins in the mid-600s B.C. They began urbanizing the settlement, improving roads, adding drainage systems, etc. They were driven out of the region in 509 B.C. during an uprising of the Latins.

56. A: James Madison, John Jay, and Alexander Hamilton published The Federalist in the Independent Journal in New York. It was a response to the Anti-Federalists in New York, who were slow to ratify the Constitution because they feared it gave the central government too much authority.

57. B: Female support for Democratic candidates has increased since the 1980s, and younger, college-age voters are more likely to vote Democrat. The 2008 election saw particularly strong support for Obama from women and young voters.

58. D: Congress did not have the authority to levy taxes under the Articles of Confederation. Without the ability to levy taxes, there was no way to finance programs, which weakened the government.

59. A: The Age of Enlightenment was a time of scientific and philosophical achievement. Also called the Age of Reason, it was a time when human thought and reason were prized.

60. C: The Constitution was not ratified immediately. Only five states accepted it in early 1788; Massachusetts, New York, Rhode Island, and Virginia were originally opposed to the Constitution. Rhode Island reluctantly accepted it in 1790.

61. D: Federalists who helped frame the Constitution believed the central government needed to be stronger than what was established under the Articles of Confederation. Anti-federalists were against this and feared a strong federal government. A system of checks and balances was established to prevent the central government from taking too much power.

62. A: The Senate and House of Representatives make up a bicameral legislature. The Great Compromise awarded seats in the Senate equally to each state, while the seats in the House of Representatives were based on population.

63. A: Checks and balances were established to keep one branch of government from taking too much authority. When Johnson violated the Tenure of Office Act by replacing Secretary of War Edwin Stanton, Johnson was impeached, but the final vote in the Senate trial came up one vote short of the number needed to convict him.

64. A: The citizens usually elect members of the local government such as mayors and city council. However, the state grants local governments their authority. State and local governments work independently and do not share authority the way the federal and state governments share power.

65. B: The Animal and Plant Health Inspection Service, the Food and Nutrition Service, and the Forest Service are agencies in the Department of Agriculture. The Department of Agriculture ensures food safety, works with farmers, promotes trade, and protects natural resources.

66. B: The House has strict rules that limit debate. A filibuster can only occur in the Senate where Senators can speak on topics other than the bill at hand and introduce amendments. A filibuster can be ended by a supermajority vote of 60 Senators.

67. C: The Government Accountability Office was originally called the General Accounting Office and was established in 1921 to audit the budget, Congress, and the Director of the Treasury. The Government Accountability Office now oversees the effectiveness of government spending in every branch.

68. C: The Civil Rights Act of 1964 affected the Jim Crowe laws in the Southern states. Many minorities suffered under unfair voting laws and segregation. President Lyndon Johnson signed the Civil Rights Act of 1964 into law after the 1963 assassination of President Kennedy, who championed the reform.

69. C: Tennessee was the only Southern state to ratify the 14th Amendment. Although Southern states that ratified this amendment could be readmitted to the Union with more reform, President Andrew Johnson, who was at odds with Congress, advised them against it.

70. C: The 17th Amendment was ratified in 1913. This amendment allowed the citizens to choose their Senators by holding elections and participating in a popular vote.

71. B: The appellant presents arguments in a brief that explains to the three judges on the panel why the trial court was wrong. The respondent explains why the trial court made the right decision. The appeals court usually makes the final decision, unless they send it back to trial.

72. A: A writ of certiorari is filed if a case is lost in appeals or the highest state court. The writ of certiorari is a request for the Supreme Court to hear the case, but it does not guarantee the case will be heard.

73. C: Nebraska does not require voter registration, but all other states do and have their own process. State and local officials administer federal elections, and though each state has its own method for holding elections, federal elections are always held at the same time.

74. B: Congress has the authority to shape the judicial branch. The Supreme Court once operated with only six members. Nine has been the standard number since 1869.

75. B: Money given directly to a party candidate is hard money. The Federal Election Commission monitors hard money because of limitations on the amount and the money's source.

76. A: Presidential candidates are eligible for a match from the federal government (with a $250 per contribution limit) if they can privately raise $5,000 per state in twenty states. Candidates who accept public money agree to limit spending. Candidates who do not accept matching funds are free to use the money they raise privately.

77. D: America is a common law country because English common law was adopted in all states except Louisiana. Common law is based on precedent, and changes over time. Each state develops its own common laws.

78. B: All states have bicameral legislatures, except Nebraska. The bicameral legislatures in states resemble the federal legislature, with an upper house and a lower house.

79. C: A caucus is a private event run by political parties, and a primary is an indirect election run by state and local governments. Voters may award delegates to candidates for the national conventions, depending on state laws.

80. A: The President has the authority to negotiate and sign treaties. A two-thirds vote of the Senate, however, is needed to ratify a treaty for it to be upheld.

81. A: Presidential candidates are nominated at each party's national convention. The Republican and Democratic Conventions have their own processes for selecting delegates. Puerto Rico, Guam, and American Samoa are also awarded PLEO (Party Leaders and Elected Officials) delegates in the Democratic National Convention.

82. C: The shortest distance between New York and Paris goes over Labrador and Greenland. This is not apparent on a projection map, in which a straight line drawn between the two cities would extend straight out across the Atlantic Ocean, roughly along the 42nd parallel. The illusion that this straight line is the shortest path is a result of the distortions inherent in projection maps. On a globe, it would be easier to see that a plane flying from New York to Paris would cover the least ground by carving an arc, first up through eastern Canada and Greenland and then back down through the British Isles and northern France. This sort of path is known as a great circle route because it looks like an arc when it is drawn on a projection map.

83. B: On a political map, countries are represented in different colors, and countries that share a border are not given the same color. This is so that the borders between countries will be distinct. Political maps are used to illustrate those aspects of a country that have been determined by people: the capital, the provincial and national borders, and the large cities. Political maps sometimes include major physical features like rivers and mountains, but they are not intended to display all such information. On a physical, climate, or contour map, however, the borders between nations are more incidental. Colors are used on these maps to represent physical features, areas with similar climate, etc. It is possible that colors will overrun the borders and be shared by adjacent countries.

84. A: A smaller box in which some part of the larger map is depicted in greater detail is known as an inset. Insets provide a closer look at parts of the map that the cartographer deems to be more important (for instance, cities, national parks, or historical sites). Often, traffic maps will include several insets depicting the roads in the most congested area of the city. Legends, also known as keys, are the boxes in which the symbols used in the map are explained. A legend, or key, might indicate how railroads and boundaries are depicted, for example. A compass rose indicates how the map is oriented along the north-south axis. It is common for cartographers to tilt a map for ease of display, such that up may not be due north.

85. D: A relative location for Milwaukee is 100 miles north of Chicago. Relative location is a description of placement in terms of some other location. The latitude and longitude of Milwaukee are its absolute location because they describe its placement relative to an arbitrary but inalterable system of positioning. To say that Milwaukee is in Wisconsin or on Lake Michigan does not provide as much detail as answer choice D because Wisconsin is a big state and because Lake Michigan is a large body of water.

86. D: On a cartogram of population, Nigeria would be bigger than Australia. Even though the area of Australia is several times greater than that of Nigeria, Nigeria has a much larger population. A cartogram is a map on which countries or regions are sized according to a certain variable. So, in a cartogram of population, the country with the most people will be the biggest. The countries would be depicted at their usual size in a contour map of elevation or in a flow-line map. On a Mercator projection, Nigeria would actually be smaller relative to Australia because it is closer to the equator.

87. D: These are all geographically parts of Southeast Asia. The countries of Myanmar (Burma), Laos, Cambodia, and Thailand (a) are considered Mainland Southeast Asia, as are Vietnam and the Malay Peninsula (b). Brunei (b), East Malaysia, Indonesia, and the Philippines (c) are considered Maritime Southeast Asia, as are Singapore and Timor-Leste. The Seven Sister States of India are also considered to be part of Southeast Asia, geographically and culturally. (The Seven Sister States of India are Arunachal Pradesh, Assam, Nagaland, Meghalaya, Manipur, Tripura, and Mizoram, which all have contiguous borders in northeastern India.)

88. B: There are four intermediate directions. They are northwest, northeast, southwest, and southeast. The intermediate directions are midway between each set of adjacent cardinal directions. The cardinal directions are north, south, east, and west. On a compass rose, the cardinal directions are typically indicated by large points, while the intermediate directions are represented by smaller points.

89. D: An isohyet is a line that connects points with equal total rainfall. On an isohyetal map then, a series of lines will indicate areas of greater or lesser rainfall. This is a form of contour map, the most common of which uses a series of lines to indicate changes in elevation. The other answer choices represent lines used in other forms of contour maps. An isotherm connects points with the same temperature. An isoline connects points with an equal value, as, for instance, on a contour map illustrating iron production. An isobar connects points with identical atmospheric pressure.

90. A: The eye wall of a hurricane has the strongest winds and the greatest rainfall. The eye wall is the tower-like rim of the eye. It is from this wall that clouds extend out, which are seen from above as the classic outward spiral pattern. A hurricane front is the outermost edge of its influence; although there will be heavy winds and rain in this area, the intensity will be relatively small. The eye of a hurricane is actually a place of surprising peace. In this area, dry and cool air rushes down to the ground or sea. Once there, the air is caught up in the winds of the eye wall and is driven outward at a furious pace.

91. B: The composite volcano, sometimes called the stratovolcano, is the most common type of volcano on earth. A composite volcano has steep sides, so the explosions of ash, pumice, and silica are often accompanied by treacherous mudslides. Indeed, it is these mudslides that cause most of the damage associated with composite volcano eruptions. Krakatoa and Mount Saint Helens are examples of composite volcanoes. A lava dome is a round volcano that emits thick lava very slowly. A shield volcano, one example of which is Mt. Kilauea in Hawaii, emits a small amount of lava over an extended period of time. Shield volcanoes are not known for violent eruptions. A cinder cone has steep sides made of fallen cinders, which themselves are made of the lava that intermittently shoots into the air.

92. D: A flow-line map describes the movement of people, trends, or materials across a physical area. The movements depicted on a flow-line map are typically represented by arrows. In more advanced flow-line maps, the width of the arrow corresponds to the quantity of the motion. Flow-line maps usually declare the span of time that is being represented. A political map depicts the man-made aspects of geography, such as borders and cities. A cartogram adjusts the size of the areas represented according to some variable. For instance, a cartogram of wheat production would depict Iowa as being much larger than Alaska. A qualitative map uses lines, dots, and other symbols to illustrate a particular point. For example, a qualitative map might be used to demonstrate the greatest expansion of the Persian Empire.

93. A: One example of the multiplier effect of large cities would be if the presence of specialized equipment for an industry attracted even more business. Large cities tend to grow even larger for a number of reasons: they have more skilled workers, they have greater concentrations of specialized equipment, and they have already-functioning markets. These factors all make it easier for a business to begin operations in a large city than elsewhere. Thus, the populations and economic productivity of large cities tend to grow quickly. Some governments have sought to mitigate this trend by clustering groups of similar industries in smaller cities.

94. C: The greatest area of corn production is in the United States, specifically in the so-called Corn Belt that runs from northern Florida and eastern Texas all the way up to Iowa and Pennsylvania. Corn has traditionally been the specialty grain of the Americas, although it is now grown as a subsistence crop all over the world. Indeed, all the incorrect answer choices are areas that produce significant amounts of corn, though not as much as the Corn Belt. Corn is useful because it can grow in various climates and can be converted into a number of different products.

95. C: The increasing popularity of Thai food in the United States is an example of cultural convergence, or the intersection of traits or customs from two distinct cultures. Thailand's cuisine has been introduced to the United States, but it has undergone subtle changes as a result of the desires and practices of the American consumer. The phenomenon of cultural

convergence is credited with much of the innovation in any society. Cultural divergence, on the other hand, is the practice of shielding one culture from the influence of another. France, for instance, seeks to limit the influence of American culture on its citizens. Assimilation is the process by which a minority group gradually adopts the culture of the majority group. For example, many Native Americans assimilated into the European-style culture of the early American settlers. Acculturation is the process of obtaining the practices and ideas of a culture. A child undergoes acculturation, wherein he or she learns to think and act appropriately for his or her setting.

96. C: The cycle of demographic transition is best illustrated by a line graph. Demographic transition is a phenomenon in which a region's growth rate increases rapidly, peaks, and then decreases slowly over a long time. In the early phase of a region's development, both the birth and death rates are high, which can cause the population to fluctuate. As the people of the region become settled, the growth rate calms down, and the region enters a period of rapid increase. Political maps are better at depicting borders and the locations of cities, while pie charts are better at representing proportions. Flow-line maps are good for illustrating the movement of people, goods, or trends across a physical area.

97. C: The death rate of Henrytown is 8. Death rate is calculated as the number of deaths every year for every thousand people. Of course, the population of Henrytown is only 500, so it requires a quick calculation to obtain the death rate. This can be accomplished with the following equation: $4 / x = 500 / 1000$. This equation basically means "4 is to 500 as x is to 1000." The equation is solved by first cross multiplying, which yields $4{,}000 = 500x$. Then, both sides are divided by 500 to isolate the variable. This indicates that x is equal to 8.

98. B: In the early expanding stage of demographic transition, the fertility rate remains high, while the mortality rate declines sharply. Demographic transition is a model for how the population growth rate of a region changes over time. It consists of four stages. In the first, the high stationary stage, fertility and mortality rates are high, so the population rate varies, and there is little growth. In the second stage, some of the problems causing mortality have been solved, but fertility continues at the same rate. This means that the population begins to expand at a greater rate. In the third stage, the late expanding stage, the fertility rate begins to decline, but because the mortality rate remains low, there is continuing growth. In the low stationary stage, there are low rates of fertility and mortality, and consequently there is a low rate of growth.

99. B: North Korea and South Korea are separated by a geometric border, meaning that the boundary between the two nations is a straight line drawn on a map, without respect to landforms. Specifically, the boundary between the Koreas is the 38th parallel. Another example of a geometric border lies between the continental United States and Canada. The Turkish Cyprus–Greek Cyprus border is anthropogeographic, or drawn according to cultural reasons. The border between France and Spain is physiographic-political, a combination of the Pyrenees Mountains and European history. The Irish Sea separates England from Ireland.

100. D: The northernmost border between India and Pakistan is represented on political maps as a broken line because the borders of the Kashmir region remain in dispute. Both nations lay claim to this mountainous region, which has great water resources. This has been just one of the issues to complicate relations between these neighbors in South Asia. Although India controls most of Kashmir at present, the boundaries have not yet been fully

resolved, and, on a political map, such undefined borders are usually represented with dotted lines.

101. A: The phenomenon of "sticky prices" refers to prices that stay the same even though it seems they should change (either increasing or decreasing).

102. B: John Maynard Keynes argued that government could help revitalize a recessionary economy by increasing government spending and therefore increasing aggregate demand. This is known as demand-side economics.

103. A: The production possibilities frontier shows the different possible combinations of goods (and/or services) a society can produce. If all other factors are even, producing more of Good A leads to a decreased production of Good B. If the PPF moves outward, that means a change in the factors of production that allows the economy to produce more goods—economic growth—has occurred. Only Answer A is an example of economic growth.

104. D: A supply shock is caused when there is a dramatic increase in input prices. This causes an increase in price levels and decreases in employment and GDP. A supply shock causes the AS curve to move to the left (in).

105. D: A change in productivity, such as workers becoming more or less productive, would affect how many goods can be supplied. No change in worker productivity would cause no change in AS. Items A, B, and C would all affect input prices and therefore would all affect AS.

106. D: When there is a lot of unemployment, the AS curve is horizontal. If AD decreases at this time, prices will tend to remain the same while GDP decreases. When there is full employment, the AS curve is vertical. If AD decreases at this time, prices will drop but GDP will tend to remain the same.

107. B: According to the theory of crowding out, when the government borrows money to increase spending, this will increase the price of money, leading to a drop in investment. That drop in investment will have a negative effect on AD, and so the government injection of funds will not have its full, desired effect (AD3), instead winding up at AD2.

108. D: If a society wants greater income equity, it can impose a progressive income tax, which taxes the wealthy at a higher rate; an inheritance tax, which prevents the wealthy from passing all their wealth on to the next generation; and a gift tax, which prevents the wealthy from simply giving their wealth away.

109. A: The input and output data illustrates the Law of Diminishing Marginal Returns, which states that as inputs are added during production, there eventually comes a time when increased inputs coincide with a decrease in marginal return.

110. B: Structural unemployment is unemployment that results from a mismatch of job skills or location. In this case, Ivy's job skill—her ability to work as a seamstress—is no longer desired by employers. Frictional and cyclical are other forms of unemployment; economists do not use the term careless unemployment.

111. D: It is believed that some level of frictional and structural unemployment will always exist, and that the best economists (and politicians) can hope for is to reduce cyclical unemployment to zero. Therefore, frictional and structural unemployment are sometimes referred to as natural unemployment, meaning unemployment that naturally exists within an economy.

112. D: While rising prices may hurt many members of an economy, those same rising prices may benefit other members of the same economy. For example, rising prices may help those who sell goods and services and are able to keep their costs of production low, increasing their profit margin. Meanwhile, rising prices can hurt consumers because their income is now able to purchase fewer goods and services than before.

113. A: Demand-pull inflation is caused when total spending is in excess of total production. This causes price levels to rise, and can lead to hyperinflation.

114. D: The business cycle includes five stages: expansion, peak, contraction, trough, and recovery. Stagflation is the name for periods when inflation and unemployment are both increasing.

115. D: Because the MPC is 0.9, the multiplier is 10 (1/0.1). Therefore, to attain an increase of $10 billion in AD, the government must increase spending by $1 billion ($1 billion x 10 = $10 billion).

116. C: Banks create money by giving out loans. For example, assume a person puts $100 into a bank. The bank will keep a percentage of that money in reserves because of the reserve requirement. If the reserve requirement is 10% then the bank will put $10 in reserves and then loan out $90 of it to a second person. The money total, which started at $100, now includes the original $100 plus the $90, or a total of $190. The bank creates $90 by loaning it.

117. D: When the FOMC sells bonds, they raise interest rates. This draws money out of the American economy, and attracts foreign investors. This causes the value of the American dollar to rise overseas, which makes American goods more expensive to overseas buyers and causes American exports to drop.

118. A: The equation of exchange is MV = PQ. This means that M1 (a measure of the supply of money) multiplied by the velocity of money (the average number of times a typical dollar is spent on final goods and services a year) = the average price level of final goods and services in GDP x real output, or the quantity of goods and services in GDP.

119. A: Answer B is a definition of gross national product, and answers C and D define other economic measures.

120. B: Humanistic. The humanistic approach to understanding human behavior is driven by the idea that a person has a need to reach self-actualization, which includes the proclivity to seek after the highest possible growth and development that is attainable. In this approach, each individual has his or her own distinctive needs, desires, talents, skills, etc.

According to the humanistic approach, a person who is well adjusted must be free to express his or her own uniqueness.

121. A: Aggression. The Big Five personality traits are agreeableness, conscientiousness, extroversion, neuroticism, and openness. This classification system is an attempt to collapse the many different traits pertaining to personality into a few foundational traits that describe consistent behavior.

122. C: Psychodynamic. The psychodynamic approach deals with the idea that a person's behavior, thoughts, and emotions come from society's restrictions on the manifestation of a person's innate drives. Freud believed that sexual and aggressive drives are the most significant in human beings. Since society limits both drives, Freud believed that people struggle with meeting their personal needs versus displeasing others. According to Freud, a person's personality is reliant on how these issues are solved during the first two years or so of childhood.

123. D: Motion parallax. Motion parallax is also known as relative motion. It is a monocular cue that causes stable objects to appear to be in motion when a person is in motion. Objects closer to the fixation point (the thing the person is looking at) appear to be moving backward. The closer the object is to the fixation point, the faster the object would seem to be moving. Things that are farther from the fixation point will appear to be moving with the person at a slower pace as the object gets farther away.

124. C: According to George Murdock, it is the preponderance of property rights, rather than property disputes, which is a characteristic of all cultural practices. It may be that property disputes arise from the characteristic of property rights, but property disputes are not, in and of themselves, one of Murdock's cultural universals.

125. A: If a father from a patriarchal society passes on his property to his youngest son, he is practicing ultimogeniture. (B) Primogeniture is incorrect because it refers to the practice of a father's passing his property to his eldest son, not his youngest. (C) Neolocality and (D) patrilocality are incorrect because they represent concepts unrelated to ultimogeniture. (E) Parsimony is incorrect because is it not a societal practice; it is merely another word for stinginess.

126. D: Race is the correct answer because it is not one of Max Weber's independent factors which form the basis for his theory of stratification. (A), (B), and (C) are all incorrect because they are among Weber's independent factors forming his theory of stratification. (E) is incorrect because there is a correct answer, (D).

127. A: Talcott Parsons is the sociologist credited with developing the action theory of society

128. B: The philosophy of history is concerned with the ultimate significance of history as a field of study and asks questions concerning how history should be studied, including what social unit is correct to use when studying history—whether it is more important to look at the individual lives of ordinary people or to concentrate on the so-called big picture, looking at the overall trends in a society or culture; only giving personal treatment to people, such as George Washington, who had particular significance to the events surrounding them. The philosophy of history also looks for broad historical trends and progress.

129. A: Bias is a form of prejudice, and a historical work is considered biased when it is unreasonably shaped by the author's personal or institutional prejudices. It is wise for a teacher to choose material that comes from reputable sources and to verify that all material used in classroom presentations is reliable and appropriate. As long as the teacher is willing to do these things and show a variety of historical opinions, this is not an example of bias.

130. D: The information in this table shows the median incomes of persons who have achieved various educational levels. Looking at the table, one can see that from 1997 to 2007, persons without a high school degree had their median income increase by less than $5,000 while persons with a high school degree had their median income increase by more than $6,000. One can also see that as a general matter, the more education a person has, the higher their income will be and that income typically increases over time.

English Practice Test

Practice Questions

Questions 1-3 refer to the following excerpts:

Had we but world enough, and time,
This coyness, lady, were no crime.
We would sit down, and think which way
To walk, and pass our long love's day.

But at my back I always hear
Time's winged chariot hurrying near;
And yonder all before us lie
Deserts of vast eternity.

1. Who is the author of this poem?
   a. John Donne
   b. Andrew Marvell
   c. George Herbert
   d. Henry Vaughan

2. This poem reflects a thematic tradition known as...
   a. Carpe diem.
   b. Classicism.
   c. Cinquain.
   d. Conceit.

3. What is the meter of the couplets in this poem?
   a. Pentameter
   b. Heptameter
   c. Hexameter
   d. Tetrameter

Questions 4-7 are based on the following excerpt:

riverrun, past Eve and Adam's, from swerve of shore to bend of bay, brings us by a commodious vicus of recirculation back to Howth Castle and Environs.

4. This is the opening sentence of...
   a. *Ulysses.*
   b. *Finnegans Wake.*
   c. *Adventures in the Skin Trade.*
   d. *A Portrait of the Artist as a Young Man.*

5. In the excerpted sentence, the word "vicus" represents which of the following?
    a. Vicinity
    b. Vico Way
    c. Giambattista Vico
    d. All of the above

6. Why does this opening sentence begin with an uncapitalized word?
    a. This is to make it stand out to the reader.
    b. It is the continuation of the author's previous novel.
    c. It forms the completion of the novel's unfinished last sentence.
    d. A typesetting error in the original edition was preserved in perpetuity.

7. The author of the excerpted work is famous for using a literary technique known as...
    a. Stream-of-consciousness.
    b. The unreliable narrator.
    c. First-person narration.
    d. The author surrogate.

Questions 8-10 refer to the following excerpt:

> Call the roller of big cigars,
> The muscular one, and bid him whip
> In kitchen cups concupiscent curds.
> Let the wenches dawdle in such dress
> As they are used to wear, and let the boys
> Bring flowers in last month's newspapers.
> Let be be finale of seem.
> The only emperor is the emperor of ice-cream.

8. The excerpted poem was written in...
    a. The 17th century.
    b. The 18th century.
    c. The 19th century.
    d. The 20th century.

9. Which literary device is shown in the third line of the excerpted stanza?
    a. Alliteration
    b. Hyperbole
    c. Onomatopoeia
    d. Metonymy

10. The line "Let be be finale of seem" can be interpreted as reflecting a concept from which of the following?
    a. Ovid's *Metamorphoses*
    b. Dante's *Divine Comedy*
    c. Plato's *Dialogues*
    d. Homer's *Iliad*

Questions 11-13 refer to the following excerpt:

> I AM assured by our Merchants, that a Boy or a Girl before twelve Years old, is no saleable Commodity; and even when they come to this Age, they will not yield above [an amount of money] at most, on the Exchange; which cannot turn to Account...to the Parents...; the Charge of Nutriment and Rags, having been at least four Times that Value.
> I SHALL now therefore humbly propose my own Thoughts; which I hope will not be liable to the least Objection.
> I HAVE been assured by a very knowing *American* of my Acquaintance in *London;* that a young healthy Child, well nursed, is, at a Year old, a most delicious, nourishing, and wholesome Food; whether *Stewed, Roasted, Baked,* or *Boiled;* and, I make no doubt, that it will equally serve in a *Fricasie,* or *Ragoust.*

11. The literary form used in the excerpted piece is...
    a. Persuasion.
    b. Satire.
    c. Exposition.
    d. Bathos.

12. The excerpted work was published in which century?
    a. 20th
    b. 19th
    c. 18th
    d. 17th

13. The author of the excerpted piece also wrote which of the following?
    a. *The Canterbury Tales*
    b. *The Faerie Queene*
    c. *Paradise Lost*
    d. *Gulliver's Travels*

Questions 14-17 refer to the following poem:

The Thought-Fox

I imagine this midnight moment's forest:
Something else is alive
Beside the clock's loneliness
And this blank page where my fingers move.

Through the window I see no star:
Something more near
Though deeper within darkness
Is entering the loneliness:

Cold, delicately as the dark snow
A fox's nose touches twig, leaf;
Two eyes serve a movement, that now

And again now, and now, and now

Sets neat prints into the snow
Between trees, and warily a lame
Shadow lags by stump and in hollow
Of a body that is bold to come

Across clearings, an eye,
A widening deepening greenness,
Brilliantly, concentratedly,
Coming about its own business

Till, with a sudden sharp hot stink of fox,
It enters the dark hole of the head.
The window is starless still; the clock ticks,
The page is printed.

14. The primary literary device used by the poet here is...
    a. Foreshadowing.
    b. Irony.
    c. Cliché.
    d. Metaphor.

15. Which of these does the poem really describe?
    a. The process of a fox's natural actions
    b. The process of being inspired by nature
    c. The process of being inspired to write
    d. The process of being attacked by a fox

16. Which of the following best characterizes how this poem portrays the creative process?
    a. The poet exercises tight control of a thought.
    b. The poet is a passive recipient of the thought.
    c. The poet carefully guides the thought to him.
    d. The poet imagines a fox to help him to write.

17. In which of the following forms is this poem written?
    a. In free verse
    b. Rhymed and metered
    c. Unrhymed and metered
    d. Rhymed and unmetered

Questions 18-20 refer to the following excerpts:

I knew I should be grateful to Mrs. Guinea, only I couldn't feel a thing. If Mrs. Guinea had given me a ticket to Europe, or a round-the-world cruise, it wouldn't have made one scrap of difference to me, because wherever I sat—on the deck of a ship or at a street café in Paris or Bangkok—I would be sitting under the same glass bell jar, stewing in my own sour air.

I sank back in the gray, plush seat and closed my eyes. The air of the bell jar wadded round me and I couldn't stir.

[Following a successful shock treatment:]
All the heat and fear had purged itself. I felt surprisingly at peace. The bell jar hung, suspended, a few feet above my head. I was open to the circulating air.

"We'll take up where we left off, Esther," she [my mother] had said, with her sweet, martyr's smile. "We'll act as if all this were a bad dream."
A bad dream.
To the person in the bell jar, blank and stopped as a dead baby, the world itself is the bad dream.

Valerie's last, cheerful cry had been "So long! Be seeing you."
"Not if I know it," I thought.
But I wasn't sure. I wasn't sure at all. How did I know that someday—at college, in Europe, somewhere, anywhere—the bell jar, with its stifling distortions, wouldn't descend again?

From *The Bell Jar* by Sylvia Plath, copyright © 1971 by Harper & Row, Publishers, Inc.

18. The bell jar the author refers to is an example of which literary device?
    a. A simile
    b. An allusion
    c. A metaphor
    d. Personification

19. In this book, Plath uses a bell jar to symbolize...
    a. The strictures of reality.
    b. Her own mental illness.
    c. A case of writer's block.
    d. A disorder of breathing.

20. Which of the following statements is accurate about Sylvia Plath?
    a. *The Bell Jar* was her last in a long series of novels, all of them successful.
    b. She ultimately recovered, lived a long life, and wrote many more novels.
    c. Plath wrote only a few poems, but *The Bell Jar* was the first of her books.
    d. She wrote *The Bell Jar* about her initial breakdown almost a decade later.

21. William Shakespeare wrote during which historical and literary period?
    a. Medieval
    b. Renaissance
    c. Restoration
    d. Enlightenment

22. Which of the following was the author of *The Pilgrim's Progress?*
   a. John Bunyan
   b. William Congreve
   c. Daniel Defoe
   d. Samuel Butler

Questions 23-24 are based on the following excerpt:

Come live with me and be my love,
And we will all the pleasures prove
That valleys, groves, hills, and fields,
Woods, or steepy mountain yields.

23. This is the first stanza of a poem written by...
   a. Andrew Marvell.
   b. Christopher Marlowe.
   c. Sir Walter Raleigh.
   d. William Shakespeare.

24. The rhyme scheme of this stanza is...
   a. ABAB.
   b. ABBA.
   c. AABB.
   d. ABCD.

25. The legend of Faust has been treated in literature by which of the following?
   a. Christopher Marlowe
   b. Johann Wolfgang von Goethe
   c. Thomas Mann
   d. All of the above

26. Of the following works by Alexander Pope, which was written in prose?
   a. "An Essay on Criticism"
   b. "The Rape of the Lock"
   c. "The Universal Prayer"
   d. None of the above

Questions 27-29 refer to the following excerpts:

[First stanza:] I wake to sleep, and take my waking slow.
I feel my fate in what I cannot fear.
I learn by going where I have to go.

[Last stanza:] This shaking keeps me steady. I should know.
What falls away is always. And is near.
I wake to sleep, and take my waking slow.
I learn by going where I have to go.

[First stanza:] I shut my eyes and all the world drops dead;
I lift my lids and all is born again.
(I think I made you up inside my head.)

[Last stanza:] I should have loved a thunderbird instead;
At least when spring comes they roar back again.
I shut my eyes and all the world drops dead.
(I think I made you up inside my head.)

From *Mad Girl's Love Song* by Sylvia Plath, copyright © 1954 by Sylvia Plath, in A Biographical Note, in *The Bell Jar,* Copyright © 1971 by Harper & Row, Publishers. *Mad Girl's Love Song* first appeared in *Mademoiselle,* August 1953 issue.

[First stanza:] Do not go gentle into that good night,
Old age should burn and rave at close of day;
Rage, rage against the dying of the light.

[Last stanza:] And you, my father, there on the sad height,
Curse, bless, me now with your fierce tears, I pray.
Do not go gentle into that good night.
Rage, rage against the dying of the light.

From *Do not go gentle into that good night* by Dylan Thomas, copyright © 1951, From *The Poems of Dylan Thomas,* Copyright © 1937-1967 the Trustees for the Copyrights of Dylan Thomas. Copyright © 1938-1971 New Directions Publishing Corp.

27. Which is true of all three excerpted poems?
    a. They are all ballads.
    b. They are all sonnets.
    c. They are all villanelles.
    d. They are all different forms.

28. Which of the excerpted poems focus on the nature of reality vs. the imagination?
    a. The second and third
    b. The first and second
    c. The first and third
    d. All three

29. Which of the excerpted poems deal(s) directly with the subject of death?
    a. The third
    b. The second and third
    c. The first and third
    d. All three

Questions 30-35 refer to the following poem:

I like to see it lap the Miles —
And lick the Valleys up —
And stop to feed itself at Tanks —
And then — prodigious step

Around a pile of Mountains —
And supercilious peer
In Shanties — by the sides of Roads -
And then a Quarry pare

To fit its Ribs
And crawl between
Complaining all the while
In horrid — hooting stanza —
Then chase itself down Hill —

And neigh like Boanerges —
Then — punctual as a Star
Stop — docile and omnipotent
At its own stable door —

30. This poem describes which of the following?
    a. An aristocratic thoroughbred horse
    b. The recently invented railroad train
    c. An incredible mythological monster
    d. The subject cannot be determined

31. This poem was written around the time of...
    a. The American Revolution.
    b. The French Revolution.
    c. The War of 1812.
    d. The Civil War.

32. An amazing feat in this poem is that the structure of the subject described is mirrored in the poem's...
    a. Vocabulary.
    b. Rhythms.
    c. Syntax.
    d. Tone.

33. The adjectives "docile and omnipotent" in the penultimate line were chosen because they are...
    a. Synonymous.
    b. Nonsensical.
    c. Mechanical.
    d. Contrasting.

34. What is the source of the phrase "And neigh like Boanerges" in the last stanza?
  a. A Greek myth about a creature that inhabits Hades (the underworld)
  b. A New Testament reference to a fiery, strong-voiced preacher/orator
  c. An Old Testament reference to a wrathful prophet seeking vengeance
  d. A Roman name for a mythological animal that lived within a labyrinth

35. This poet famously used dashes for _______ and capitals for _______.
  a. Punctuation; honor
  b. Separation; names
  c. Prosody; emphasis
  d. Continuity; names

Questions 36-38 refer to the following poem:

Because I could not stop for Death —
He kindly stopped for me —
The Carriage held but just Ourselves —
And Immortality.

We slowly drove — He knew no haste
And I had put away
My labor and my leisure too,
For His Civility —

We passed the School, where Children strove
At Recess — in the Ring —
We passed the Fields of Gazing Grain —
We passed the Setting Sun —

Or rather — He passed Us —
The Dews drew quivering and chill —
For only Gossamer, my Gown —
My Tippet — only Tulle —

We paused before a House that seemed
A Swelling of the Ground —
The Roof was scarcely visible —
The Cornice — in the Ground —

Since then — 'tis Centuries — and yet
Feels shorter than the Day
I first surmised the Horses' Heads
Were toward Eternity —

36. The descriptions of Death, of the "Fields of Gazing Grain," and of the setting sun all employ which literary device?
  a. Analogy
  b. Hyperbole
  c. Alliteration
  d. Personification

37. Irrespective of its topic, the tone of this poem would best be described as...
   a. Serious, grave, and portentously dark
   b. Detached, alienated, and numb of feeling
   c. Lighthearted, humorous, and gently ironic
   d. Frantic, agitated, and with a frenzy of fear

38. What is described in the fifth stanza?
   a. A home
   b. A grave
   c. A church
   d. A school

39. A distinguishing feature of the form known as haiku is...
   a. 5/7/5 syllables per line
   b. An ABA rhyme scheme
   c. Perfectly regular meter
   d. Lengthy epic narratives

40. Which of the following accurately identifies *The Diary of a Young Girl* by Anne Frank?
   a. A fictional novel of a 1920s American debutante's diary
   b. A non-fictional Dutch journal influenced by World War II
   c. A long, episodic poem depicting childhood schizophrenia
   d. A British record documenting a sociological diary project

Question 41 refers to the following excerpt:

> When I got to camp I warn't feeling very brash, there warn't much sand in my craw; but I says, this ain't no time to be fooling around. So I got all my traps into my canoe again so as to have them out of sight, and I put out the fire and scattered the ashes around to look like an old last-year's camp, and then clumb a tree.

41. This passage is taken from which of the following?
   a. *The Mysterious Stranger*
   b. *The Adventures of Tom Sawyer*
   c. *The Adventures of Huckleberry Finn*
   d. *The Prince and the Pauper*

42. Which of the following statements is most accurate regarding the characters of Drouet and Hurstwood in Theodore Dreiser's novel *Sister Carrie?*
   a. Drouet has the awareness to be decent, but he lacks the morality.
   b. Hurstwood has the morality, but not the awareness, for decency.
   c. Only one of these characters is representative of the middle class.
   d. Drouet is morally decent but unaware; Hurstwood is the opposite.

Questions 43- 45 refer to the following excerpt:

I bequeath myself to the dirt to grow from the grass I love,
If you want me again look for me under your boot-soles.

43. What is the title of the poem from which this is taken?
    a. "To You"
    b. "Thou Reader"
    c. "Song of Myself"
    d. "One's-Self I Sing"

44. Which of the following is the best interpretation of the excerpted lines?
    a. The poet means that he will be dead and buried in the future.
    b. The poet means he is one with and an integral part of nature.
    c. The poet means the person addressed is above him in station.
    d. The poet means the recipient stepped on/walked all over him.

45. The excerpted work was published in which century?
    a. 18th
    b. 19th
    c. 20th
    d. 21st

Questions 46-50 refer to the following excerpts:

I should have been a pair of ragged claws
Scuttling across the floors of silent seas.

Shall I part my hair behind? Do I dare to eat a peach?
I shall wear white flannel trousers, and walk upon the beach.
I have heard the mermaids singing, each to each.

I do not think that they will sing to me.

We have lingered in the chambers of the sea
By sea-girls wreathed with seaweed red and brown
Till human voices wake us, and we drown.

46. What is the title of the work from which these excerpts are taken?
    a. "The Waste Land"
    b. "The Love Song of J. Alfred Prufrock"
    c. "Notes Toward the Definition of Culture"
    d. "The Hollow Men"

47. The second excerpt is speaking about...
    a. Indecision.
    b. A vacation.
    c. Mortality.
    d. Drowning.

48. Which of the following is/are the best interpretation(s) of the meaning in the first excerpt?
  a. The speaker's existence is as significant as the life of a crab.
  b. The speaker loves the sea and wishes he could live under it.
  c. The scavenger can create beauty by reconstructing garbage.
  d. The answers choices in (A) and (C) are valid interpretations.

49. Why does the speaker say, "I do not think that they will sing to me"?
  a. Because he feels the despair of existence.
  b. Because he is becoming deaf with old age.
  c. Because he knows mermaids are not real.
  d. Because he is on the beach, not in the sea.

50. Which of the following is the best interpretation of the final line?
  a. Mermaids protect us from drowning; humans ruin it.
  b. The dream of art is ruined by the intrusion of reality.
  c. Dreaming of mermaids is part of death by drowning.
  d. Mermaids bewitch us from knowing that we drown.

51. Which of Chaucer's *Canterbury Tales* is an example of the literary form known as the fabliau?
  a. "The Physician's Tale"
  b. "The Wife of Bath's Tale"
  c. "The Miller's Tale"
  d. "The Pardoner's Tale"

52. Which of the following pairs are NOT both written in the form of frame tales?
  a. *The Canterbury Tales* by Geoffrey Chaucer and *The Decameron* by Giovanni Bocaccio
  b. The *Mahabharata* by Veda Vyasa and *The Parlement of Foules* by Geoffrey Chaucer
  c. *Frankenstein* by Mary W. Shelley and *Wuthering Heights* by Emily Brontë
  d. *The Great Gatsby* by F. Scott Fitzgerald and *To the Lighthouse* by Virginia Woolf

53. Which of the following works was the first ever published in vernacular Italian?
  a. *De re publica (On the Republic)* by Marcus Tullius Cicero
  b. *Il Decameron* (*The Decameron*) by Giovanni Bocaccio
  c. *La Divina Commedia (The Divine Comedy)* by Dante Alighieri
  d. *Il Nome della Rosa* (*The Name of the Rose*) by Umberto Eco

Questions 54-56 are based on the following poem:

Leda and the Swan

A sudden blow: the great wings beating still
Above the staggering girl, her thighs caressed
By the dark webs, her nape caught in his bill,
He holds her helpless breast upon his breast.

How can those terrified vague fingers push
The feathered glory from her loosening thighs?
And how can body, laid in that white rush,
But feel the strange heart beating where it lies?

A shudder in the loins engenders there
The broken wall, the burning roof and tower
And Agamemnon dead.
                    Being so caught up,
So mastered by the brute blood of the air,
Did she put on his knowledge with his power
Before the indifferent beak could let her drop?

William Butler Yeats, 1923

54. "The broken wall, the burning roof and tower/And Agamemnon dead" refer to...
   a. The Punic Wars.
   b. The Trojan War.
   c. The Peloponnesian War.
   d. A murder but no war.

55. In what form is this poem?
   a. A sonnet
   b. Villanelle
   c. Free verse
   d. A sestina

56. The poet's final question best suggests which of the following ideas?
   a. Humans get godlike knowledge and power from the gods.
   b. Human knowledge and power are necessarily incomplete.
   c. Humans in ancient Greece interacted differently with gods.
   d. Humans interacting with gods got power, not knowledge.

57. In the Three Cueing Systems model of word recognition in reading instruction, which system most relates to how words are assembled into meaningful language?
   a. Phonological
   b. Semantic
   c. Syntactic
   d. Pragmatic

58. In the word-recognition model of the Three Cueing Systems used in teaching reading, which of the following is most associated with the meanings of words?
   a. Using pragmatic cues
   b. Phonological system
   c. The syntactic system
   d. The semantic system

59. In the model known in reading instruction as the Three Cueing Systems, which of these relate most to how sounds are used to communicate meaning?
   a. Syntactic cues
   b. Semantic cues
   c. Phonological cues
   d. Pragmatic cues

60. In reading instruction, the Three Cueing Systems is one model used. Which of the following represent a valid reading strategy that is NOT a system in the Three Cueing Systems model?

a. Syntactic cues
b. Pragmatic cues
c. Semantic cues
d. Phonological cues

61. When should students be taught to activate their prior knowledge?

a. Before reading
b. During reading
c. After reading
d. All of the above

62. Which choice most appropriately fills the blanks in this statement? "Teaching children which thinking strategies are used by ______ and helping them use those strategies ______ creates the core of teaching reading." (*Mosaic of Thought,* Keene and Zimmerman, 1997)

a. Reading teachers; in different ways
b. Beginning students; with assistance
c. Proficient readers; independently
d. Published writers; more creatively

63. Scholars have identified three kinds of major connections that students make when reading: connecting text to self, text to the world, and text to text. Which of the following student statements best reflect(s) the connection of text to the world?

a. "These mythic gods have more power, but feel and act like humans."
b. "This novel is set during a period I learned about in my history class."
c. "I can relate to how the main character felt about being controlled."
d. All three statements equally reflect connection of text to the world.

64. When students are taught to use effective reading comprehension strategies, they not only achieve deeper understanding, but they also learn to think about how they think when reading. This is known as...

a. Schemata.
b. Scaffolding.
c. Metacognition.
d. Metamorphosis.

65. Activity settings (Tharp and Gallimore, 1988) are aspects of the sociocultural context that affect how students learn and read. Of five activity settings, one is participant identity, or who the students are. Of the other four, which is most related to motivation?

a. When the activity is done
b. Why the activity is done
c. Where the activity is done
d. How the activity is done

66. Some experts maintain that teaching reading comprehension entails not only the application of skills, but also the process of actively constructing meaning. This process they describe as *interactive, strategic,* and *adaptable.* Which of the following best defines the *interactive* aspect of this process?

a. The process involves the text, the reader, and the context in which reading occurs.
b. The process involves readers using a variety of strategies in constructing meaning.
c. The process involves readers changing their strategies to read different text types.
d. The process involves changing strategies according to different reasons for reading.

67. In first-language (L1) and second-language (L2) acquisition, which of the following is true about developmental stages?

a. L2 learners do not undergo the first stage called the Silent Period as L1 learners do.
b. L2 learners undergo all stages, but are urged to skip the first stage more than L1s.
c. L2 learners do not undergo the second stage of Formulaic Speech as L1 learners do.
d. L2 learners undergo the third stage of Structural and Semantic Simplifications later.

68. Which statement is most accurate about social contexts of L1 and L2 acquisition?

a. Both L1 and L2 learning can occur in equally varied natural and educational contexts.
b. L1s are only learned in natural contexts, while L2s are learned in educational contexts.
c. Variations in L2 proficiency can result from the different contexts of learning the L2s.
d. L2s are not a speaker's natural language and so are never learned in natural contexts.

69. Which of the following is unique to second-language learning?

a. Zone of proximal development
b. The critical period hypothesis
c. Marked/unmarked features
d. The process of fossilization

70. An ESL student whose L1 is Chinese tends to omit plural endings and articles before nouns. Of the following, which is the best explanation for these errors?

a. The student has not yet learned these English grammatical forms.
b. Omission avoids having to choose among irregular English forms.
c. Incompatible nature and rules of the L1 are transferring to the L2.
d. The student does not understand how the L1 and L2 forms relate.

71. Which of the following is the most accurate characterization of dialects?

a. They are non-standard versions of any language.
b. They are often seen as less socially acceptable.
c. They include linguistic features that are incorrect.
d. They indicate poor/incomplete language learning.

72. Of the following, which statement is correct regarding Standard English?

a. The formal Standard English applies to written language.
b. Standard English is universal in English-speaking nations.
c. Speech communities use the Standard English of writing.
d. The Standard English construct does not include dialects.

73. The Great Vowel Shift occurred during which time span?
a. 10th to 13th centuries
b. 12th to 15th centuries
c. 15th to 18th centuries
d. 16th to 19th centuries

74. The Great Vowel Shift caused the pronunciation of long vowels in English to shift:
a. Farther back in the mouth.
b. Higher in the mouth.
c. Lower in the mouth.
d. Farther to the front of the mouth.

75. Of the following authors, whose English existed *during* the Great Vowel Shift?
a. William Shakespeare
b. Geoffrey Chaucer
c. Emily Dickinson
d. The Pearl Poet

76. Linguists generally analyze the Great Vowel Shift as having transpired in _____ steps.
a. Ten
b. Eight
c. Six
d. Four

77. Which of the following areas has been affected in the long term by the Great Vowel Shift?
a. Written spelling
b. Teaching reading
c. Text comprehension
d. All the above

78. The source of the silent *b* in the English word *debt* was originally...
a. A Middle English word.
b. A voiced Old English *b.*
c. From Latin etymology.
d. From Greek etymology.

79. We are familiar with the modern English meanings of the word "disaster." But in the 16th century, this word meant...
a. Catastrophe.
b. Star-crossed.
c. A misfortune.
d. Unflowerlike.

80. The English word "salary" has a 2,000-year-old etymology to a word meaning...
a. Salt.
b. Celery.
c. Money.
d. Earnings.

81. Which of the following is an example of a portmanteau?
  a. Fax
  b. Brunch
  c. Babysitter
  d. Saxophone

82. The English language word "quark" is an example of the result of which linguistic process?
  a. Blending
  b. Conversion
  c. Neologisms
  d. Onomatopoeia

83. The questions in this test can give you an idea of what kinds of questions you might find on the actual test; however, they are not duplicates of the actual test questions, which cover the same subject material but may differ in form and content.
The preceding sentence is which of the following sentence types?
  a. Simple
  b. Complex
  c. Compound
  d. Compound-complex

84. A patient dies in surgery and the reporting doctor describes the death as a "negative patient outcome." This is *best* identified as an example of...
  a. Jargon.
  b. Ambiguity.
  c. Euphemism.
  d. Connotation.

85. Which of the following is NOT typically categorized as a prewriting process?
  a. Planning
  b. Reflection
  c. Visualization
  d. Brainstorming

86. Which of the following correctly represents the sequence of stages or steps in the writing process?
  a. Prewriting, drafting, revising, editing, publishing
  b. Prewriting, drafting, editing, publishing, revising
  c. Prewriting, editing, drafting, revising, publishing
  d. Prewriting, drafting, editing, revising, publishing

87. Research has found that which of the following occur for students during revision and rewriting?
  a. Students only correct their mechanical errors in revisions.
  b. Students often incorporate new ideas when they rewrite.
  c. Students retain their original writing goals during revision.
  d. Students' planning in prewriting is unaffected in rewriting.

88. Which of the following have researchers learned about children's writing?
  a. Children's writing reflects as much knowledge as they have on any given topic.
  b. Children stop writing when they have run out of things they want to articulate.
  c. Children stop writing when they cannot adequately articulate their knowledge.
  d. Children's writing commonly covers more than they actually know about a topic.

89. Arthur writes a paper. One classmate identifies ideas and words that resonated with her when she read it. Another describes how reading the paper changed his thinking. A third asks Arthur some questions about what he meant by certain statements in the paper. A fourth suggests that a portion of the paper needs more supporting information. This description is most typical of...
  a. A portfolio assessment.
  b. A holistic scoring.
  c. A scoring rubric.
  d. A peer review.

90. Which of the following is the best definition of Information Literacy?
  a. It is the set of skills required for reading and comprehending different information.
  b. It is the cognitive skill set necessary to amass a comprehensive base of knowledge.
  c. It is the skill set required for the finding, retrieval, analysis, and use of information.
  d. It is the set of skills necessary for effectively communicating information to others.

91. What is the primary reason the early 21st century has been referred to as the Information Age?
  a. Because educational and governmental agencies require greater information
  b. Because there are more sources and outputs of information than ever before
  c. Because students can now learn all they need to know in four years of college
  d. Because college students today are much more interested in new information

92. Of the following statements, which adheres to Information Literacy standards?
  a. Students accessing information must critically evaluate it and its sources before using it.
  b. Students accessing information can ascertain how much of it they need after they find it.
  c. Students accessing information efficiently sacrifice broader scope and incidental learning.
  d. Students accessing information ethically must eschew using it to attain specific purposes.

93. According to the MLA system for documenting sources in literature, which of the following typically combines signal phrases and parenthetical references?
  a. An MLA list of the works cited
  b. MLA in-text citations in a paper
  c. Adding MLA information notes
  d. All of the above

94. According to MLA guidelines for writing research papers, which of the following is correct regarding citations of web sources if you do not quickly see the author's name?

a. Assume the author is not named, as this is a common occurrence on the Web.
b. Do not name an agency or corporation as author if it is the sponsor of the source.
c. Author names are often on websites, but need additional looking to discover.
d. It is not permissible to cite the book or article title in lieu of an author's name.

95. When making in-text citations in a research paper, which of the following reflects MLA guidelines for citing Web sources with regard to page numbers?

a. If a Web source does not include pagination, you are advised to avoid citing that source.
b. If page numbers appear on a printout from a website, include these numbers in citations.
c. In-text citations of online sources in research papers should never include page numbers.
d. If the Web source is a PDF file, it is recommended to cite page numbers in your citations.

96. The MLA guidelines for citing multiple authors of the same source in the in-text citations of a research paper are to use the first author's name and "et al" for the other(s) in the case of...

a. More than one author.
b. Two or three authors.
c. Three or more authors.
d. Four or more authors.

97. A movie review is one example of what type and purpose of writing?

a. Narration
b. Description
c. Persuasion
d. Exposition

98. Of the following writing types and purposes, which can often be the hardest to write?

a. Expository
b. Persuasive
c. Descriptive
d. Narrative

99. Which of the following do *The Adventures of Huckleberry Finn* by Mark Twain, *The Diary of a Young Girl* by Anne Frank, and "The Fall of the House of Usher" by Edgar Allan Poe have in common?

a. They are all examples of the narrative type and purpose of writing.
b. They are all examples of a purely descriptive writing type/purpose.
c. They are all examples of works of primarily expository writing type.
d. They are all examples of writing of the persuasive type and purpose.

100. When you have a writing assignment, which of the following is true about your audience?

a. You need not identify the audience because it is the teacher who gave the assignment.
b. You should consider how your readers are likely to use what you write.
c. You should know your writing purpose more than a reader's purposes.
d. You are overthinking to wonder about readers' likely attitude/reaction.

101. Which statement is correct regarding the relationship of your audience profile to the decisions you make in writing?

a. How much time you spend on research is unrelated to your audience.
b. Your audience does not influence how much information you include.
c. The writing style, tone and wording you use depend on your audience.
d. How you organize information depends on structure, not on audience.

102. Which of the following statements is most accurate about writing the introduction to an essay?

a. The introduction should use the technique of starting essays with dictionary definitions.
b. The introduction should leave the most attention-getting material for later in the work.
c. The introduction should move from the focused and specific to the broad and general.
d. The introduction should move from the broad and general to the focused and specific.

103. When writing an essay, which part of the introduction should come first?

a. Your thesis statement for the essay
b Background on the essay's purpose
c. Something original to engage reader attention
d. A "road map" of how you will present the thesis

104. Which of the following is true about effective ways to open the introduction of an essay?

a. You should summarize your position with your own words, not with a quote.
b. Citing a surprising statistic related to the topic can grab readers' attention.
c. Opening with a story or anecdote is counter to the purposes of an essay or paper.
d. Asking rhetorical questions to open an essay or paper will only frustrate readers.

105. Which of the following is the *worst* way to view the conclusion of an essay?

a. As a means of including all material that would not fit elsewhere
b. As a means of reiterating the thesis you stated in the introduction
c. As a means of synthesizing and/or summarizing your main points
d. As a means of clarifying the context of your discussion/argument

106. In writing, _____ is the overall written expression of the writer's attitude, and _____ is the individual way in which the writer expresses the former.

a. Voice; tone
b. Tone; voice
c. Style; tone
d. Voice; style

107. ________ is the overall choice of language you make for your writing; ________ refers to the words that you use when writing within or about a specific discipline.

a. Vocabulary; diction
b. Vocabulary; jargon
c. Diction; vocabulary
d. Style; vocabulary

108. Which of the following is most accurate regarding writing style?

a. The kind of diction you use does not affect style.
b. Add style later in the writing process to give personality.
c. Style is unrelated to your control of your content.
d. Your purpose for writing guides your style.

109. When considering strategies for writing assignments, it helps to know the cognitive (or learning) objectives your teacher intends for an assignment. If the assignment asks you to "describe," "explain," "summarize," "restate," "classify," or "review" some material you read, what is the cognitive objective?

a. Knowledge recall
b. Application
c. Comprehension
d. Evaluation

110. Your writing assignment asks you to "organize," "plan," "formulate," "assemble," "compose," "construct," and/or "arrange" some material. Which of the following cognitive (learning) objectives is the teacher aiming to meet with this assignment?

a. Analysis
b. Synthesis
c. Evaluation
d. Application

111. Which of the following processes used in writing is the most complex?

a. Evaluation
b. Application
c. Comprehension
d. Knowledge recall

112. Of the following learning and writing processes, which strategy/strategies is (or are) the most common forms of analysis in college-level writing?

a. Comparing and contrasting
b. Explaining cause and effect
c. Giving support to an opinion
d. Options A and B

113. Which of the following writing strategies is (or are) among the most commonly used forms of synthesis in college-level writing?

a. Explaining cause and effect
b. Comparing and contrasting
c. Proposing a solution
d. Using persuasion

114. Among writing projects that can develop from research, which of the following discourse aims is represented by a white paper, an opinion survey, an annotated bibliography, and a problem solution?
a. Expressive
b. Exploratory
c. Informative
d. Persuasive

115. "This treatise developed from an initial idea about the way a plant develops from a seed." The preceding sentence is an example of which literary device and argument method?
a. Analogy
b. Allegory
c. Allusion
d. Antithesis

116. In the famous balcony scene of William Shakespeare's *Romeo and Juliet,* Romeo says:

> But soft! What light through yonder window breaks?
> It is the east, and Juliet is the sun.
> Arise, fair sun, and kill the envious moon,
> Who is already sick and pale with grief,
> That thou her maid art far more fair than she:
> Be not her maid, since she is envious;
> Her vestal livery is but sick and green
> And none but fools do wear it; cast it off.

The literary device Shakespeare used here is also used in all *except* which of the following?
a. T. S. Eliot's description of the fog in "The Love Song of J. Alfred Prufrock" (1915)
b. Robert Frost's entire poem "The Road Not Taken" (1916)
c. Carl Sandburg's whole short poem "Fog" (1916)
d. All of these use the same device as Shakespeare

117. Of the following sentences, which one appeals to emotion?
a. It is dangerous to use a cell phone while driving because you steer one-handed.
b. Statistics of accident risk show that cell-phone use while driving is dangerous.
c. It is really stupid to use a cell phone when you drive because it is so dangerous.
d. Many state laws ban cell-phone use when driving due to data on more accidents.

118. Which of the following gives an example of a fallacy of inconsistency?
a. "There are exceptions to all general statements."
b. "Please pass me; my parents will be upset if I fail."
c. "He is guilty; there is no evidence that he is innocent."
d. "Have you stopped cheating on your assignments?"

119. In the 1984 comedy movie *All of Me,* a character from another country, who has no experience with either telephones or flush toilets, flushes a toilet and then a phone rings. He flushes again and the phone rings again. After this occurs several times, the character concludes that pulling the toilet's flush handle causes the ringing. This is an example of which type of cognitive bias?

a. An above-average effect
b. A clustering illusion
c. A confirmation bias
d. A framing bias

120. Archie says, "Asian people are all terrible drivers." The *most precise* definition of this statement is...

a. A stereotype.
b. An inference.
c. An assumption.
d. A generalization.

Answers and Explanations

1. B: The author of the excerpted poem, "To His Coy Mistress," is Andrew Marvell. Marvell, Donne (A), Herbert (C), and Vaughan (D) were all members of a group of mainly 17th-century poets known as the Metaphysical Poets for their common time period, themes, content, and style.

2. A: Carpe diem is Latin for "seize the day." This tradition reflects the theme that time flies and that life is fleeting, and thus we should take advantage of the present moment. The tradition of classicism (B) reflects ancient Greek and Roman ideals of beauty and principles of form and discipline (as opposed to Romanticism's principles of emotional impact), as reflected in the works of Alexander Pope and John Dryden. The cinquain (C) is a five-line type of poem in which line 1 is a one-word title, line 2 contains two words describing the title, line 3 has three words telling the action, line 4 contains four words expressing the feeling, and line 5 reverts back to one word that recalls the title. The conceit (D) type of poetry uses a metaphor, simile, or image comparing two very dissimilar things, such as Shakespeare's Sonnet # 18, "Shall I compare thee to a summer's day?"

3. D: Tetrameter means four beats per line, which is the meter of the rhymed couplets in this poem. Pentameter (A) means five beats per line. Heptameter (B) means seven beats per line. Hexameter (C) means six beats per line. Also, beats are only the stressed syllables, not total syllables.

4. B: This is the opening sentence of James Joyce's last novel, *Finnegans Wake* (1939). He published *Ulysses* (A) previously, in 1922; and *A Portrait of the Artist as a Young Man* (D) even earlier, in 1916. *Adventures in the Skin Trade* (C) was not written by Joyce but by Dylan Thomas (1938).

5. D: Joyce used the word "vicus" because it means "vicinity" (A) or "lane" in Latin; to refer to Vico Way (B), the name of the shore road running alongside of Dublin Bay; and to allude to Giambattista Vico (C), an Italian philosopher (1688-1744) who espoused the cyclic theory of history, a theme in Joyce's novel.

6. C: The lower-case initial letter of the first word was not an error (D). It did not continue Joyce's previous novel (B). And he did not use it to make the opening stand out as different to the reader (A). Rather, it is uncapitalized to show that it completes the book's last sentence fragment, "A way a lone a last a loved a long the—." By writing the end of the book to be completed and continued only by the beginning, Joyce embodied the cyclical nature of history and of the novel within its sentence structure.

7. A: Joyce is famous for using stream-of-consciousness in his novels, as in *Ulysses* and *Finnegans Wake.* The unreliable narrator (B) is a technique used often in murder mysteries, as by Edgar Allan Poe in "The Tell-Tale Heart," "The Cask of Amontillado," and many other stories and by Agatha Christie in *The Murder of Roger Ackroyd*. Joyce is not famous for using it. He used third-person narration and often included soliloquies, but is not famous for using first-person narration (C). An example of the author surrogate (D) is Socrates in Plato's works; Joyce is not known for using this technique.

8. D: "The Emperor of Ice-Cream" was written by Wallace Stevens in 1922. The style of the excerpted stanza is typical of modern poetry and does not reflect the conventions of 17th-century (A), 18th-century (B), or 19th-century (C) poems.

9. A: "In kitchen cups concupiscent curds" makes use of alliteration, the repetition of the same initial sound and/or letter in adjoining or nearby words—in this case, the sound /k/ from the letter "c." Hyperbole (B) is the device of exaggeration. Onomatopoeia (C) is the device of words sounding like what they mean (for example, "the clang of the bell" or "the gun went bang"). Metonymy (D) is the device of referring to a noun by an associated thing (such as using "the White House" to mean the U.S. government, or "Hollywood" to mean the American film and television industry).

10. C: Plato's *Dialogues* expound the philosophy of Socrates, including the concept that the mortal life of humanity and the world of the human senses and perception are an illusion, while the eternal life of the divine and the world of the ideal are reality, rather than vice versa. Stevens refers to this concept with "Let be be finale of seem"—meaning that "seem" is what we perceive, and is followed by "be," which is the reality found after life—as the first stanza's boys bringing flowers is continued in the second (final) stanza with references to shrouding a dead woman's body. A main theme in option (A) is the creation of the world; an allegorical journey through Hell, Purgatory, and Heaven in choice (B); and, in option (D), a journey home from war, which is also an allegory for every man's life journey.

11. B: The author, Jonathan Swift, wrote the excerpted piece, "A Modest Proposal," as a satire. He was not literally suggesting that children be cooked and eaten, but lampooning the way the British looked down on the Irish with his "proposal" as an ironic example of a "solution" to the poverty and overpopulation in Ireland. Persuasion (A) is a form of argument to sway the reader rather than make fun of something. Exposition (C) is also a straightforward method of giving information. Bathos (D) is a literary mood of overstated emotion that moves suddenly from the sublime to the ridiculous or pedestrian to create an anticlimactic effect.

12. C: "A Modest Proposal" was published in 1729, i.e., the 18th century. It does not have the modern style of the 20th (A) century. The bulk of Swift's work was published in the 1700s, with several pieces published in the late 1690s (D)—but not this one. Swift died in 1745 and even *A Journal to Stella,* published posthumously, was published in 1766, so the 19th century (B) is incorrect.

13. D: Jonathan Swift, author of the excerpted satirical essay "A Modest Proposal," also wrote *Gulliver's Travels* (1726, 1735), a novel satirizing human behavior and parodying the travel genre. *The Canterbury Tales* (A) were written by Geoffrey Chaucer in the 14th century. *The Faerie Queene* (B) was written by Edmund Spenser in the 16th century. *Paradise Lost* (C) was written by John Milton in the 17th century.

14. D: Hughes uses (extended) metaphor by describing the concrete presence of a fox to represent the abstract concept of a poet's inspiration. From beyond the blank window, starless sky, and dark forest, the fox, as a totem for the writer's imagination, approaches from without to inspire, its pawprints in the snow symbolizing print appearing on the blank page. Foreshadowing (A) is the literary device of hinting earlier in a work at something that will become more apparent later. Irony (B) is the device of creating a discrepancy between

what is expected and what really occurs (verbal, dramatic, or situational irony). Hughes's work is notable for NOT including any overused expressions known as clichés (C).

15. C: The poem describes how the poet is inspired to write, using the fox to embody the thought that enters the poet's mind (hence the title "The Thought-Fox"). The fox's natural actions (A) are thus symbolic rather than literal. The poet is not inspired by nature (B); in this poem, he uses an element of nature (the fox) to represent the thought that he receives and writes. The fox's entering "the head" is not a literal attack (D) but a symbolic representation of having or getting that thought.

16. B: The poet's passivity and lack of control over the thought, or content, of his writing can be interpreted from Hughes's separation of the thought, which does not arise from within his head, but approaches symbolically in the form of a fox from outside of his head, his body, and even his house. This separation is emphasized by the description of the Thought-Fox as "Coming about its own business." The poet as passive recipient is further shown in the last stanza, where the fox "enters the dark hole of the head." This passivity is further reflected in the last line, "The page is printed," as Hughes uses passive voice to represent the writing process, rather than saying that he himself prints the page.

17. A: This poem is written in free verse, meaning it has no regular rhyme scheme (options B and D) or metrical pattern (choices B and C). There is some partial rhyming, as in the sight rhyme of "snow" and "now" in stanza 3; the near rhymes of "star" with "near" in stanza 2 and "lame" with "come" in stanza 3; the rhymes of "darkness" and "loneliness" in stanza 2, "snow" and "hollow" in stanza 4, and "greenness" with "business" in stanza 5; and the off rhyme of "fox" with "ticks" in the last stanza. However, these are not regular, like the repeated rhymes of an established rhyme scheme. There is also no regular meter or number of beats per line. Hence the overall form of this poem is free verse.

18. C: The bell jar is a metaphor, an implied comparison between two things. A simile (A) is an overtly stated comparison; it would be a simile if she had written, "It was *like* a bell jar." An allusion (B) is an implied, indirect, or incidental reference, usually to a real or fictional person, place, or event. Personification (D) or anthropomorphism is attributing human characteristics to non-human animals or things.

19. B: The bell jar is Plath's metaphor for her mental illness. She describes feeling confined, not by reality (A), but by her own depression and its attendant alienated feelings and distorted perceptions. Writer's block (C) was not the bell jar but a symptom of it (her illness), as when she wrote about fearing she would never be able to write again. Moreover, though Plath did experience inability to write at times and her fear was genuine, she also produced many great poems as well as this novel during and in spite of her illness. Her references to "stewing in my own sour air," being unable to stir with the "air of the bell jar wadded round me," closed off from the "circulating air," being "blank and stopped as a dead baby," and "the bell jar, with its stifling distortions," do not signify any literal breathing disorder (D), but rather a metaphorical lack of the fresh air of reality and sanity.

20. D: Sylvia Plath underwent a serious breakdown and hospitalization in 1953; she wrote about this experience in *The Bell Jar* around 1961 (published in England in 1963 and America in 1971.) *The Bell Jar* was Plath's only novel (A). Plath wrote many poems, not a few (C). She did not recover to live a long life or write more novels (B); she committed suicide in 1963, a month after *The Bell Jar*'s London publication. (There is some evidence

she intended to have the suicide attempt discovered and be rescued from it. She recounts a number of suicide attempts in *The Bell Jar,* which were either discovered in time or she found she could not complete.) While she wrote other prose pieces early in her career, *The Bell Jar* was, she wrote, "my world... as seen through the distorting lens of a bell jar." Before her death at age 30, she had intended to write a second novel about "that same world as seen through the eyes of health."

21. B: Shakespeare (1564-1616) wrote during the Renaissance. The Medieval (A) era (also known as the Middle Ages) was earlier, ending before the 16th century (circa 1485), and included authors like Geoffrey Chaucer, Dante Alighieri, the Pearl Poet and author of *Sir Gawain and the Green Knight,* and Sir Thomas Malory. The Restoration (C) period followed the Renaissance, circa 1660-1700, and included authors like John Dryden, who wrote poetry, satire, and criticism. The Enlightenment (D) occurred from 1700-1785, and included the authors Jonathan Swift, Alexander Pope, Dr. Samuel Johnson and James Boswell.

22. A: John Bunyan (1628-1688) was the author of *The Pilgrim's Progress,* a religious allegory. William Congreve (B) (1670-1729) wrote *The Way of the World,* originally a play not successful on the theatre stage, but subsequently highly regarded as a literary exemplar of the comedy of manners. Daniel Defoe (C) (circa 1660-1731) is known for *Robinson Crusoe* and other adventure novels. Samuel Butler (D) (1612-1680), one of the Augustan poets, wrote the burlesque poem "Hudibras."

23. B: This is the first stanza of "The Passionate Shepherd to His Love" by Christopher Marlowe (1564-1593). Andrew Marvell (A) also included poems on pastoral themes in his oeuvre, including "The Garden"; however, he lived later (1621-1678) than Marlowe and was one of the Metaphysical Poets. Sir Walter Raleigh (C) was more contemporary (1552-1618) with Marlowe and wrote "The Nymph's Reply to the Shepherd," among others. William Shakespeare (D) was a contemporary (1564-1616) of Raleigh and Marlowe and also included pastoral themes in his songs and sonnets, including "Shall I compare thee to a summer's day?"

24. C: The rhyme scheme of this stanza, and the rest of the poem, is AABB: The second line rhymes with the first, and the fourth line rhymes with the third. This use of rhyming couplets was popular in the poetry of the time.

25. D: All of the above. The legend of Faust, who sold his soul to the devil in exchange for knowledge (echoing Adam and Eve's fall from grace in Eden caused by their desire for knowledge), has been popular throughout the various literary eras. Marlowe (A) wrote *Dr. Faustus* near the end of the 1500s. Goethe (B) wrote his German dramatic masterpiece *Faust* in the 19th century. Mann (C), also German, wrote the novel *Doktor Faustus* in the 20th century.

26. D: None of the above. These are all titles of poems written by Pope. "An Essay on Criticism" (A) is a didactic poem discussing literary theory, modeled after the style, language, and tone of the ancient Roman poet Horace. "The Rape of the Lock" (B) is a satirical poem, like "The Dunciad" and many others; Pope became famous for his satires. "The Universal Prayer" (C) is also a poem from Pope's *Moral Essays,* stating his beliefs. Pope wrote in a variety of styles on diverse subjects, including romantic, philosophical, political, pastoral, and others as well as satires, but all of his works were poetry.

27. C: The poems excerpted are all villanelles (D). The villanelle has nineteen lines with five tercets (three-line stanzas) and an ending quatrain (four-line stanza). The first and third line of the first stanza are alternately quoted in the last line of each subsequent stanza and both lines are repeated as a refrain at the end of the last stanza. Villanelles typically have ABA rhyme schemes. The quoted excerpts are not in ballad (A) form, which often uses quatrains, and rhymes either all alternating lines or second and fourth lines. (A famous example is "The Rime of the Ancient Mariner" by Samuel Taylor Coleridge.) Sonnet (B) form also differs from villanelle form. The Petrarchan sonnet has 14 lines, with a major shift in thinking or *volta* between the octave and sestet. The Shakespearean sonnet's 14 lines are three quatrains with ABAB/CDCD/EFEF rhymes and ending with a pivotal GG couplet. Sonnets also lack the repetition characteristic of villanelles.

28. B: The first poem excerpted, "The Waking" by Theodore Roethke, is a meditation on the nature of waking reality vs. dreaming imagination and which is which; life vs. death, mortality vs. immortality, process/journey vs. product/destination, world vs. self; the constancy of change; and the inability to control or even understand the mysteries of life, nature, and eternity. The second poem excerpted, "Mad Girl's Love Song" by Sylvia Plath (options A and B), also contemplates the nature of reality vs. imagination via the existentialist argument that we construct and destroy our own realities, and nothing objective exists beyond these. The third excerpted poem, "Do not go gentle into that good night" by Dylan Thomas (options A and C), focuses instead on how the dying should approach death.

29. A: Dylan Thomas' "Do not go gentle into that good night," addressed to his dying father, expresses the idea that death should be approached with spirited resistance rather than serene acceptance. The second poem, Sylvia Plath's "Mad Girl's Love Song," despite its use of the words "drops dead" and "born again," is not dealing with death but rather with the existentialist idea that reality is only what we perceive, imagine, or create and does not exist objectively outside of our own constructs. The first poem, Theodore Roethke's "The Waking," explores the nature of both reality vs. dreaming and life vs. death, but does not deal directly with the subject of death as Thomas' poem does.

30. B: This poem was written around 1862, during the Industrial Revolution when the railroad had recently been invented. (The poet's father was one of the owners of a local railroad.) The poet describes this "iron horse" by appropriately using the extended metaphor of a horse, but is not describing an actual horse (A) or a mythic monster (C). Thus it is not true that the subject of the poem cannot be determined (D).

31. D: This poem was written circa 1862. The American Revolution (A) was 1775-1783, the French Revolution (B) was 1789-1799, and the War of 1812 (C) was 1812-1815. The Civil War (D) was 1861-1865. Therefore, this poem was written during the Civil War period.

32. C: The poet performs an amazing structural feat in reflecting the composition of a railroad train in the composition of the poem's single, 17-line sentence. The first two words "I like" are the only subject and predicate; everything after the object "it" is a series of verbs complementing that object: "lap," "lick," "stop," "step," "peer," "pare," "crawl," "chase," "neigh," and "stop." This syntax mirrors the engine (subject and predicate) pulling the train behind it. The train's structure is not as specifically mirrored in vocabulary (A). The poem's rhythms (B) are typical of this poet, who very often wrote in iambic lines of alternating

tetrameter and trimeter. The tone (D), a childlike kind of enthusiasm, is deliberately used to suggest its role as a powerful toy, satirizing the "progress" of the modern invention.

33. D: The poet, Emily Dickinson, chose these words because they both contrast with one another and typify characteristics of domesticated horses, thus carrying out her horse metaphor for the "iron horse" of the railroad train. In this sense, they are not contradictory: horses have great physical power, are larger than humans and could easily kill a human, but domesticated horses, when treated well, are also typically obedient and gentle with humans. Thus these words are contrasting rather than synonyms (A). They are not nonsense words (B). While they describe a mechanical object, they are not mechanical (C) words.

34. B: Dickinson compares the train's whistle, first metaphorically to a horse's neigh, and then in the simile "like Boanerges," the last name/nickname given by Jesus to disciples James and John, sons of Zebedee, in Mark 3:17. This name has since come to mean a fiery and/or vociferous preacher or orator, especially one with a powerful voice. One creature inhabiting Hades in Greek myth (A) was Cerberus, the three-headed guardian dog. A mythological animal in a labyrinth (D) was the Minotaur, slain by Theseus. This was a Greek myth, not a Roman one. (Like most Greek culture, it was later appropriated by the Romans.) One Old Testament prophet who was angry at opponents and prayed for vengeance (C) was Jeremiah.

35. C: Dickinson habitually used dashes as a kind of musical mechanism to establish the prosody of her poems and habitually capitalized the initials of certain words to lend them additional emphasis. The dashes were not simply punctuation (A); she used other punctuation marks conventionally in places, and the dashes were more a rhythmic device. She did not capitalize to honor (A) the capitalized words. The dashes were not to separate words (B) and the capitals were not used only with names (B, D). The dashes added control to her prosody rather than providing continuity (D).

36. D: The author of this poem, Emily Dickinson, uses personification by attributing human qualities to nonhuman entities, a practice also known as anthropomorphism. She describes how Death "kindly stopped for me" and "knew no haste." She also describes the grain as "gazing," and notes that the setting sun "passed Us," using pronouns ("He") and human actions ("stopped," "drove," "knew," "gazing," "passed," "paused") to describe nonhumans. Analogy (A) is a comparison of different things, like saying that the human heart is like a pump. Hyperbole (B) is exaggeration. Alliteration (C) is repetition of sounds in adjacent or close words. Although "gazing grain" and "setting sun" both use brief alliteration in the poem, the descriptions of Death do not.

37. C: While the topic of this poem is death, it is treated with a lighthearted tone, finding humor in death with a gentle kind of irony. The diction, word choice, rhythms, and conclusion do not convey gravity, portent or darkness (A). The descriptive details of the journey to Eternity, slow yet seemingly over within a day in retrospect, do not convey detachment, alienation, or numbness (B). The deliberate, placid narrative has no frantic, agitated, frenzied, or fearful (D) qualities. Rather, the poet seems to welcome "Immortality" even as she quietly observes Death's "kindly" character and "Civility"—examples of the aforementioned gentle irony regarding death's inevitability, in that even if we cannot "stop for Death," death will still stop for us.

38. B: The fifth stanza about "a House that seemed/A Swelling of the Ground" is an oblique description of a grave. Its cornice is "in the Ground" and the roof is "scarcely visible," indicating that this "House" was underground. This is not a literal description of a home (A) or a church (C). A school (D) with children at recess is literally described as one of the aspects of life they pass in their journey, in the third stanza. The fifth stanza's description of a grave is in keeping with the whole poem's light, gentle, indirect, yet spiritually accepting treatment of death.

39. A: The haiku, originating in Japanese poetry and since adopted in English-language poetry, is a short poem of only three lines, often with 17 syllables, with the first and third lines having five syllables and the second line having seven syllables. (In Japanese there are many other rules, which become very complicated.) Haiku are typically unrhymed, so they do not have a rhyme scheme (B). Similarly, they do not employ any regular meter (C). Because haiku are typically 17 syllables or fewer, they do not involve long narratives (D).

40. B: This book was the actual diary kept by Anne Frank, a Dutch Jewish teenager whose family and others spent two years hiding in another family's attic before being sent to concentration camps by Nazis during World War II. Frank, 14-15 years old at the time, was intelligent and wrote articulately, depicting both the everyday details and the unusual difficulties of life in hiding and constant fear. The book is invaluable today, not only for its personal perspective on history and details of first-hand experiences with war and Nazism, but also as a testament to a young girl's unshakeable faith in human nature, even in the face of horrible inhumanity: she wrote near the end of her entries (July 15, 1944, only weeks before being arrested by Nazis) in one of the book's most often-quoted passages, "I still believe, in spite of everything, that people are truly good at heart."

41. C: All answer choices are novels by Mark Twain. However, while *The Mysterious Stranger* (A) is also a first-person narrative written in the literate language of its narrator, while *The Adventures of Huckleberry Finn* is written in its narrator's uneducated and Southern regional dialect. *The Adventures of Huckleberry Finn* followed and referred to *The Adventures of Tom Sawyer* (B), which is a third-person narrative rather than in first person. *The Prince and the Pauper* (D) is also a third-person narrative. The use of a first-person narrative in dialect differentiates the correct choice from the others. (*Tom Sawyer* contains similar dialects as *Huckleberry Finn,* but only in dialogue spoken by characters, not in the actual narration, which is third-person and not narrated by a character.) Also, the subject matter of the excerpt does not fit choices A or D.

42. D: In *Sister Carrie* (1900), Drouet is basically a decent person but is deficient in the intelligence or awareness for moral behavior. Therefore, choice A is incorrect. Hurstwood, by contrast, has the intelligence to understand moral behavior, and his awareness allows him to reject his family's superficial values. However, the moral deficiencies of his own character allow him to behave immorally. Therefore, option B is incorrect. In their attitudes toward women, both characters represent the middle class of the time; therefore, choice C is incorrect.

43. C: All choices are titles of poems by the same author, Walt Whitman, and all are published in the volume *Leaves of Grass.* This particular excerpt is taken from "Song of Myself," Whitman's longest and perhaps most famous poem.

44. B: Whitman's masterpiece is his celebration ("singing") of a mystical experience revealing, among other themes, his unity with the universe and nature. This is reflected in the title, *Leaves of Grass,* that he gave his collection of poems including "Song of Myself." The meaning of the excerpt is not simply literal (A). It is also not a metaphor for social classes or roles (C), and it does not refer to mistreatment in a personal relationship (D).

45. B: *Leaves of Grass,* the book of poems containing "Song of Myself," was first published in 1855, and Whitman continued to make revisions over 36 years, releasing subsequent editions through 1891. Hence all editions were published in the 19th century.

46. B: These excerpts are from "The Love Song of J. Alfred Prufrock" by T. S. Eliot. The other choices are also by Eliot. "Prufrock" was one of his earliest poems (published in *Poetry* magazine in 1915 and in a collection, *Prufrock and Other Observations*, in 1917). "The Waste Land" (A), often considered his masterwork, was published in 1922. While these two share several similar themes, "The Waste Land" is far longer and is not written as a dramatic monologue. "Notes Toward the Definition of Culture" (C) is by Eliot, but it is an essay, not a poem. Eliot published his poem "The Hollow Men" (D) in 1925.

47. C: The persona in the poem is speaking about his mortality. His rhetorical questions about parting his hair and eating a peach do not indicate indecision (A) but rather allude to conditions of old age (balding and diarrhea), and the imagery of his dress and the beach allude to retirement—not a vacation (B). This excerpt does not mention drowning (D). (The third excerpt does, but is not literal.)

48. D: Options (A) and (C) both express meanings that can be interpreted from this verse. The speaker compares his existence to that of a crab to show his own sense of unimportance, which is consistent with other parts of the poem expressing his sense of low status (e.g., "No! I am not Prince Hamlet, nor was meant to be... Almost, at times, the Fool"). Moreover, the poet has chosen the image of a crab not only to fit with the poem's other sea imagery, but also because it is a scavenger. Eliot's essay "Tradition and the Individual Talent" suggests that art can rescue the bleakness of modern life by creating beauty from its refuse. The imagery ("ragged," "scuttling," "silent") reinforces this bleak view rather than expressing a simple, literal wish (B).

49. A: This line is an expression of the despair felt by the speaker, characterizing the poet's view of modern life as broken, fragmented, and both alienating and isolating to the individual. While the speaker often mourns his aging throughout the poem ("I grow old... I grow old"), the statement about the mermaids is not literal as in options B and D. The mermaids represent the beautiful dream of the world of art; the speaker feels he cannot be included in or belong to it, even though he can perceive it. He is not saying the mermaids are not real (C) as in the previous line, he has said, "I have heard the mermaids singing." But they only sing to one another ("each to each"), not to him.

50. B: Hearing the mermaids singing to each other is part of Eliot's imagery, symbolizing the beauty found in art and in the beautiful dreams that both inspire it and are created by it. Prufrock's hearing them singing can also symbolize his glimpses of eternity, immortality, the ideal, and/or Paradise—things that art can portray or even achieve, but which he despairs of experiencing. His hearing them singing to each other but thinking they will not sing to him emphasizes his feelings of isolation and futility, which reflect Eliot's desolate view of the modern condition. The meaning is not primarily literal as in options A, C and D.

51. C: The fabliau is a humorous story including an incident that is nearly always indecent. In "The Miller's Tale," the cuckolded husband hangs his rear end out of the window and flatulates into the face of his wife's lover. "The Reeve's Tale," "The Shipman's Tale," "The Summoner's Tale," and others are additional instances of fabliau in *The Canterbury Tales.* "The Physician's Tale" (A) is an example of the literary form of the classical legend. "The Wife of Bath's Tale" (B), an Arthurian story, is an example of one version of the literary form of the romance. "The Pardoner's Tale" (D) is an example of the literary form of the *exemplum*, a type of instructional anecdote or story often used by preachers in sermons to illustrate moral points or principles.

52. D: *The Great Gatsby* by F. Scott Fitzgerald (1925) and *To the Lighthouse* by Virginia Woolf (1927) are both novels, but neither is a frame tale (a story or stories set within a story). Chaucer's *Canterbury Tales* is a 14th-century work that is rather famous for, among other things, being a frame tale containing multiple stories. Bocaccio's *Decameron* is likewise a 14th-century frame tale containing 100 tales. Each story-within-a-story is told by a different character in both *The Canterbury Tales* and *The Decameron* (A). Vyasa's Sanskrit epic the *Mahabharata* (circa 4th century) and Chaucer's 14th-century *The Parlement of Foules (Parliament of Fowls)* also use the frame tale structure—the former for historical, geographical, religious, and moral instruction and the latter framed in the form of a dream. The Gothic-Romantic novel *Frankenstein* (1818) by Mary W. Shelley and the Victorian novel *Wuthering Heights* by Emily Brontë (1847) also use the narrative structure of the frame tale (C).

53. C: Dante wrote his *Divine Comedy* between 1308 and 1321, consisting of three *canticas* (songs or chants): *Inferno* (Hell), *Purgatorio* (Purgatory) and *Paradiso* (Heaven). It was the first work ever published in vernacular Italian, the everyday language actually spoken by the people. Previously, all publications in Italy were issued in Latin, the language of the Roman Catholic Church. This was also true in other countries dominated by the Roman Empire; throughout the Middle Ages, as vernacular languages developed, books began to be published in the local languages. Cicero wrote *De re publica (On the Republic)* (A) between 54 and 51 BCE, an ancient Roman work published in Latin. Bocaccio finished writing *Il Decameron* (*The Decameron*) (B) around 1351-1353, after Dante's *Divine Comedy.* Umberto Eco's *Il nome della rosa* (*The Name of the Rose*) (D) is a novel published in modern Italian in 1980.

54. B: In this line, Yeats refers to the Trojan War, which has been indirectly attributed to the rape of Leda by the god Zeus in the form of a swan. This union produced the war-gods Castor and Polydeuces and also Helen of Troy and Clytemnestra. Helen's elopement with Paris triggered the Trojan War, a conflict powered by the war-gods. In the war, Agamemnon killed Clytemnestra's first husband and infant and took Clytemnestra as his wife. After his 10-year absence in the war, Clytemnestra killed Agamemnon. As such, this part of Yeats's poem refers to both a murder *and* a war (D). The Trojan War occurred roughly around the 11th-12th century BCE. The Peloponnesian War (C) between Athens and Sparta occurred from 431-404 BCE, ending the Golden Age of Greece. The Punic Wars (A) between Rome and Carthage occurred from 264-246 BCE, establishing Roman dominance. Hence these both occurred far later than the Trojan War.

55. A: This poem is a sonnet. Specifically, it is the Petrarchan (Italian) sonnet form, composed of an octave (eight lines) and a sestet (six lines), with the transition from former

to latter signaling a major change. (The Shakespearean or English sonnet is composed of three quatrains followed by a couplet.) The third line of the sestet is broken for emphasis. It is not a villanelle (B), which has 19 lines rather than the sonnet's 14 and uses a convention of repetition. This poem uses rhyme schemes of ABAB repeated in the octave and ABC repeated in the sestet, and is in iambic pentameter, hence it is not free verse (C). It is not a sestina (D), which dates back to 12th-century Provençal troubadours and has 39 lines rather than 14.

56. B: Yeats' question at the end of the poem best suggests the poignancy of the human condition, which is necessarily incomplete as we do not and cannot have the power or knowledge of the divine. Yeats asks whether, but does not state that, Leda "put on his knowledge with his power" (A). While certainly ancient Greece portrayed humans interacting differently with divinity than modern Western culture does (C), this is not Yeats's point. He uses this mythological event as a device for telescoping sex and history, showing how it generated ("engenders there") forces dominating the Western world, and musing about what Leda might have experienced in the moment. Line 13, "...his knowledge with his power" does not indicate she gained the latter but not the former (D). It asks if she "put on" the two together.

57. C: The Syntactic Cueing System is that set of cues available in the syntax. Syntax is the sentence structure and word order of language. The Phonological (A) Cueing System is that set of cues available in the phonological structure of language. Phonological structure is the language's speech sounds and the letters representing them. The Semantic (B) Cueing System is that set of cues available in the semantics. Semantics are the meaning (and meanings) of words and the morphemes (smallest units of meaning) that comprise words. The Three Cueing Systems model does not include a Pragmatic (C) system. However, it recognizes, as all linguists and reading instructors do, that pragmatic cues involve reader understanding of their reasons for reading and of how text structures operate. (In linguistics, pragmatics is the study of how language is used for social communication.)

58. D: Semantics refers to the meanings of words and language. The semantic system in the Three Cueing Systems model is the set of cues (including words, phrases, sentences, discourse, and complete text) that readers can use to recognize words based on meanings. Pragmatic cues (A) are based on reader purposes for reading and reader understanding of text structure. The phonological system (B) consists of cues related to the phonemic (or sound) structure of language. The syntactic system (C) consists of cues related to the sentence structure and word order of language.

59. C: Phonological cues are based on the speech sounds in words and their alphabetic representations in print. Readers can identify words by knowing sound-to-letter correspondences. Syntactic cues (A) are based on how words are arranged and ordered to create meaningful phrases, clauses and sentences. Semantic cues (B) are based on the meanings of morphemes and words and how they combine to create additional meanings. Pragmatic cues (D) are based on the readers' purposes for reading and their understanding of how textual structures function in the texts that they read.

60. B: Pragmatics is the study of how language is used socially for communication. In reading instruction, pragmatic cues relate to the reader's purposes for reading and the reader's understanding of the workings of textual structures. Although pragmatic cues are valid and important, the Three Cueing Systems model does not include a pragmatic

"system." The three cueing systems named in this theory are the phonological system of sound cues (D), the Semantic system of meaning cues (C), and the Syntactic system of sentence-structure cues (A).

61. D: Reading instructors should teach students to activate their prior knowledge because it will improve their reading comprehension. Before reading (A), teachers should discuss and model connections with existing knowledge to prepare students by helping them consider what they already know about the subject of the text. While they read (B), students can make better sense of the text by considering how it fits with what they already know. After reading (C), teachers can lead discussions helping students focus on how the connections they made between the text and their previous knowledge informed their understanding of the text, and on how the text helped them build on their foundations of existing knowledge.

62. C: Certain cognitive strategies used by good readers have been identified through research. Teaching children these strategies and helping them apply these until they can do so independently are found to support mastery of reading comprehension. Good readers who use such successful strategies are not necessarily reading teachers, and it is not necessary for students to find different ways (A) to apply them. Such strategies are less likely to be used by beginning students, and always applying them with assistance (B) without ever graduating to independent application is less effective. These strategies are used by all proficient readers, not just published writers (D). Finally, creativity is important to many kinds of writing, but not necessary to understand what one reads.

63. A: The student making this observation is connecting reading of a mythological text (presumably Greek or Roman) s/he reads to the world—in this instance, to human nature—by noting that despite greater powers, the gods' emotional reactions and behaviors are like those of humans. The student statement in option B reflects a connection of text to text—fiction (a novel) to historical accounts of a period (for example, see Dickens's *A Tale of Two Cities)*. The student statement in option C reflects a connection of text to self: the student can relate to the feelings of a character in the text. Because each choice reflects a different one of the three kinds of student connections named, option D is incorrect.

64. C: Thinking about thinking, or understanding our own cognitive processes, is known as metacognition. Explicitly teaching effective reading comprehension strategies does more than deepen student understanding of reading: it also promotes the higher-order, abstract cognitive skill of metacognition. Schemata (A) (plural; singular is *schema*) is Piaget's term for mental constructs we form to understand the world. Piaget said we either assimilate new information into an existing schema or alter an existing schema to accommodate the new knowledge. Reading instruction experts may refer to experience or background knowledge as schemata because students undergo this cognitive process when they fit what they read to their existing knowledge/experience. Scaffolding (B), a term coined by Jerome Bruner, refers to the temporary support given to students as needed while they learn, which is gradually reduced as they become more independent. Reading instruction experts may also describe students' connections of text to prior experience as scaffolding. Metamorphosis (D) is a term meaning a transformation—literally in biology as with caterpillars into butterflies, or figuratively, as in Franz Kafka's *The Metamorphosis,* wherein protagonist Gregor Samsa becomes a cockroach.

65. B: Why the students participate in a reading/learning activity refers to the motivation for the activity. Option A refers to the timing of the reading/learning activity. Option C refers to the place or physical setting of the learning activity. Option D refers to the way(s) in which the learning activity is defined and executed. All of these activity settings are factors that influence learning differently according to the different cultural, social, and economic factors involved in each specific situation.

66. A: The process of actively constructing meaning from reading is interactive, in that it involves the text itself, the person reading it, and the setting in which the reading is done: the reader interacts with the text, and the text interacts with the reader by affecting him/her; the context of reading interacts with the text and the reader by affecting them both; and the reader interacts with the reading context as well as with the text. Choice B is a better definition of the *strategic* aspect of the process. Options C and D are better definitions of the *adaptable* aspect of the process.

67. B: Researchers find that learners of both their native language (L1) and a second language (L2) go through all three developmental stages, which means that choices A and C are both incorrect. However, learners of a second language are often urged by teachers and others to skip the Silent Period, whereas young children acquiring their native languages are not similarly expected to speak immediately. L2 learners are not likely to undergo the third stage later (D) but sooner than or at a similar time as L1 learners, due either to having not yet learned all linguistic forms of the L2 or to being unable to access all of the L2's forms as they produce language.

68. C: L2s can be learned in a number of educational contexts, such as being segregated from the L1, formally taught via the medium of the L1, through submersion, or within the language classroom but not used to communicate outside it, among many others. They can also be taught/learned in several natural contexts: as the majority language to members of ethnic minority groups, as the official language of a country where learners are non-natives, or for international communication purposes separate from the L1 or official language. Therefore, it is not accurate that L2s are never learned in natural contexts (B and D). Unlike L2s, L1s are always first acquired in natural contexts, meaning choice A is inaccurate.

69. D: The process of fossilization occurs when some of the incorrect forms a learner of a second language has developed are not corrected over time, but become permanently fixed. (When a learner's L2 contains many such fossilized forms, it is termed an interlanguage.) Vygotsky's Zone of Proximal Development (A), in which a learner can accomplish tasks with assistance that s/he could not yet achieve independently, applies to the acquisition of both first and second languages. The hypothesis that there is a critical period for learning language (B) has also been applied to both L1 and L2 acquisition. In the same way, proponents of linguistic universals—both the typological universals proposed by Greenberg and the Universal Grammar described by Chomsky—find that in both first- and second-language learning, marked (language-specific) features do not transfer and are harder to learn, while unmarked (universal across most languages) features conform to general linguistic principles and are easier to learn. Fossilization is the only choice that occurs exclusively in second-language acquisition.

70. C: Omitting articles (for example, *a/an, the, these*) and plural endings (*-s*), which is common among Chinese ESL students, is not because they have not yet learned the English forms (A) or words for these. Nor are these omissions a way to avoid having to choose the

correct form among various English irregularities (C). Nor are these errors due to the student's lack of understanding of the relationship between the Chinese and English versions of the forms (D). Rather, Chinese does not include articles or plural endings the way English does, so the student has no frame of reference or comparison. Therefore, the student's ESL pattern of absent articles and plurals reflects the nature and rules of the L1, which have transferred to the L2 but are incompatible with it.

71. B: As linguists have long pointed out, dialects are NOT non-standard versions of a language (A). In linguistics, dialects are *differing* varieties of any language, but these may be vernacular (nonstandard) OR standard versions of a language. They are often considered less socially acceptable, especially in educational, occupational and professional settings, than whichever standard version is most accepted. The linguistic features of dialects are not incorrect (C), but simply different. Their use does not indicate poor or incomplete language learning (D).

72. A: The formal version of Standard English is reflected in dictionaries and grammar books and applied in written language. In speech, Standard English is NOT universal (B): it differs in pronunciation between the regions of North America and between native English speakers in England, Ireland, Australia, India, and other English-speaking areas. Speech communities use a more flexible variety of *informal* Standard English rather than the Standard English of writing (C). The construct of Standard English actually includes a range of dialects (D) because formal Standard English is used in writing and not speech, which by nature dictates a less formal, more flexible version.

73. C: The Great Vowel shift was a huge shift in the phonemics of English pronunciation that occurred from the 15th to 18th centuries in all places where English was spoken and written.

74. B: During the Great Vowel shift, the location of the tongue in the mouth where the long vowels in English were produced eventually shifted to a higher position, altering the sounds of their pronunciation. For example, the letter "e," pronounced /e/ (the sound spelled as "-ay" by Modern English speakers) in Chaucer's day (as it is still pronounced in Romance languages), gradually changed to be pronounced /i/ (the sound spelled as "ee" in Modern English). The tongue's movement back (A), down (C), or front (D) in the mouth would produce respectively different phonemes.

75. A: Shakespeare lived from circa 1564-1616 and wrote most of his known plays and poems between 1589 and 1613, or in the late 16th and early 17th centuries. The Great Vowel Shift occurred from the 15th to 18th centuries. Thus, Shakespeare wrote his Elizabethan English during this major language change. Geoffrey Chaucer (B) lived from circa 1343-1400 and wrote his known works between roughly 1369 and 1399. Therefore, his Middle English was the form that existed *before* the Great Vowel Shift took place. Emily Dickinson (C) wrote her poetry during the 19th century, *after* the Great Vowel Shift. The Pearl Poet (D), author of the *Pearl* poem, *Sir Gawain and the Green Knight,* and other works was a contemporary of Chaucer, meaning his works were also written *before* the Great Vowel Shift.

76. B: Linguists generally analyze the Great Vowel Shift as having consisted of eight steps: Step 1 = /i/ and /u/ → /əI/ and /əU/; Step 2 = /e/ and /o/ →/i/ and /u/; Step 3 = /a/ →/æ/; Step 4 = /ɛ/ → /e/, /ɔ/ → /o/; Step 5 = /æ/ → /ɛ/; Step 6 = /e/ → /i/; Step 7 = /ɛ/ →/e/; and Step 8 = / əI/ and / əU/ → /aI/ and /aU/. Step 1 involved downward shifts, Step

3 a forward shift, and Step 8 downward shifts. However, the overall effect of the Great Vowel Shift across all of its steps was an upward shift in the placement of the tongue in the mouth in the pronunciation of all long English vowels.

77. D: The Great Vowel Shift ultimately changed the pronunciation of the long vowels in English completely. Consequently, it has affected orthographic conventions and rules (A), instruction in reading (B), and how easily the modern readers of English texts can comprehend literature written before the GVS (C), as in the works of Chaucer and others. The sources of difficulty (in addition to changes in vocabulary and usage) for modern readers include not only the earlier spellings, but also the pronunciations that affected those spellings, as well as rhymes.

78. C: The etymology, or origin, of the English word *debt* is the Latin word *debitum*. It came into English during the Middle English form of the language. Therefore, this word was not originally a Middle English word (A) but a Latin word. Because it came from Latin into Middle English, it did not exist as an Old English word with a voiced *b* (B) as Old English preceded Middle English. The origin of this word was not Greek (D) but Latin. NOTE: Early scribes and printers, described by some as "inkhorn scholars," introduced many silent letters to English spellings to indicate their Latin or Greek roots, as in this case.

79. B: In Old Italian, the word *disastro* meant unfavorable in one's stars. It was commonplace to attribute bad fortune to the influences of the stars in the Medieval and Renaissance eras. The Old Italian word came into English in the late 1500s as "disaster" and was used by Shakespeare (cf. *King Lear)*. The word's Latin root is *astrum*, meaning "star," and the Latin prefix *dis-*, meaning "apart" and signifying negation. *Catastrophe* (A) and *misfortune* (C) are both Modern English meanings of the word "disaster," whereas the "ill-starred" meaning used in Elizabethan times has now become archaic or obsolete. The root means "star," not the aster flower (D).

80. A: The Latin word *sal* meant "salt." According to the famous ancient historian Pliny the Elder, "in Rome, a soldier was paid in salt," as it was a means of preserving food in the days before refrigeration and was thus a very valuable commodity. The Latin term *salarium,* from the root *sal,* originally meant the salt paid to soldiers but eventually became generalized to mean any kind of payment. (The expression "worth your salt" also derives from this origin.) "Salary" may sound similar to "celery" (B), but their roots and meanings are not the same. While salt eventually referred to any kind of payment including money or other kinds, it never originally meant *money* (C). "Earnings" (D) is a Modern English synonym for "salary" rather than the original meaning of its root word.

81. B: The word "brunch" is a blend of "breakfast" and "lunch". Blends of two or more words are known as portmanteau words. (*Portmanteau* is a French word meaning a suitcase.) "Fax" (A) is an example of clipping, or shortening a word, from its original "facsimile." "Babysitter" (C) is an example of compounding, or combining two or more words into one. "Saxophone" (D) is an example of proper noun transfer: A Belgian family that built musical instruments had the last name of Sax, and this wind instrument was named after them. These represent some of the ways that new words have entered—and still do enter—the English language.

82. C: Neologisms (from *neo-* meaning "new"), also known as "creative coinages," are new words sometimes invented by people which then become parts of our vocabulary. The word

"quark" was first coined by the great Irish author James Joyce; he used it in his last novel, *Finnegans Wake.* The physicist Murray Gell-Mann then chose this word from Joyce's work to name the model of elementary particles he proposed (also proposed concurrently and independently by physicist George Zweig) in 1964. Blending (A) is another way new words come into our language; for example, "moped" is a blend of the respective first syllables of "motor" and "pedal." Conversion (B), also called functional shift, changes a word's part of speech. For example, the common nouns "network," "microwave," and "fax," along with the proper noun "Google" have all been converted to verbs in modern usage. Onomatopoeia (D) means words that imitate associated sounds, such as "meow" and "click."

83. D: This is an example of a compound-complex sentence. A simple (A) sentence contains a subject and a verb and expresses a complete thought. Its subject and/or verb may be compound (e.g., "John and Mary" as subject and "comes and goes" as verb). A complex (B) sentence contains an independent clause and one or more dependent clauses. The independent and dependent clauses are joined by a subordinating conjunction or a relative pronoun. A compound (C) sentence contains two independent clauses—two simple sentences—connected by a coordinating conjunction. A compound-complex (also called complex-compound) sentence, as its name implies, combines both compound and complex sentences: it combines more than one independent clause with at least one dependent clause. In the example sentence given, the first two clauses, joined by "however," are independent, and the clause modifying "actual test questions," beginning with "which cover," is a relative, dependent clause.

84. C: A euphemism is an expression used instead of more literal words to make a harsh expression sound softer, to make an impolite description sound more polite, or to make a description less polite (such as saying "bit the dust" instead of "died" in a formal setting). Jargon (A) is the specialized terminology of a specific field or group. This example, however, is NOT medical jargon; a better example might be "expired" or "deceased." Ambiguity (B) means unclear and/or open to multiple interpretations. A better example of ambiguity in this scenario might be, "The surgery did not obtain all of the desired outcomes." This can mean a greater number of things than that the patient died. A connotation (D) is a suggested meaning associated with the literal meaning of a word. For example, "The surgery was abortive" does not state that the patient died, but if the surgery was meant to save the patient's life, the adjective "abortive," meaning unsuccessful or failing to obtain the desired result, could connote that the patient died.

85. B: Typically, after students write something, teachers may ask them to reflect on what they wrote, which would mean that this is NOT a prewriting activity. In writing exercises, teachers will typically ask students to plan (A) what they will write in order to clearly define their main topic and organize their work. Many teachers find it helps students to visualize (C) what they are reading and/or want to write about, and make drawings of what they visualize as preparation for writing. Brainstorming (D) is another common prewriting activity designed to generate multiple ideas from which students can select.

86. A: After prewriting (planning, visualizing, brainstorming), the correct sequence of steps in the writing process are drafting, in which the writer takes the material generated during prewriting work and makes it into sentences and paragraphs; revising, where the writer explores to improve the quality of the writing; editing, in which the writer examines his or her writing for factual and mechanical (grammar, spelling, punctuation) errors and

correcting them; and publishing, when the writer finally shares what he or she has written with others who will read it and give feedback.

87. B: Researchers have found that the writing processes both form a hierarchy and are observably recursive in nature. Moreover, they find that when students continually revise their writing, they are able to consider new ideas and to incorporate these ideas into their work. Thus they do not merely correct mechanical errors when revising (A), they also add to the content and quality of their writing. Furthermore, research shows that writers, including students, not only revise their actual writing, during rewrites, they also reconsider their original writing goals rather than always retaining them (C), and they revisit their prewriting plans rather than leaving these unaffected (D).

88. C: Researchers have found that children know a great deal more about a given topic than what their writing usually reflects. Therefore, options A and D are incorrect. Furthermore, researchers have concluded that when children stop writing, they do not do so because they have run out of things to write about the topic (B), but rather because they have not yet developed the means to articulate their knowledge adequately. Educational experts find that these research findings inform writing instruction in that the process of continually rewriting helps children to access and articulate more of the knowledge they actually have.

89. D: This description is most typical of the process of peer review. Classmates read a peer's paper and then identify values in it, describe it, ask questions about it, and suggest points for revision. These are types of helpful feedback identified by experts on writing and collaborative writing. The other choices, however, are not typically collaborative. For a portfolio assessment (A), the teacher collects finished work products from a student over time, eventually assembling a portfolio of work. This affords a more authentic assessment using richer, more multidimensional, and more visual and tactile products for assessment instead of using only standardized test scores for assessment. Holistic scoring (B) is a method of scoring a piece of writing for overall quality (evaluating general elements such as focus, organization, support, and conventions) rather than being overly concerned with any individual aspect of writing. A scoring rubric (C) is a guide that gives examples of the levels of typical characteristics in a piece of writing that correspond to each available score (for example, scores from 1-5).

90. C: According to the Association of College and Research Libraries, Information Literacy is the set of skills that an individual must have for finding, retrieving, analyzing, and using information. It is required not just for reading and understanding information (A). Information Literacy does not mean learning and retaining a lot of information (B), or only sharing it with others (D), but rather knowing how to find information one does not already have and how to evaluate that information critically for its quality and apply it judiciously to meet one's purposes.

91. B: The early 21st century has been dubbed the Information Age primarily because, with widespread Internet use and other innovations in electronic communications and publishing, there are more sources of information and greater output of available information than ever before. While some agencies might require more information (A), this is only possible because such information is more readily available now. Professionals in higher education and research find that with this new explosion of information, college students cannot possibly gain enough information literacy by just reading texts and writing research papers, and cannot learn all they need to know in four years (C). This period is also

not called the Information Age due to an increased student interest in acquiring information (D), but due to the increased access to information.

92. A: It is a standard of Information Literacy (IL) that students must use their own critical thinking skills to evaluate the quality of the information and its sources before they use it. Another standard is that the student should ascertain how much information s/he needs for his/her purposes first, deciding this after uncovering excessive information is inefficient (B). An additional IL standard is to access necessary information in an efficient and effective way. However, none of these standards include the idea that students will lose incidental learning or broadness of scope by doing so (C). IL standards include the principle that students *should* use the information they find in ways that are effective for attaining their specific purposes (D).

93. B: The MLA (Modern Language Association) system for documenting literary sources defines in-line citations in a paper as combining signal phrases, which usually include the author's name and introduce information from a source via a fact, summary, paraphrase, or quotation; parenthetical references following the material cited, frequently at the end of the sentence; and, except for web sources that are unpaginated, page number(s). MLA defines a list of works cited (A) as an alphabetized list found at the end of a research paper that gives the information sources referenced in the paper, including each source's publication information, quotations, summaries, and paraphrases. Guidelines for preparing the list of works cited are provided in the *MLA Handbook.* MLA information notes (C) are an optional addition to the MLA parenthetical documentation system. These notes can be used to add important material without interrupting the paper's flow, and/or to supply comments about sources or make references to multiple sources. They may be endnotes or footnotes. Because only one of the answers is correct, Option D is not possible.

94. C: On the Internet, the name of an author is usually provided but may not be visible at first glance. Web sources frequently include the author's name on another page of the same site, such as the website's home page, or in a tiny font at the very end of the web page, rather than in a more conspicuous location. In such cases, students doing online research may have to search more thoroughly than usual to find the author's name. Therefore, they should not immediately assume the author is not named (A). Also, many Web sources are sponsored by government agencies or private corporations and do not give individual author names. In these cases, the research paper *should* cite the agency or corporation name as author (B). Finally, it is much more common for online sources to omit an author's name than it is in print sources. In these cases, it is both permitted and advised by the MLA to cite the article or book title instead (D).

95. D: When online sources you are citing in your research paper are in PDFs and other file formats that have stable pagination, the MLA advises including the page number in the research paper's in-text citation because these numbers are valid and do not change. If a Web source has no pagination, as often happens, the MLA does NOT advise avoiding the citation (A), it advises simply making the citation without a page number because there is not one available. Unlike in PDFs (above), when citing a source from a printout, the MLA advises NOT including page numbers even if you see them because the same page numbers are not always found in all printouts (B). It is not true that in-text citations should never include page numbers (C).

96. D: The MLA guidelines for citing multiple authors of the same work in in-text citations (for both print and online sources) dictate using the first author's name plus "et al" for the other authors when there are four or more authors. If there are two (options A and B) or three (options B and C) authors, the guidelines say to name each author, either in a signal phrase [for example, "Smith and Jones note that... (45)" or "Smith, Jones, and Gray have noted... (45)"] or in a parenthetical reference ["(Smith, Jones, and Gray 45)."].

97. C: Persuasive writing has the purpose of expressing the writer's opinion and/or of convincing the reader of something. A movie review is one example of this writing purpose and type. Other examples include advertisements, editorials, book and music reviews, and literary essays. Narration (A) is a type of writing for telling stories. Description (B) is a type of writing for creating a picture using words that evoke imagery for the reader. Exposition (D) is a type of writing for informing and/or explaining.

98. B: Persuasive writing tries to convince readers to agree with the author's opinion or position regarding a topic. To convince others, writers must have sufficient knowledge about the topic, logical thinking skills, strong beliefs about the topic, and enough technical skill for making logical points, supporting one's opinions, and swaying the reader's emotions. Expository (A) writing aims to give information and/or explanations. It requires sufficient knowledge, practicality, and the technical skill for writing clarity, but it is not as hard as persuasion because it seeks not to convince the reader of anything, only to inform or explain. Descriptive (C) writing seeks to paint verbal pictures that make the described things real to readers through sensory details. This requires imagination and strong creative writing skills, but is not as difficult as persuading the reader to agree with the author's viewpoint. Narrative (D) writing tells a story and can be the easiest, as storytelling and enjoying stories are natural for most people.

99. A: *The Adventures of Huckleberry Finn* by Mark Twain is a fictional novel. *The Diary of a Young Girl* by Anne Frank is a non-fictional journal. "The Fall of the House of Usher" by Edgar Allan Poe is a fictional short story in the horror genre. Novels, personal narratives like diaries/journals, and short stories, as well as biographies and anecdotes are all types of narrative. Narration tells a story, often (but not always) advances chronologically, and has a beginning, middle, and end. Descriptive writing (B) paints a word picture using sensory imagery to make an event, scene, thing, or person more real to the imagination of the reader. Other than character sketches, picture captions, and some kinds of advertising, most writing is not completely descriptive: narrative works typically include descriptive parts. Exposition (C) is found in news stories, encyclopedias, research papers, informational essays, and instruction manuals rather than fiction or journals. Persuasion (D) is more characteristic of editorials, reviews, ads, and literary essays than novels, short stories or diaries.

100. B: For any writing assignment, you should first target an audience, perform an audience analysis, and develop an audience profile to determine what you should include in and omit from your writing. Even though the assigning teacher may be the only one to read your writing, you should not assume s/he is your main audience (A) because the teacher may expect you to write for other readers. In addition to first knowing your purpose for writing before beginning, you should also consider what purpose your writing will meet for your readers (C) and how they are likely to use it. Considering your audience's attitude toward what you will write and their likely reactions are also important to shaping your writing and is NOT overthinking (D).

101. C: The kind of audience for your writing, as well as your purpose, will determine what style, tone, and wording you choose. Knowing your audience will enable you to select writing strategies, style and tone, and specific word choices that will be most understandable and appealing to your readers. Knowing the type of audience will also dictate how much time to spend on research (A). Some readers will expect more supporting evidence, while others will be bored or overwhelmed by it. Similarly, you will want to include more or less information depending on who will be reading what you write (B). And while the structure of your piece does inform how you organize your information, you should also vary your organization according to who will read it (D).

102. D: It is best to begin an essay or paper with a broader, more general introduction to the topic, and move to a more focused and specific point regarding the topic—not vice versa (C)—by the end of the introduction. This point is your thesis statement. Writing experts advise *against* the technique of beginning an essay with a dictionary definition (A) because it has been so overused that it has become ineffective and uninteresting. To engage the reader's interest in your topic, it is best to begin with some very attention-getting material rather than leaving it for later (B).

103. C: The first part of the introduction to an essay or paper should be some original, fresh material that will engage the attention of readers enough so they are interested in continuing to read. Following this should be the transitional portion of the introduction, which gives some pertinent background information about the piece's particular purpose (B). This informs the reader of your reason for focusing on your paper or essay's specific topic. The transitional portion moves the piece to the third part of the introduction: the thesis statement (A), which is a clear expression of the main point you are trying to make in your essay or paper. An optional part of the introduction is an explanation of how you will defend your thesis, giving readers a general idea of how your essay or paper's various points will be organized. This is sometimes described as a "road map" (D).

104. B: One recommended technique for beginning an essay is to cite a surprising statistic related to your essay's topic. This will get the readers' attention, while also giving some information about the topic to be discussed in the rest of the piece. Another effective technique is to begin with an interesting quotation that summarizes your position. This adds interest, support, and power; it is not true that you should use only your own words instead of quoting another's (A). It is also untrue that opening with a story or anecdote is contrary to the purposes of an essay or paper (C); when you have some personal interest in your topic, this technique is useful for emotionally engaging the readers in the subject matter. It is not true that asking rhetorical questions will only frustrate readers (D): this is a technique that helps readers imagine being in different situations so they can consider your topic in new ways.

105. A: While students may sometimes regard the conclusion of their essay or paper as simply the last paragraph that includes all the pieces that they could not fit into earlier parts of the piece, this is an inadequate treatment of the conclusion. Because the conclusion is the last thing the audience reads, they are more likely to remember it. Also, the conclusion is an excellent opportunity to reinforce your main point, remind readers of the importance of your topic, and prod readers to consider the effects of the topic in their own lives and/or in the world at large. A good conclusion should restate your original thesis statement (B), pull

together and/or summarize the main points you made (C), and make clear(er) your discussion's or argument's context (D).

106. B: Tone is the writer's overall way of expressing his or her attitude. Voice is who the reader hears speaking in the writing, the individual way the writer uses to express his or her tone—not vice versa (A). Style (options C and D) is the effect a writer creates through language, mechanics, and attitude or the sound (formal or informal) or impressions (seriousness, levity, grace, fluency) of the writing.

107. C: Diction refers to your overall choice of language for your writing, while vocabulary refers to the specific words in a discipline that you use when writing in or about that discipline—not vice versa (A). Jargon (B) is very specialized terminology used in a discipline that is not readily understood by readers outside of that discipline. It is hence less accessible than the vocabulary of the discipline, and only used in writing intended only for those who are already familiar with it. Style refers to the writer's effect through language and technique (D).

108. D: Knowing your purpose for writing means knowing what you want to achieve with the content of your writing, and thus what writing style to use. Your choice of words and how formal or informal your writing is—your diction—*does* affect your style (A). Diction and tone should be consistent in your writing style, and should reflect vocabulary and writing patterns that suit your writing purpose best. Style is not added later to give writing personality (B). It develops from your purpose for writing, or what you want to accomplish with your writing. Style *is* directly related to your control of the content (C) of your writing.

109. C: The verbs quoted all refer to interpreting information in your own words. This task targets the cognitive objective of comprehension. Tasks targeting knowledge recall (A) would ask you to name, label, list, define, repeat, memorize, order, or arrange the material. Tasks targeting application (B) would ask you to calculate, solve, practice, operate, sketch, use, prepare, illustrate, or apply the material. Tasks targeting evaluation (D) would ask you to judge, appraise, evaluate, conclude, predict, score, or compare the material.

110. B: The verbs quoted all refer to taking pieces or parts of information or knowledge and bringing them together to create a whole, and to building relationships among the parts to fit new or different circumstances. Analysis (A) is the opposite of synthesis—breaking information down into its component parts and demonstrating the relationships among those parts. An assignment for analysis would ask you to compare, distinguish, test, categorize, examine, contrast, or analyze information. Evaluation (C) is making judgments based on given criteria, confirming or supporting certain preferences, and persuading the reader. An assignment targeting evaluation would use words like evaluate, predict, appraise, conclude, score, judge, or compare. Application (D) is using knowledge in new contexts. The assignment would ask you to apply, prepare, practice, use, operate, sketch, calculate, solve, or illustrate.

111. A: Evaluation is the most complex of the thinking/writing strategies listed in these choices because it commonly incorporates the other thinking strategies. Knowledge recall (D) requires showing mastery of information learned. Comprehension (C) requires showing understanding of the information learned. Application (B) requires taking the information learned and using it in new or different circumstances. These processes are not as complex as evaluating (or making critical judgments about) the information learned. Analysis and

synthesis are also more complex than knowledge recall, comprehension, and application, though less so than evaluation.

112. D: Comparing and contrasting, explaining cause and effect relationships, and analyzing are the most commonly used forms of analysis in college-level writing. Supporting an opinion (C) you have stated in your writing is one of the most commonly used forms of *synthesis*, not analysis, in college-level writing.

113. C: Proposing a solution to some problem or situation is one of the most commonly used forms of synthesis strategies in college-level writing. The other most commonly used synthesis writing strategy is stating an opinion and supporting it with evidence. Explaining cause and effect (A) and comparing and contrasting (B) are two of the most commonly used *analysis* (not synthesis) writing strategies. Using persuasion (D) to convince the reader is typically combined with the other strategies named to add credibility and acceptance to the position stated by the writer.

114. B: A white paper, opinion survey, annotated bibliography, and problem solution are all examples of the exploratory discourse aim. So are definitions, diagnoses, marketing analyses, feasibility studies, and literature (*not* literary) reviews. The expressive (A) discourse aim is reflected in vision statements, mission statements, proposals, constitutions, legislative bills, etc. Examples of writing reflecting the informative (C) discourse aim include news and magazine articles, reports, and encyclopedia articles. Examples of writing reflecting the persuasive (D) discourse aim include political speeches; editorials; ad campaigns; and works of artistic, social, or political criticism.

115. A: This sentence is an analogy, which compares similarities between two concepts to establish a relationship. Analogy can enhance comprehension of a new concept via comparison to an older/more familiar concept. Allegory (B) uses symbolism to represent a more abstract concept with a more concrete concept. Allusion (C) is a passing reference to a specific work/place/person/event. For example, saying "Susan loves to help and care for other people so much that her friends call her Mother Teresa" is an allusion to a famous person for effectiveness. Antithesis (D) juxtaposes words/phrases/sentences with opposite meanings, balancing these to add insight. A good example is Neil Armstrong's statement during the moon landing: "That's one small step for man, one giant leap for mankind."

116. D: All these choices use the literary device of an extended metaphor, as does the quoted Shakespeare passage wherein Romeo describes Juliet as the sun. In option A, Eliot describes the fog as a cat ("...rubs its back... rubs its muzzle... licked its tongue... Let fall upon its back the soot... curled once about the house, and fell asleep.") Similarly, Carl Sandburg's (1916) poem "Fog" (C) describes the fog that "comes on little cat feet." In option B, Frost uses the extended metaphor of two roads that "diverged in a wood" to describe the journey of life.

117. C: This sentence appeals to the reader's emotions by stating simply that it is dangerous and "really stupid" to use a cell phone while driving; it does not provide any evidence or logic to support the statement. Choice A offers a logical, common-sense argument in that steering one-handed makes driving more dangerous. Choice B refers to statistics of greater accident risk to support the statement that cell phone use while driving is dangerous. Such supporting evidence is an appeal to logic. Choice D cites the fact that many state laws ban cell phone use while driving to support the idea that it is dangerous, and also refers to data

on more accidents from doing so. These pieces of supporting evidence also appeal to logic rather than emotion.

118. A: A fallacy of inconsistency exists in a statement that contradicts itself or defeats itself. Saying there are exceptions to all general statements is itself a general statement; therefore, according to the content, this statement must also have an exception, implying there are NOT exceptions to all general statements. Option B is an example of a fallacy of irrelevance: passing or failing is determined by course performance, so asking to pass because parents will be upset if one fails is an irrelevant reason for appealing to a teacher for a passing grade. Option C is an example of a fallacy of insufficiency: a statement is made with insufficient supporting evidence. A lack of evidence of innocence is not enough to prove one is guilty because there could also be an equal lack of evidence of guilt. Option D is an example of a fallacy of inappropriate presumption: asking someone if s/he has stopped cheating presumes that s/he has cheated in the past. The person being asked this question cannot answer either "yes" or "no" without confirming that s/he has indeed been cheating. If the person being asked has not been cheating, then the person asking the question is making a false assumption.

119. B: A clustering illusion is a cognitive bias of attributing cause and effect and patterns to unrelated or random events. The character described considers the phone's ringing an effect caused by flushing the toilet, when in reality the two are unrelated. It was mere coincidence that the first ring occurred after he flushed; subsequent rings always occur at preset time intervals, and his repeated flushes simply coincided with these. The above-average effect (A) is the cognitive bias of overestimating our own abilities. The confirmation bias (C) is our tendency to focus on information confirming our pre-existing beliefs while overlooking conflicting information. In comparing ourselves with other people, we notice others' errors more and our own errors less. The framing bias (D) is being influenced by how information is framed rather than the facts. For example, whether a doctor presents the success or failure rate of an operation can influence the patient's decision to undergo it, even if both rates reflect identical data.

120. A: The statement reflects a stereotype. A stereotype is an assumption or generalization made about everybody in an identified group. Assumptions (C) can be made about many things, not just about the members of a certain group. Generalizations (D) also apply to a great many subjects, not just to the characteristics of a specific group of people. An inference (B) is a conclusion based on available evidence rather than on an overt statement of fact. For example, if Archie said, "That man is Asian, so he must be a terrible driver," he would be making an inference based on his stereotype of Asian people. Therefore, stereotype is the most precise definition of the statement.

Secret Key #1 - Time is Your Greatest Enemy

Pace Yourself

Wear a watch. At the beginning of the test, check the time (or start a chronometer on your watch to count the minutes), and check the time after every few questions to make sure you are "on schedule."

If you are forced to speed up, do it efficiently. Usually one or more answer choices can be eliminated without too much difficulty. Above all, don't panic. Don't speed up and just begin guessing at random choices. By pacing yourself, and continually monitoring your progress against your watch, you will always know exactly how far ahead or behind you are with your available time. If you find that you are one minute behind on the test, don't skip one question without spending any time on it, just to catch back up. Take 15 fewer seconds on the next four questions, and after four questions you'll have caught back up. Once you catch back up, you can continue working each problem at your normal pace.

Furthermore, don't dwell on the problems that you were rushed on. If a problem was taking up too much time and you made a hurried guess, it must be difficult. The difficult questions are the ones you are most likely to miss anyway, so it isn't a big loss. It is better to end with more time than you need than to run out of time.

Lastly, sometimes it is beneficial to slow down if you are constantly getting ahead of time. You are always more likely to catch a careless mistake by working more slowly than quickly, and among very high-scoring test takers (those who are likely to have lots of time left over), careless errors affect the score more than mastery of material.

Secret Key #2 - Guessing is not Guesswork

You probably know that guessing is a good idea. Unlike other standardized tests, there is no penalty for getting a wrong answer. Even if you have no idea about a question, you still have a 20-25% chance of getting it right.

Most test takers do not understand the impact that proper guessing can have on their score. Unless you score extremely high, guessing will significantly contribute to your final score.

Monkeys Take the Test

What most test takers don't realize is that to insure that 20-25% chance, you have to guess randomly. If you put 20 monkeys in a room to take this test, assuming they answered once per question and behaved themselves, on average they would get 20-25% of the questions correct. Put 20 test takers in the room, and the average will be much lower among guessed questions. Why?

1. The test writers intentionally write deceptive answer choices that "look" right. A test taker has no idea about a question, so he picks the "best looking" answer, which is often wrong. The monkey has no idea what looks good and what doesn't, so it will consistently be right about 20-25% of the time.
2. Test takers will eliminate answer choices from the guessing pool based on a hunch or intuition. Simple but correct answers often get excluded, leaving a 0% chance of being correct. The monkey has no clue, and often gets lucky with the best choice.

This is why the process of elimination endorsed by most test courses is flawed and detrimental to your performance. Test takers don't guess; they make an ignorant stab in the dark that is usually worse than random.

$5 Challenge

Let me introduce one of the most valuable ideas of this course—the $5 challenge:

You only mark your "best guess" if you are willing to bet $5 on it.
You only eliminate choices from guessing if you are willing to bet $5 on it.

Why $5? Five dollars is an amount of money that is small yet not insignificant, and can really add up fast (20 questions could cost you $100). Likewise, each answer choice on one question of the test will have a small impact on your overall score, but it can really add up to a lot of points in the end.

The process of elimination IS valuable. The following shows your chance of guessing it right:

If you eliminate wrong answer choices until only this many remain:	Chance of getting it correct:
1	100%
2	50%
3	33%

However, if you accidentally eliminate the right answer or go on a hunch for an incorrect answer, your chances drop dramatically—to 0%. By guessing among all the answer choices, you are GUARANTEED to have a shot at the right answer.

That's why the $5 test is so valuable. If you give up the advantage and safety of a pure guess, it had better be worth the risk.

What we still haven't covered is how to be sure that whatever guess you make is truly random. Here's the easiest way:

Always pick the first answer choice among those remaining.

Such a technique means that you have decided, **before you see a single test question**, exactly how you are going to guess, and since the order of choices tells you nothing about which one is correct, this guessing technique is perfectly random.

This section is not meant to scare you away from making educated guesses or eliminating choices; you just need to define when a choice is worth eliminating. The $5 test, along with a pre-defined random guessing strategy, is the best way to make sure you reap all of the benefits of guessing.

Secret Key #3 - Practice Smarter, Not Harder

Many test takers delay the test preparation process because they dread the awful amounts of practice time they think necessary to succeed on the test. We have refined an effective method that will take you only a fraction of the time.

There are a number of "obstacles" in the path to success. Among these are answering questions, finishing in time, and mastering test-taking strategies. All must be executed on the day of the test at peak performance, or your score will suffer. The test is a mental marathon that has a large impact on your future.

Just like a marathon runner, it is important to work your way up to the full challenge. So first you just worry about questions, and then time, and finally strategy:

Success Strategy

1. Find a good source for practice tests.
2. If you are willing to make a larger time investment, consider using more than one study guide. Often the different approaches of multiple authors will help you "get" difficult concepts.
3. Take a practice test with no time constraints, with all study helps, "open book." Take your time with questions and focus on applying strategies.
4. Take a practice test with time constraints, with all guides, "open book."
5. Take a final practice test without open material and with time limits.

If you have time to take more practice tests, just repeat step 5. By gradually exposing yourself to the full rigors of the test environment, you will condition your mind to the stress of test day and maximize your success.

Secret Key #4 - Prepare, Don't Procrastinate

Let me state an obvious fact: if you take the test three times, you will probably get three different scores. This is due to the way you feel on test day, the level of preparedness you have, and the version of the test you see. Despite the test writers' claims to the contrary, some versions of the test WILL be easier for you than others.

Since your future depends so much on your score, you should maximize your chances of success. In order to maximize the likelihood of success, you've got to prepare in advance. This means taking practice tests and spending time learning the information and test taking strategies you will need to succeed.

Never go take the actual test as a "practice" test, expecting that you can just take it again if you need to. Take all the practice tests you can on your own, but when you go to take the official test, be prepared, be focused, and do your best the first time!

Secret Key #5 - Test Yourself

Everyone knows that time is money. There is no need to spend too much of your time or too little of your time preparing for the test. You should only spend as much of your precious time preparing as is necessary for you to get the score you need.

Once you have taken a practice test under real conditions of time constraints, then you will know if you are ready for the test or not.

If you have scored extremely high the first time that you take the practice test, then there is not much point in spending countless hours studying. You are already there.

Benchmark your abilities by retaking practice tests and seeing how much you have improved. Once you consistently score high enough to guarantee success, then you are ready.

If you have scored well below where you need, then knuckle down and begin studying in earnest. Check your improvement regularly through the use of practice tests under real conditions. Above all, don't worry, panic, or give up. The key is perseverance!

Then, when you go to take the test, remain confident and remember how well you did on the practice tests. If you can score high enough on a practice test, then you can do the same on the real thing.

General Strategies

The most important thing you can do is to ignore your fears and jump into the test immediately. Do not be overwhelmed by any strange-sounding terms. You have to jump into the test like jumping into a pool—all at once is the easiest way.

Make Predictions

As you read and understand the question, try to guess what the answer will be. Remember that several of the answer choices are wrong, and once you begin reading them, your mind will immediately become cluttered with answer choices designed to throw you off. Your mind is typically the most focused immediately after you have read the question and digested its contents. If you can, try to predict what the correct answer will be. You may be surprised at what you can predict.

Quickly scan the choices and see if your prediction is in the listed answer choices. If it is, then you can be quite confident that you have the right answer. It still won't hurt to check the other answer choices, but most of the time, you've got it!

Answer the Question

It may seem obvious to only pick answer choices that answer the question, but the test writers can create some excellent answer choices that are wrong. Don't pick an answer just because it sounds right, or you believe it to be true. It MUST answer the question. Once you've made your selection, always go back and check it against the question and make sure that you didn't misread the question and that the answer choice does answer the question posed.

Benchmark

After you read the first answer choice, decide if you think it sounds correct or not. If it doesn't, move on to the next answer choice. If it does, mentally mark that answer choice. This doesn't mean that you've definitely selected it as your answer choice, it just means that it's the best you've seen thus far. Go ahead and read the next choice. If the next choice is worse than the one you've already selected, keep going to the next answer choice. If the next choice is better than the choice you've already selected, mentally mark the new answer choice as your best guess.

The first answer choice that you select becomes your standard. Every other answer choice must be benchmarked against that standard. That choice is correct until proven otherwise by another answer choice beating it out. Once you've decided that no other answer choice seems as good, do one final check to ensure that your answer choice answers the question posed.

Valid Information

Don't discount any of the information provided in the question. Every piece of information may be necessary to determine the correct answer. None of the information in the question is there to throw you off (while the answer choices will certainly have information to throw you off). If two seemingly unrelated topics are discussed, don't ignore either. You can be confident there is a relationship, or it wouldn't be included in the question, and you are probably going to have to determine what is that relationship to find the answer.

Avoid "Fact Traps"

Don't get distracted by a choice that is factually true. Your search is for the answer that answers the question. Stay focused and don't fall for an answer that is true but irrelevant. Always go back to the question and make sure you're choosing an answer that actually answers the question and is not just a true statement. An answer can be factually correct, but it MUST answer the question asked. Additionally, two answers can both be seemingly correct, so be sure to read all of the answer choices, and make sure that you get the one that BEST answers the question.

Milk the Question

Some of the questions may throw you completely off. They might deal with a subject you have not been exposed to, or one that you haven't reviewed in years. While your lack of knowledge about the subject will be a hindrance, the question itself can give you many clues that will help you find the correct answer. Read the question carefully and look for clues. Watch particularly for adjectives and nouns describing difficult terms or words that you don't recognize. Regardless of whether you completely understand a word or not, replacing it with a synonym, either provided or one you more familiar with, may help you to understand what the questions are asking. Rather than wracking your mind about specific detailed information concerning a difficult term or word, try to use mental substitutes that are easier to understand.

The Trap of Familiarity

Don't just choose a word because you recognize it. On difficult questions, you may not recognize a number of words in the answer choices. The test writers don't put "make-believe" words on the test, so don't think that just because you only recognize all the words in one answer choice that that answer choice must be correct. If you only recognize words in one answer choice, then focus on that one. Is it correct? Try your best to determine if it is correct. If it is, that's great. If not, eliminate it. Each word and answer choice you eliminate increases your chances of getting the question correct, even if you then have to guess among the unfamiliar choices.

Eliminate Answers

Eliminate choices as soon as you realize they are wrong. But be careful! Make sure you consider all of the possible answer choices. Just because one appears right, doesn't mean that the next one won't be even better! The test writers will usually put more than one good answer choice for every question, so read all of them. Don't worry if you are stuck between two that seem right. By getting down to just two remaining possible choices, your odds are now 50/50. Rather than wasting too much time, play the odds. You are guessing, but guessing wisely because you've been able to knock out some of the answer choices that you know are wrong. If you are eliminating choices and realize that the last answer choice you are left with is also obviously wrong, don't panic. Start over and consider each choice again. There may easily be something that you missed the first time and will realize on the second pass.

Tough Questions

If you are stumped on a problem or it appears too hard or too difficult, don't waste time. Move on! Remember though, if you can quickly check for obviously incorrect answer choices, your chances of guessing correctly are greatly improved. Before you completely give up, at least try to knock out a couple of possible answers. Eliminate what you can and then guess at the remaining answer choices before moving on.

Brainstorm

If you get stuck on a difficult question, spend a few seconds quickly brainstorming. Run through the complete list of possible answer choices. Look at each choice and ask yourself, "Could this answer the question satisfactorily?" Go through each answer choice and consider it independently of the others. By systematically going through all possibilities, you may find something that you would otherwise overlook. Remember though that when you get stuck, it's important to try to keep moving.

Read Carefully

Understand the problem. Read the question and answer choices carefully. Don't miss the question because you misread the terms. You have plenty of time to read each question thoroughly and make sure you understand what is being asked. Yet a happy medium must be attained, so don't waste too much time. You must read carefully, but efficiently.

Face Value

When in doubt, use common sense. Always accept the situation in the problem at face value. Don't read too much into it. These problems will not require you to make huge leaps of logic. The test writers aren't trying to throw you off with a cheap trick. If you have to go beyond creativity and make a leap of logic in order to have an answer choice answer the question, then you should look at the other answer choices. Don't overcomplicate the problem by creating theoretical relationships or explanations that will warp time or space. These are normal problems rooted in reality. It's just that the applicable relationship or explanation may not be readily apparent and you have to figure things out. Use your common sense to interpret anything that isn't clear.

Prefixes

If you're having trouble with a word in the question or answer choices, try dissecting it. Take advantage of every clue that the word might include. Prefixes and suffixes can be a huge help. Usually they allow you to determine a basic meaning. Pre- means before, post- means after, pro - is positive, de- is negative. From these prefixes and suffixes, you can get an idea of the general meaning of the word and try to put it into context. Beware though of any traps. Just because con- is the opposite of pro-, doesn't necessarily mean congress is the opposite of progress!

Hedge Phrases

Watch out for critical hedge phrases, led off with words such as "likely," "may," "can," "sometimes," "often," "almost," "mostly," "usually," "generally," "rarely," and "sometimes." Question writers insert these hedge phrases to cover every possibility. Often an answer choice will be wrong simply because it leaves no room for exception. Unless the situation calls for them, avoid answer choices that have definitive words like "exactly," and "always."

Switchback Words

Stay alert for "switchbacks." These are the words and phrases frequently used to alert you to shifts in thought. The most common switchback word is "but." Others include "although," "however," "nevertheless," "on the other hand," "even though," "while," "in spite of," "despite," and "regardless of."

New Information

Correct answer choices will rarely have completely new information included. Answer choices typically are straightforward reflections of the material asked about and will directly relate to the question. If a new piece of information is included in an answer choice that doesn't even seem to relate to the topic being asked about, then that answer choice is likely incorrect. All of the information needed to answer the question is usually provided for you in the question. You should not have to make guesses that are unsupported or choose answer choices that require unknown information that cannot be reasoned from what is given.

Time Management

On technical questions, don't get lost on the technical terms. Don't spend too much time on any one question. If you don't know what a term means, then odds are you aren't going to get much further since you don't have a dictionary. You should be able to immediately recognize whether or not you know a term. If you don't, work with the other clues that you have—the other answer choices and terms provided—but don't waste too much time trying to figure out a difficult term that you don't know.

Contextual Clues

Look for contextual clues. An answer can be right but not the correct answer. The contextual clues will help you find the answer that is most right and is correct. Understand the context in which a phrase or statement is made. This will help you make important distinctions.

Don't Panic

Panicking will not answer any questions for you; therefore, it isn't helpful. When you first see the question, if your mind goes blank, take a deep breath. Force yourself to mechanically go through the steps of solving the problem using the strategies you've learned.

Pace Yourself

Don't get clock fever. It's easy to be overwhelmed when you're looking at a page full of questions, your mind is full of random thoughts and feeling confused, and the clock is ticking down faster than you would like. Calm down and maintain the pace that you have set for yourself. As long as you are on track by monitoring your pace, you are guaranteed to have enough time for yourself. When you get to the last few minutes of the test, it may seem like you won't have enough time left, but if you only have as many questions as you should have left at that point, then you're right on track!

Answer Selection

The best way to pick an answer choice is to eliminate all of those that are wrong, until only one is left and confirm that is the correct answer. Sometimes though, an answer choice may immediately look right. Be careful! Take a second to make sure that the other choices are not equally obvious. Don't make a hasty mistake. There are only two times that you should stop before checking other answers. First is when you are positive that the answer choice you have selected is correct. Second is when time is almost out and you have to make a quick guess!

Check Your Work

Since you will probably not know every term listed and the answer to every question, it is important that you get credit for the ones that you do know. Don't miss any questions through careless mistakes. If at all possible, try to take a second to look back over your answer selection and make sure you've selected the correct answer choice and haven't made a costly careless mistake (such as marking an answer choice that you didn't mean to mark). The time it takes for this quick double check should more than pay for itself in caught mistakes.

Beware of Directly Quoted Answers

Sometimes an answer choice will repeat word for word a portion of the question or reference section. However, beware of such exact duplication. It may be a trap! More than likely, the correct choice will paraphrase or summarize a point, rather than being exactly the same wording.

Slang

Scientific sounding answers are better than slang ones. An answer choice that begins "To compare the outcomes…" is much more likely to be correct than one that begins "Because some people insisted…"

Extreme Statements

Avoid wild answers that throw out highly controversial ideas that are proclaimed as established fact. An answer choice that states the "process should used in certain situations, if…" is much more likely to be correct than one that states the "process should be discontinued completely." The first is a calm rational statement and doesn't even make a definitive, uncompromising stance, using a hedge word "if" to provide wiggle room, whereas the second choice is a radical idea and far more extreme.

Answer Choice Families

When you have two or more answer choices that are direct opposites or parallels, one of them is usually the correct answer. For instance, if one answer choice states "x increases" and another answer choice states "x decreases" or "y increases," then those two or three answer choices are very similar in construction and fall into the same family of answer choices. A family of answer choices consists of two or three answer choices, very similar in construction, but often with directly opposite meanings. Usually the correct answer choice will be in that family of answer choices. The "odd man out" or answer choice that doesn't seem to fit the parallel construction of the other answer choices is more likely to be incorrect.

Special Report: How to Overcome Test Anxiety

The very nature of tests caters to some level of anxiety, nervousness, or tension, just as we feel for any important event that occurs in our lives. A little bit of anxiety or nervousness can be a good thing. It helps us with motivation, and makes achievement just that much sweeter. However, too much anxiety can be a problem, especially if it hinders our ability to function and perform.

"Test anxiety," is the term that refers to the emotional reactions that some test-takers experience when faced with a test or exam. Having a fear of testing and exams is based upon a rational fear, since the test-taker's performance can shape the course of an academic career. Nevertheless, experiencing excessive fear of examinations will only interfere with the test-taker's ability to perform and chance to be successful.

There are a large variety of causes that can contribute to the development and sensation of test anxiety. These include, but are not limited to, lack of preparation and worrying about issues surrounding the test.

Lack of Preparation

Lack of preparation can be identified by the following behaviors or situations:

Not scheduling enough time to study, and therefore cramming the night before the test or exam
Managing time poorly, to create the sensation that there is not enough time to do everything
Failing to organize the text information in advance, so that the study material consists of the entire text and not simply the pertinent information
Poor overall studying habits

Worrying, on the other hand, can be related to both the test taker, or many other factors around him/her that will be affected by the results of the test. These include worrying about:

Previous performances on similar exams, or exams in general
How friends and other students are achieving
The negative consequences that will result from a poor grade or failure

There are three primary elements to test anxiety. Physical components, which involve the same typical bodily reactions as those to acute anxiety (to be discussed below). Emotional factors have to do with fear or panic. Mental or cognitive issues concerning attention spans and memory abilities.

Physical Signals

There are many different symptoms of test anxiety, and these are not limited to mental and emotional strain. Frequently there are a range of physical signals that will let a test taker know that he/she is suffering from test anxiety. These bodily changes can include the following:

Perspiring
Sweaty palms
Wet, trembling hands
Nausea
Dry mouth
A knot in the stomach
Headache
Faintness
Muscle tension
Aching shoulders, back and neck
Rapid heart beat
Feeling too hot/cold

To recognize the sensation of test anxiety, a test-taker should monitor him/herself for the following sensations:

The physical distress symptoms as listed above
Emotional sensitivity, expressing emotional feelings such as the need to cry or laugh too much, or a sensation of anger or helplessness
A decreased ability to think, causing the test-taker to blank out or have racing thoughts that are hard to organize or control.

Though most students will feel some level of anxiety when faced with a test or exam, the majority can cope with that anxiety and maintain it at a manageable level. However, those who cannot are faced with a very real and very serious condition, which can and should be controlled for the immeasurable benefit of this sufferer.

Naturally, these sensations lead to negative results for the testing experience. The most common effects of test anxiety have to do with nervousness and mental blocking.

Nervousness

Nervousness can appear in several different levels:

The test-taker's difficulty, or even inability to read and understand the questions on the test
The difficulty or inability to organize thoughts to a coherent form
The difficulty or inability to recall key words and concepts relating to the testing questions (especially essays)
The receipt of poor grades on a test, though the test material was well known by the test taker

Conversely, a person may also experience mental blocking, which involves:

Blanking out on test questions
Only remembering the correct answers to the questions when the test has already finished.

Fortunately for test anxiety sufferers, beating these feelings, to a large degree, has to do with proper preparation. When a test taker has a feeling of preparedness, then anxiety will be dramatically lessened.

The first step to resolving anxiety issues is to distinguish which of the two types of anxiety are being suffered. If the anxiety is a direct result of a lack of preparation, this should be considered a normal reaction, and the anxiety level (as opposed to the test results) shouldn't be anything to worry about. However, if, when adequately prepared, the test-taker still panics, blanks out, or seems to overreact, this is not a fully rational reaction. While this can be considered normal too, there are many ways to combat and overcome these effects.

Remember that anxiety cannot be entirely eliminated, however, there are ways to minimize it, to make the anxiety easier to manage. Preparation is one of the best ways to minimize test anxiety. Therefore the following techniques are wise in order to best fight off any anxiety that may want to build.

To begin with, try to avoid cramming before a test, whenever it is possible. By trying to memorize an entire term's worth of information in one day, you'll be shocking your system, and not giving yourself a very good chance to absorb the information. This is an easy path to anxiety, so for those who suffer from test anxiety, cramming should not even be considered an option.

Instead of cramming, work throughout the semester to combine all of the material which is presented throughout the semester, and work on it gradually as the course goes by, making sure to master the main concepts first, leaving minor details for a week or so before the test.

To study for the upcoming exam, be sure to pose questions that may be on the examination, to gauge the ability to answer them by integrating the ideas from your texts, notes and lectures, as well as any supplementary readings.

If it is truly impossible to cover all of the information that was covered in that particular term, concentrate on the most important portions, that can be covered very well. Learn these concepts as best as possible, so that when the test comes, a goal can be made to use these concepts as presentations of your knowledge.

In addition to study habits, changes in attitude are critical to beating a struggle with test anxiety. In fact, an improvement of the perspective over the entire test-taking experience can actually help a test taker to enjoy studying and therefore improve the overall experience. Be certain not to overemphasize the significance of the grade - know that the result of the test is neither a reflection of self worth, nor is it a measure of intelligence; one grade will not predict a person's future success.

To improve an overall testing outlook, the following steps should be tried:

Keeping in mind that the most reasonable expectation for taking a test is to expect to try to demonstrate as much of what you know as you possibly can.
Reminding ourselves that a test is only one test; this is not the only one, and there will be others.
The thought of thinking of oneself in an irrational, all-or-nothing term should be avoided at all costs.
A reward should be designated for after the test, so there's something to look forward to. Whether it be going to a movie, going out to eat, or simply visiting friends, schedule it in advance, and do it no matter what result is expected on the exam.

Test-takers should also keep in mind that the basics are some of the most important things, even beyond anti-anxiety techniques and studying. Never neglect the basic social, emotional and biological needs, in order to try to absorb information. In order to best achieve, these three factors must be held as just as important as the studying itself.

Study Steps

Remember the following important steps for studying:

Maintain healthy nutrition and exercise habits. Continue both your recreational activities and social pass times. These both contribute to your physical and emotional well being.
Be certain to get a good amount of sleep, especially the night before the test, because when you're overtired you are not able to perform to the best of your best ability.
Keep the studying pace to a moderate level by taking breaks when they are needed, and varying the work whenever possible, to keep the mind fresh instead of getting bored.
When enough studying has been done that all the material that can be learned has been learned, and the test taker is prepared for the test, stop studying and do something relaxing such as listening to music, watching a movie, or taking a warm bubble bath.

There are also many other techniques to minimize the uneasiness or apprehension that is experienced along with test anxiety before, during, or even after the examination. In fact, there are a great deal of things that can be done to stop anxiety from interfering with lifestyle and performance. Again, remember that anxiety will not be eliminated entirely, and it shouldn't be. Otherwise that "up" feeling for exams would not exist, and most of us depend on that sensation to perform better than usual. However, this anxiety has to be at a level that is manageable.

Of course, as we have just discussed, being prepared for the exam is half the battle right away. Attending all classes, finding out what knowledge will be expected on the exam, and knowing the exam schedules are easy steps to lowering anxiety. Keeping up with work will remove the need to cram, and efficient study habits will eliminate wasted time. Studying should be done in an ideal location for concentration, so that it is simple to become interested in the material and give it complete attention. A method such as SQ3R (Survey, Question, Read, Recite, Review) is a wonderful key to follow to make sure that the study habits are as effective as possible, especially in the case of learning from a textbook. Flashcards are great techniques for memorization. Learning to take good notes will mean that notes will be full of useful information, so that less sifting will need to be done to seek out what is pertinent for studying. Reviewing notes after class and then again on occasion will keep the information fresh in the mind. From notes that have been taken summary sheets and outlines can be made for simpler reviewing.

A study group can also be a very motivational and helpful place to study, as there will be a sharing of ideas, all of the minds can work together, to make sure that everyone understands, and the studying will be made more interesting because it will be a social occasion.

Basically, though, as long as the test-taker remains organized and self confident, with efficient study habits, less time will need to be spent studying, and higher grades will be achieved.

To become self confident, there are many useful steps. The first of these is "self talk." It has been shown through extensive research, that self-talk for students who suffer from test anxiety, should be well monitored, in order to make sure that it contributes to self confidence as opposed to sinking the student. Frequently the self talk of test-anxious students is negative or self-defeating, thinking that everyone else is smarter and faster, that they always mess up, and that if they don't do well, they'll fail the entire course. It is important to decreasing anxiety that awareness is made of self talk. Try writing any negative self thoughts and then disputing them with a positive statement instead. Begin self-encouragement as though it was a friend speaking. Repeat positive statements to help reprogram the mind to believing in successes instead of failures.

Helpful Techniques

Other extremely helpful techniques include:

Self-visualization of doing well and reaching goals
While aiming for an "A" level of understanding, don't try to "overprotect" by setting your expectations lower. This will only convince the mind to stop studying in order to meet the lower expectations.
Don't make comparisons with the results or habits of other students. These are individual factors, and different things work for different people, causing different results.
Strive to become an expert in learning what works well, and what can be done in order to improve. Consider collecting this data in a journal.
Create rewards for after studying instead of doing things before studying that will only turn into avoidance behaviors.
Make a practice of relaxing - by using methods such as progressive relaxation, self-hypnosis, guided imagery, etc - in order to make relaxation an automatic sensation.
Work on creating a state of relaxed concentration so that concentrating will take on the focus of the mind, so that none will be wasted on worrying.
Take good care of the physical self by eating well and getting enough sleep.
Plan in time for exercise and stick to this plan.

Beyond these techniques, there are other methods to be used before, during and after the test that will help the test-taker perform well in addition to overcoming anxiety.

Before the exam comes the academic preparation. This involves establishing a study schedule and beginning at least one week before the actual date of the test. By doing this, the anxiety of not having enough time to study for the test will be automatically eliminated. Moreover, this will make the studying a much more effective experience, ensuring that the learning will be an easier process. This relieves much undue pressure on the test-taker.

Summary sheets, note cards, and flash cards with the main concepts and examples of these main concepts should be prepared in advance of the actual studying time. A topic should never be eliminated from this process. By omitting a topic because it isn't expected to be on the test is only setting up the test-taker for anxiety should it actually appear on the exam. Utilize the course syllabus for laying out the topics that should be studied. Carefully go over the notes that were made in class, paying special attention to any of the issues that the professor took special care to emphasize while lecturing in class. In the textbooks, use the chapter review, or if possible, the chapter tests, to begin your review.

It may even be possible to ask the instructor what information will be covered on the exam, or what the format of the exam will be (for example, multiple choice, essay, free form, true-false). Additionally, see if it is possible to find out how many questions will be on the test. If a review sheet or sample test has been offered by the professor, make good use of it, above anything else, for the preparation for the test. Another great resource for getting to know the examination is reviewing tests from previous semesters. Use these tests to review, and aim to achieve a 100% score on each of the possible topics. With a few exceptions, the goal that you set for yourself is the highest one that you will reach.

Take all of the questions that were assigned as homework, and rework them to any other possible course material. The more problems reworked, the more skill and confidence will form as a result. When forming the solution to a problem, write out each of the steps. Don't simply do head work. By doing as many steps on paper as possible, much clarification and therefore confidence will be formed. Do this with as many homework problems as possible, before checking the answers. By checking the answer after each problem, a reinforcement will exist, that will not be on the exam. Study situations should be as exam-like as possible, to prime the test-taker's system for the experience. By waiting to check the answers at the end, a psychological advantage will be formed, to decrease the stress factor.

Another fantastic reason for not cramming is the avoidance of confusion in concepts, especially when it comes to mathematics. 8-10 hours of study will become one hundred percent more effective if it is spread out over a week or at least several days, instead of doing it all in one sitting. Recognize that the human brain requires time in order to assimilate new material, so frequent breaks and a span of study time over several days will be much more beneficial.

Additionally, don't study right up until the point of the exam. Studying should stop a minimum of one hour before the exam begins. This allows the brain to rest and put things in their proper order. This will also provide the time to become as relaxed as possible when going into the examination room. The test-taker will also have time to eat well and eat sensibly. Know that the brain needs food as much as the rest of the body. With enough food and enough sleep, as well as a relaxed attitude, the body and the mind are primed for success.

Avoid any anxious classmates who are talking about the exam. These students only spread anxiety, and are not worth sharing the anxious sentimentalities.

Before the test also involves creating a positive attitude, so mental preparation should also be a point of concentration. There are many keys to creating a positive attitude. Should fears become rushing in, make a visualization of taking the exam, doing well, and seeing an A written on the paper. Write out a list of affirmations that will bring a feeling of confidence, such as "I am doing well in my English class," "I studied well and know my material," "I enjoy this class." Even if the affirmations aren't believed at first, it sends a positive message to the subconscious which will result in an alteration of the overall belief system, which is the system that creates reality.

If a sensation of panic begins, work with the fear and imagine the very worst! Work through the entire scenario of not passing the test, failing the entire course, and dropping out of school, followed by not getting a job, and pushing a shopping cart through the dark alley where you'll live. This will place things into perspective! Then, practice deep breathing and create a visualization of the opposite situation - achieving an "A" on the exam, passing the entire course, receiving the degree at a graduation ceremony.

On the day of the test, there are many things to be done to ensure the best results, as well as the most calm outlook. The following stages are suggested in order to maximize test-taking potential:

Begin the examination day with a moderate breakfast, and avoid any coffee or beverages with caffeine if the test taker is prone to jitters. Even people who are used to managing caffeine can feel jittery or light-headed when it is taken on a test day.
Attempt to do something that is relaxing before the examination begins. As last minute cramming clouds the mastering of overall concepts, it is better to use this time to create a calming outlook.
Be certain to arrive at the test location well in advance, in order to provide time to select a location that is away from doors, windows and other distractions, as well as giving enough time to relax before the test begins.
Keep away from anxiety generating classmates who will upset the sensation of stability and relaxation that is being attempted before the exam.
Should the waiting period before the exam begins cause anxiety, create a self-distraction by reading a light magazine or something else that is relaxing and simple.

During the exam itself, read the entire exam from beginning to end, and find out how much time should be allotted to each individual problem. Once writing the exam, should more time be taken for a problem, it should be abandoned, in order to begin another problem. If there is time at the end, the unfinished problem can always be returned to and completed.

Read the instructions very carefully - twice - so that unpleasant surprises won't follow during or after the exam has ended.

When writing the exam, pretend that the situation is actually simply the completion of homework within a library, or at home. This will assist in forming a relaxed atmosphere, and will allow the brain extra focus for the complex thinking function.

Begin the exam with all of the questions with which the most confidence is felt. This will build the confidence level regarding the entire exam and will begin a quality momentum. This will also create encouragement for trying the problems where uncertainty resides.

Going with the "gut instinct" is always the way to go when solving a problem. Second guessing should be avoided at all costs. Have confidence in the ability to do well.

For essay questions, create an outline in advance that will keep the mind organized and make certain that all of the points are remembered. For multiple choice, read every answer, even if the correct one has been spotted - a better one may exist.

Continue at a pace that is reasonable and not rushed, in order to be able to work carefully. Provide enough time to go over the answers at the end, to check for small errors that can be corrected.

Should a feeling of panic begin, breathe deeply, and think of the feeling of the body releasing sand through its pores. Visualize a calm, peaceful place, and include all of the sights, sounds and sensations of this image. Continue the deep breathing, and take a few minutes to continue this with closed eyes. When all is well again, return to the test.

If a "blanking" occurs for a certain question, skip it and move on to the next question. There will be time to return to the other question later. Get everything done that can be done, first, to guarantee all the grades that can be compiled, and to build all of the confidence possible. Then return to the weaker questions to build the marks from there.

Remember, one's own reality can be created, so as long as the belief is there, success will follow. And remember: anxiety can happen later, right now, there's an exam to be written!

After the examination is complete, whether there is a feeling for a good grade or a bad grade, don't dwell on the exam, and be certain to follow through on the reward that was promised...and enjoy it! Don't dwell on any mistakes that have been made, as there is nothing that can be done at this point anyway.

Additionally, don't begin to study for the next test right away. Do something relaxing for a while, and let the mind relax and prepare itself to begin absorbing information again.

From the results of the exam - both the grade and the entire experience, be certain to learn from what has gone on. Perfect studying habits and work some more on confidence in order to make the next examination experience even better than the last one.

Learn to avoid places where openings occurred for laziness, procrastination and day dreaming.

Use the time between this exam and the next one to better learn to relax, even learning to relax on cue, so that any anxiety can be controlled during the next exam. Learn how to relax the body. Slouch in your chair if that helps. Tighten and then relax all of the different muscle groups, one group at a time, beginning with the feet and then working all the way up to the neck and face. This will ultimately relax the muscles more than they were to begin with. Learn how to breathe deeply and comfortably, and focus on this breathing going in and out as a relaxing thought. With every exhale, repeat the word "relax."

As common as test anxiety is, it is very possible to overcome it. Make yourself one of the test-takers who overcome this frustrating hindrance.

Additional Bonus Material

Due to our efforts to try to keep this book to a manageable length, we've created a link that will give you access to all of your additional bonus material.

Please visit http://www.mometrix.com/bonus948/westemlhuman to access the information.